Making Sense of the Bible

Making Sense of the Bible

REDISCOVERING THE POWER
OF SCRIPTURE TODAY

Adam Hamilton

HarperOne

An Imprint of HarperCollins*Publishers*

HarperOne

MAKING SENSE OF THE BIBLE. Copyright © 2014 by Adam Hamilton.
All rights reserved. Printed in the United States of America. No part of
this book may be used or reproduced in any manner whatsoever without
written permission except in the case of brief quotations embodied in critical
articles and reviews. For information address HarperCollins Publishers,
195 Broadway, New York, NY 10007.

HarperCollins books may be purchased for educational, business, or sales
promotional use. For information please e-mail the Special Markets
Department at SPsales@harpercollins.com.

HarperCollins website: http://www.harpercollins.com

FIRST HARPERCOLLINS PAPERBACK EDITION PUBLISHED IN 2016

Maps by Beehive Mapping

Library of Congress Cataloging-in-Publication Data is available upon request.

ISBN 978–0–06–223498–8

16 17 18 19 20   RRD(H)   10 9 8 7 6 5 4 3 2 1

To my first grandchild, whose birth will occur about the day this book is published, in the hope that she will come to love the Bible, and that in it she will find her defining story.

Contents

Section One:

The Nature of Scripture

A Disturbing, Wonderful, Perplexing, and Inspiring Book

I love the Bible. I've read it many times through over the last thirty-five years. Each morning, I begin by reading one of its passages and reflecting upon it. I study it in depth each week as I prepare my sermon expounding a passage or theme from it. I have committed to memory many of its verses. When I open its pages, I hear God speaking to me. Its story, particularly the story of Jesus, is the one story I hope will define my life. The Bible captures my deepest hopes and highest aspirations.

I love this book . . . and I wrestle with it. There are parts, if I'm honest, that I have questions about. There are statements on its pages that I don't believe capture the character and will of God. I'm guessing that if you're honest, you have questions too. We're not alone. As a pastor, I regularly hear from people who are perplexed, confused, or disturbed by something they've read in the Bible.

A couple of years ago, I received a call from a man I love dearly, whose pastor I have been for more than twenty years. He said he'd accepted my challenge to read the Bible cover to cover, but now he had questions. There were passages that he found troubling. Could we get together to talk? We sat on my back porch, glasses of iced tea in hand. He began, "I'm drawn to the God of Jesus Christ, who loved sinners and tax collectors and who laid down his life for the lost. But I'm disturbed by the picture of God in the Old Testament. He seems petty and vindictive. He commands the Israelites to slaughter entire cities. Abraham and Moses both plead with him to show mercy to those he would destroy. This same God says adulterers, Sabbath violators, homosexuals, and children who curse their parents should be put to death. He hardly seems like the God Jesus came to make known."

A science major in college wrote me to say that she was unsettled by the fact that the Bible's creation accounts could not be reconciled with modern science. She'd heard from other Christians that she had to reject contemporary scientific explanations for origins of life on our planet if she wished to be a faithful Christian.

An attorney in the church I serve is troubled by the fact that the Gospels disagree with one another at various points. He notes, "In a courtroom, when witnesses disagree like this, I know there is a problem with their testimony. How can I trust what the Gospels say about Jesus?"

These are just the tip of the iceberg. Does everything really happen for a reason? Does God will the death of babies or natural disasters that leave thousands dead and tens of thousands homeless?

And what of the fate of people of other religions? Jesus said, "I am the way, the truth and the life. No one comes to the Father except through me." Peter said, "There is salvation in no one else, for there is no other name under heaven given among mortals by which we must be saved" (John 14:6 and Acts 4:12). Do these verses mean that everyone who is not a Christian will be damned, as many believe? Is there any other way to understand these statements?

Among the thorniest issues in society today are those that have to do with sexuality, particularly homosexuality. While much of society is becoming more accepting of gay and lesbian people, and a number of states in the United States have approved "gay marriage," a significant number of American Christians believe that same-sex intimacy is a sin. Ask them why and they'll tell you that the Bible says it is a sin, noting that both Moses and Paul were clear on this (Leviticus 20:13 and Romans 1:26–27). Do these verses express God's final word and will regarding sexuality? Leviticus 20:13 calls for the execution of gay men. Do we believe this captures God's will? Or is humiliation and condemnation enough?

As you can see, there is no shortage of questions that might be raised about the "clear teaching of scripture." Here's what I hope to do on the pages of this book you hold in your hand: I envision having a conversation with you, the reader, sitting on my back porch, each of us with a glass of iced tea. Each chapter will be a short discussion related to one of these questions. My aim is not to give you all the answers. I don't have all the answers. Part of the reason for writing this book is to sort through the issues for myself. Am I right in everything I say in this book? I'm certain I'm not. But the book is an attempt to honestly wrestle with the difficult questions often raised by thoughtful Christians and non-Christians concerning things taught in the Bible.

If you are looking for a scholarly work or you want to go deeper, I include a bibliography at the end with books I've read that will take you deeper still. But the aim of this book is not to offer a scholarly treatise on each of these questions. Instead I'm hoping to distill down (not dumb down but rather summarize and express the essence of) the work of scholars, while offering my own reflections as one who preaches and teaches the Bible and who regularly engages with questions from laity and pastors alike.

I've divided the book into two parts. In the first section, we'll start with some foundational questions: What is the Bible, exactly? In what sense is it God's word, and in what sense is it human reflections on God? What do we mean by calling it "inspired"? Is it inerrant or infallible, as many Christians believe? We'll also consider how the Bible was written and when it was written, as well as the various types of writings found in it. And we'll talk about who decided what books made it into the Bible, which ones were left out, and why.

In the second section, we'll dig into the kinds of questions I've described above. We'll talk about the different pictures of God found in the Old and New Testaments. We'll ponder science and the Bible. We'll think together about sex and the Bible, as well as the Second Coming, and a few other questions you might not have thought to ask—upon hearing them, I think you'll agree they are important for us to consider. We'll end this section, and the book, by looking at various ways to read the Bible, so that in reading it, you may hear God speak through it and find its words to be life-changing and life-giving.

I hear God speak through the Bible. Its words convict me, challenge me, and comfort me. And some of them disturb me. In this book, I'd like to share with you how I and many others have wrestled with the Bible and have come to make sense of its thorny passages while listening carefully for the One to whom all scripture bears witness.

So, grab a glass of iced tea, and let's begin . . .

CHAPTER I

What the Bible Is Not

Let's begin our conversation by answering a seemingly simple question: "What exactly is the Bible?" I've heard people describe the Bible as the "Owner's Manual." I'm looking at the owner's manual for my Ford Mustang as I write these words. It begins with a table of contents that starts with the basic safety features of my car, then moves to how to operate my vehicle, then how to do routine maintenance and repairs. Near the end it offers troubleshooting.

Sitting next to my owner's manual is my Bible. I wish it were written like my Ford manual. Instead, its table of contents begins with stories of people who lived in the ancient Near East thousands of years ago. Next come books of poetry, followed by books written by fiery prophets warning about the wrath of the Assyrian and Babylonian armies. Next are the New Testament Gospels telling stories about what Jesus said and did, about his Crucifixion and resurrection. These are followed by twenty-one letters, called the

Epistles, written by people called apostles, to Christians living in the Roman Empire two thousand years ago. Finally, about where the troubleshooting guide should be, there's the Book of Revelation with stories of multiheaded beasts and dragons. This is definitely not written like an owner's manual.

I've heard people refer to the Bible as an acronym for

Basic
Instructions
Before
Leaving
Earth

As fun as the acronym is, the Bible is neither basic nor simply instructions for what to do before you die.

Some treat the Bible as though it were a Magic 8 Ball—do you remember the Magic 8 Ball? It looks like a regular billiards ball, but on the bottom is a glass window. Inside there is mysterious blue fluid and a die with twenty sides and twenty different sayings. You ask the Magic 8 Ball a question—"Should I quit my job to find something better?"—and shake the ball. One side of the die comes up with your answer: "Signs point to yes." Many treat the Bible the same way. We ask God a question, "Should I quit my job to find something better?" and then we flip open the Bible to some random page and read, "He makes Lebanon skip like a calf, and Sirion like a young wild ox" (Psalm 29:6—yes, I actually flipped my Bible open to see what would happen with a random verse!). Hmm. Perhaps it's not meant to work like the Magic 8 Ball.

Some expect the Bible to be a book of systematic theology, carefully laying out doctrine and dogma in each verse. But while Christian systematic theology is grounded in the Bible, you'll seldom find doctrine carefully spelled out in the biblical text. Try searching for an explanation of the Trinity, or a comprehensive explanation of atonement theories, or how it is that Jesus is both human and divine. Even a chapter giving a complete explanation of the meaning of baptism would be great, but you won't find this either.)

I attended a meeting of the Young Earth Creationists in Kansas City several years ago. Nice folks but very intense. Evolution is a lie. The evidence points to an earth that is less than ten thousand years old. Amid the comments was this one: "There is only one eyewitness account of Creation. It is found in Genesis 1 and 2. God knows what he did, and he told us in his Word. And God does not lie." For them at least, Genesis 1 and 2 contain an eyewitness account of what happened at Creation, dictated by God to Moses, and therefore the most accurate account, upon which all scientific theories must be built. Yet the Bible doesn't read like a science textbook, and even its Creation accounts do not read like treatises on cosmology or physics or biology.

Some read the Bible as though it were a book of promises from God. I met a woman several years ago who was angry with God. She had gone to church her whole life. She was part of a women's Bible study for years. Her son became gravely ill, and the women in her Bible study agreed with her to "stand upon the Word" and to trust its promises. They "claimed" certain scriptures like Psalm 91:3, "Surely he will save you from the fowler's snare and from the deadly pestilence" and James 5:14, "Is any among you sick? Let them call the elders of the church pray over them and anoint them with oil in the name of the Lord. And the prayer offered in faith will make the sick person well" (NIV). Yet her son died. The Bible now seemed to her a book of broken promises.

I'd suggest that each of the above concepts about the Bible is flawed, and when the Bible is read while holding these assumptions the reader will, at some point, become confused, misguided, or profoundly disappointed. While I've described what the Bible is not, in the remainder of this section, I'd like to help you think about what the Bible *is*. That answer is a bit more complex and rich than our pat answers might imply.

CHAPTER 2

A Biblical Geography and Timeline

You may or may not have enjoyed geography or history when you were in school, but it can be really helpful to know just a little geography as you dig deeper into the Bible. And I find most people appreciate having some frame of reference for when biblical events occurred relative to each other and to other world events. Before we consider how and when the Bible was written and those places where we have questions related to its teachings, let's consider the biblical story's place in history and its timeline, and take a look at a couple of maps that will help you understand the biblical story better.

First, because the Bible starts with the Creation story, let's note the current consensus view of science regarding the origins of our universe, the world, and the human race (I'm using "consensus" to capture the view held by a majority of mainstream scientists in the fields of cosmology, astrophysics, geology, and paleontology). The consensus view is that the universe as we know it had its beginning 13.77 billion years ago. The earth is approximately 4.5 billion years old. Dinosaurs as we typically think of them were around from 230 million to about 66 million years ago. The first anatomically modern humans are seen in the fossil record about 200,000 years ago. Art begins to show up on cave walls about 40,000 years ago. The last Ice Age ended about 12,000 years ago.[1] This led to a period called the Neolithic, sometimes called the "Agricultural Revolution," when humans began to move from being hunter-gatherers to raising livestock and farming. Cities begin to emerge around 9000 BC in the region of Mesopotamia and the rest of the Fertile Crescent (the Fertile Crescent included modern-day Iraq, Syria, Lebanon, Israel, and the Nile River basin of Egypt, where there were sufficient rain and floods to support agriculture). The ancient oasis city of Jericho was founded in this period, around 9000 BC.

Around the year 3000 BC, the wheel became more widely adopted, and the smelting of bronze meant stone tools gave way to bronze. Humans in the Fertile Crescent left behind the Stone Age. With bronze tools came more productive harvests and surpluses for trade. The wheel created the opportunity for trade. And bronze weapons created the tools for empires to emerge. It was during this period, starting around 2600 BC, that the Egyptians began building their pyramids.

The biblical story focuses on a man named Abraham and his descendants, who become known as the Israelites and later the Jews. We don't know exactly when Abraham lived, but he's typically ascribed to the middle Bronze Age, with dates for his birth ranging from 2250 BC to 1800 BC. Let's take a look at the timeline for biblical events. I've included on the left the "traditional" dates for biblical events and people, and in the column on the right other events, people, and empires. (There is debate among biblical scholars as to when to date Abraham, the period the Israelites were slaves in Egypt, and Moses and the Exodus. The dates for these three people/events are within two hundred years of the dates shown. Dates become much more accurate starting with King David. Dates for New Testament events are also subject to debate, but are accurate to within a few years.)

Events Described in the Bible	World Events, Empires, and People
4004 BC (TRADITIONAL DATING)	
Creation/universe/earth/people	
2349 BC (TRADITIONAL DATING)	
Worldwide flood	
1900 BC (APPROXIMATE)	
Abraham and Sarah	
1600S BC (APPROXIMATE)	
Israelites enslaved in Egypt	Rigveda—oldest collection of Hindu prayers/hymns written 1700–1100 BC (?)
1300S BC (APPROXIMATE)	
Moses, the Exodus, the Law	
1010 BC	
King David, some of the Psalms written	
970 BC	
King Solomon builds temple to God	
930 BC	
Israel divided into Israel and Judah	
	Homer's *Iliad* and *Odyssey* written in the 800s or 700s BC (?)
722 BC	
Northern Kingdom of Israel destroyed	Assyrian Empire

Events Described in the Bible	*World Events, Empires, and People*
587 BC	
Judah destroyed—the Babylonian Exile	Babylonian Empire
	The Buddha born in 563 BC
	Confucius born in 551 BC
538 BC	
Jews allowed to return to Jerusalem	Persian Empire
516 BC	
Temple rebuilt	Classical Greek period 500–323 BC in politics, literature, arts, democracy in Athens
400S BC	
Old Testament period ends	Socrates and Plato in Greece
	Aristotle 384 BC, Alexander the Great 356–323 BC
300–100 BC	
Septuagint Greek translation of OT	146 BC Rome conquers Greece
	Julius Caesar 100–44 BC
37 BC	
King Herod the Great reigns	Augustus Caesar 63 BC–AD 14
Herod rebuilds the temple	
4 BC	
Jesus is born	
AD 26–30	
Jesus's public ministry	Tiberius Caesar rules Empire, including Judea AD 14–37

Events Described in the Bible	World Events, Empires, and People
AD 34	
Apostle Paul converted	
AD 48	
Council at Jerusalem, Law set aside	
AD 48–65	
Paul's Letters written	
AD 65	
Peter and Paul martyred	Nero Caesar brings localized persecution of Christians, blames them for fire of Rome
AD 66	
Jews revolt against Rome	
AD 70	
Rome destroys Jerusalem and temple	
AD 70–85	
Gospels written	
AD 70–100	
Paul's letters circulating	Mt. Vesuvius destroys Pompeii
AD 95	
Revelation written	Persecutions under Emperor Domitian
AD 110	
Final epistle of NT written (?)	

As a postscript to the timeline above, Mohammed was born 570 years *after* the birth of Christ, and he died in the year AD 632.

Now for a bit of biblical geography. Let's start with a map that shows Europe, Africa, and Asia.

Israel's Location in Context

You can make out Africa, Europe, and of course Asia. Notice what a small place the Holy Land appears on the map. Yet this is where most of the Bible's story takes place. Let's take a closer look . . .

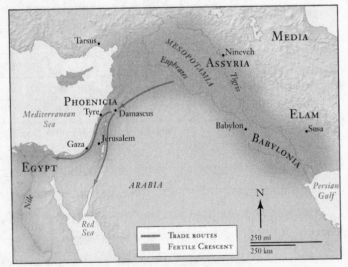

The Ancient Near East

The area marked is the Fertile Crescent. The area between the Tigris and Euphrates Rivers was known as Mesopotamia (which means "the land between the rivers"). Today this is modern-day Iraq. Abraham was from this region. This land was home to the Babylonian Empire, the Assyrian Empire, and later the Persian Empire, all three of which loom large in the biblical story.

At the bottom left of the map is the great Egyptian Empire. Throughout the biblical period, the Egyptian Empire would vie with the Assyrian and later the Babylonian Empires for control of the Holy Land. Why did they care so much about controlling this little piece of ground? Remember the area in the center of the map is the Arabian Desert, and it was treacherous to pass through it. For this reason the ancient highways and trade routes linking Asia to Africa passed along Israel's eastern border, and at least one of these routes passed through the Holy Land. This was the primary land route for trade between two continents. It was also the narrow strip of land through which invading armies from competing empires would need to pass. It held significant strategic importance.

In the time of Abraham, the Holy Land was the land of the Canaanites. Five hundred years later, just after Moses's death, Joshua and the Israelites conquered it. Over time the region was unified under Israel's first king, Saul, who was followed by Israel's great shepherd king, David, and then by the wise Solomon, who built a great temple to God in Jerusalem. Following Solomon's reign, the northern half of the nation rebelled against Solomon's son, and the kingdom was split in two. The northern half retained the name Israel. The southern half retained the capital city, Jerusalem, and the temple but was henceforth called Judah. On the map on the next page, you can see the two nations of Israel and Judah.

The Divided Kingdom of Israel and Judah

Finally, take a look at the map opposite, of the Holy Land in the time of Jesus. To the west is the Mediterranean Sea. On the north side of the map is the Sea of Galilee. To the south is the Dead Sea. The Jordan River connects these two bodies of water. The northern region is called the Galilee, where Jesus grew up. Most of the stories in Matthew, Mark, and Luke occur there. In the center of the country was Samaria. The Samaritans considered themselves to be the true Israelites. The Jewish people considered them a mixed race, Israelites who had intermarried with the people forcibly relocated to the region in the eighth century before Christ. The Samaritans were treated with disdain by the Jews, and they treated the Jews with disdain. Interestingly, today Samaria is known as the West Bank. The people who live there are the Palestinians, and the relationship between Jews and Palestinians is not much different from the relationship between Jews and Samaritans in Jesus's day. Finally, to the south of Samaria was Judea. Jerusalem with its temple was located here. Bethlehem, where Jesus was born, was just southwest of Jerusalem.

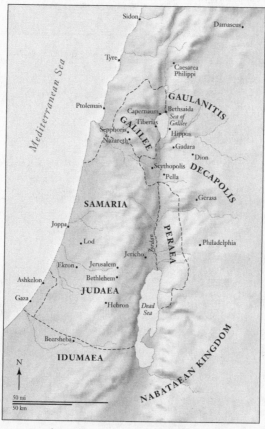

The Holy Land in the Time of Jesus

I'd like to encourage you to actually visit the Holy Land. I've been there on many occasions, filming small group studies on the life of Jesus, leading groups, and once hiking on my own with nothing but a backpack and a Bible. The scriptures come alive when you actually see the places described in them. It is for this reason the Holy Land has been described as the "fifth gospel."

With this historical and geographical background, it's time for us to take a quick walk through the entire Old Testament. Grab a Bible—you're going to need it. We're going to walk through the entire Old Testament in fifteen minutes.

❧ *The Old Testament*

CHAPTER 3

The Old Testament in Fifteen Minutes

If you've always wanted to read straight through the Old Testament but never quite made it, this chapter is for you. I'm going to summarize the entire Old Testament in fifteen minutes (ten if you are a fast reader!). Grab your Bible and let's walk through the Old Testament together.

Allow me to preface our journey through the Old Testament by mentioning that what Christians consider the Old Testament is simply "The Bible" for Jews. It is not "old." It represents their defining story. The Jewish Bible, often referred to as the Hebrew Bible, contains the same books as the Protestant Old Testament, but in a different arrangement. We'll discuss the arrangement later, but for now it is helpful to know that the Jewish Bible is divided into three sections: The Torah (or Law), the Prophets, and the Writings. The Christian Old Testament changes the order to the Torah, the Writings and then the Prophets.

Open to Genesis chapter 1, keeping your finger there, and then turn to Genesis chapter 11. The stories that appear in these eleven chapters are primeval and archetypal (they date to before recorded history, and they are stories that point to something bigger—they tell us about the persons named in them, but their real point is to tell us about ourselves). There are parallels to some of these stories that appear in other ancient Near Eastern religions—particularly the Creation stories and the story of the Flood, which likely share a common source—but the biblical stories make a very different point, and they offer a very different picture of God. The stories in Genesis 1–11 are not merely (or perhaps not at all) meant to teach ancient history; they are meant to teach us about ourselves, about the human condition. They teach us about our universal struggle to resist temptation, the lure of forbidden fruit, the human propensity toward violence, and pride.

From Genesis 12 on, the Old Testament becomes the story of the Israelites and their unique relationship with God. It is a story of God's call for them to be his people, and the story of the covenant he makes with them. But it also recounts how God's people struggled, and often failed, to fulfill the covenant.

The biblical story also involves a narrow strip of land about the size of New Hampshire that God gave to this people. This is the Promised Land, and it was home for the Jewish people. It is a very valuable piece of land because, as we learned in the last chapter, the major trade routes from Africa to Asia pass through it. Hence there's always a larger kingdom or empire wanting to control it, and this is part of the drama of Israel's story.

The Book of Exodus tells the story of God graciously delivering the Israelites from slavery in Egypt by way of a man named Moses, a stuttering goatherder and a fugitive from the law—precisely the kind of guy God chooses for great things! (No, really!) God gives the people the Ten Commandments and the Law to order their new society. Their new kingdom is meant to be a light to the nations, and God himself is their king. God (along with Moses) leads them to the Promised Land—the Land of Canaan—and delivers the land into their hands. We've just covered Exodus, Leviticus, Numbers, Deuteronomy, and Joshua.

Once in the land, the people struggle, repeating in their own way the story of Adam and Eve. When things are going well, they tend to forget about God. They focus on gaining wealth or on their own pleasure. They worship the idols their own hands have made. They no longer demonstrate love and justice. They stop helping the poor. God withholds his protection, and Israel's enemies begin to attack. Israel cries out to God for help. God delivers them (through Judges, then Kings), and all is well again, until they forget God once more, focus on wealth and pleasure, and practice injustice and idolatry, so God withholds his hand again.

During this time, the kings who are meant to shepherd the people on behalf of God instead lead them away from God. After the cycle of turning from God, attack, repentance, and deliverance has been repeated multiple times, the northern half of the country is eventually captured by the Assyrians in 722 BC. The ten northern tribes of Israel are forcibly relocated to other parts of the Assyrian Empire. They intermarried with those living where they are scattered, and thus largely became assimilated into the Assyrian Empire. One hundred and thirty years later, the same thing happens in the southern half of the country, only this time the Babylonians defeat the Jews. Jerusalem and its temple are destroyed. The people are taken into exile in Babylon. This time the people of Judah seek to preserve their national identity and refuse to be assimilated. We've just covered the books of Joshua, Judges, 1 and 2 Samuel, 1 and 2 Kings, and 1 and 2 Chronicles.

After fifty years in exile, God once more delivers his people from bondage, brings them back to the Promised Land, and calls them to rebuild their temple and the city walls. (This is the story of Ezra and Nehemiah and, tangentially, Esther, and with this we've completed what Christians view as the historical books of the Old Testament.) Thus Genesis through Esther review Israel's history from the Creation of the world to the return from exile in Babylon. The story is told chronologically and covers, not counting Genesis 1–11, a period from around 2000 BC to about 430 BC.[1] It is one sweeping story of "covenant making and covenant breaking," in the words of theologian Albert Outler. If you put one finger in your Bible at Genesis 1, another at the end of Esther, and then another at the end of the Old Testament, you'll see that roughly the first half of the Old Testament is devoted to recounting Israel's story.

Let's pause for a minute and recognize something about history. Ask a Republican and a Democrat to each tell you the history of America for the last hundred years and you'll likely hear the same names but very different stories. The same is true for biblical authors. If you were to read the account of King David in 2 Samuel and then look at how the writer of 1 Chronicles tells his story, you'd find that they are very different accounts. The history of Israel told in the Old Testament is told from the particular theological and historical perspective of each of the writers and final editors. The writers of the books of Samuel and Kings had one slant, the writer of Chronicles another. The human authors and editors of the Old Testament brought their own experiences and presuppositions to the task of writing. We don't often think about this when we read the Bible. We tend to focus on God's role in inspiring scripture, but we value scripture when we also recognize the contributions and ideas of scripture's human authors. (This will help us as we seek to resolve some of the questions and conflicts we mentioned in the first chapter.) Let's continue our walk through the Old Testament.

Now put your finger at the beginning of the Book of Job, then find the end of the Song of Songs (or Song of Solomon). What you have here is the poetry and wisdom literature of the Old Testament. Start at Song of Solomon and flip backward to Job. Notice that the words on your pages are not prose but poetry. Hebrew poetry doesn't rhyme—it repeats. What I mean is that the poetry of the Jews starts with a statement, then the next line either repeats the first statement in different words or states its opposite—either way, the aim is to drive the point home. Hebrew poetry has a rhythm all its own.

These Writings appear in the middle (the heart) of the Old Testament, and this is appropriate because they capture the heart and soul of the Jewish people—both the joyful moments in life, as when the psalmist cries out, "Shout for joy to the Lord, all the earth!" (Psalm 100:1, NIV), and the difficult moments when faith is shattered: "My God, my God, why have you forsaken me?" (Psalm 22:1).

Job begins these writings. It is an epic poem addressing the question of suffering. In some ways, Job is a counterbalance to the historical books we've just looked at. They routinely suggest that suffering comes from unfaithfulness to God. But the Book of Job stands against all those books, both in its location in the Bible (butting right up against them in the Old Testament) and in its message, which makes clear that Job was a righteous man, and yet he suffered—thus countering the idea that suffering is always a punishment for sin.

From Job, we enter the Psalms—Israel's hymn and prayer book—composed across the course of Israel's history, during the good times and the bad, with joyful songs of praise and not a small number of laments, cries for help in times of trouble. Next comes Proverbs, short pithy sayings that communicate the kind of knowledge that is gained by life experience. Similar pithy sayings were found throughout the ancient Near East. Here's a great one: "A generous person will be blessed, for he shares his food with the poor" (Proverbs 22:9).

Ecclesiastes is the existential wrestling of a wealthy man at the end of his life who recognizes the futility of all he has worked for his entire life. Finally there's the Song of Songs, which rounds out the wisdom books, offering a tribute to romantic love and intimacy. Despite the church's best effort at trying to see this book as an allegory of God's love for the church, most scholars see it as a bit of erotic poetry to remind us that God invented sexual desire, and it is a good gift.

With that, you've completed the Writings, or the poetic and wisdom books, of the Old Testament. Which leaves only the Prophets. The Prophets are organized into two groups, the major prophets and the minor prophets (the designation relates to the length of the book). Within these groups, they are organized roughly—not exactly but roughly—chronologically. The earliest prophets in both the major and minor groups date from the 700s BC, and the last prophets around the year 400 BC.[2] In biblical times, prophets were not soothsayers or fortune-tellers. They were not interested in telling the future. They were social critics sounding the alarm that if the Jews continued walking away from God, God would withhold his protection, and one or another empire or some natural disaster would inevitably come and bring destruction. The prophets were the spiritual and ethical conscience of the nation.

Turn to Isaiah chapter 1 and read verses 10–20. These perfectly capture the message of the prophets. The first two-thirds of Isaiah relates to the 700s BC, when people were going through the motions of religiosity. They brought their sacrifices and observed the holy days, but they ignored justice; they didn't care for the widows and orphans or help the oppressed. But even then, in that moment, if the people would only repent, "though your sins are like scarlet, they shall be like snow" (Isaiah 1:18). Typically the people did not repent, and the warnings became more and more dire, foretelling national catastrophes. But nearly always, near the end of the prophet's writings, there would come words of comfort and hope promising that God would one day redeem his people and bring them back. It was in this context that some prophets foretold a future king who would rule with righteousness and justice—one who would be anointed by God to lead the people. The Hebrew word for "anointed one" is *Messiah*. The Greek word is *Christ*. What I've just described captures the general tenor of the Prophets.

Put your finger at Isaiah 1 and another finger at Malachi 4, and you can see that the section devoted to the Prophets is slightly longer than the Writings. Taken together, they are roughly equal to the story of Israel's history from Genesis to Esther. And with that, you've taken a journey through the entire Old Testament in fifteen minutes or less.

With all this in mind, let's come back to the question "What is the Bible?" You've seen that it is not an owner's manual, a Magic 8 Ball, a systematic theology textbook, nor a book of promises. It is first the story of the people of Israel and their faith in God. It is also a story about their God and his will and purposes for his people. It does not read like a book dictated by God. It reads like a diverse set of writings—short stories, law codes, court histories, poetry, and prophetic warnings and promises—written by people who were reflecting upon their story in the light of their faith. In the midst of reading Israel's story, we find our own story. And through their stories, and their experiences and reflections about God, we hear God speaking to us.

In the next chapter, we'll consider when and how the Old Testament came to be written.

CHAPTER 4

Who Wrote the Old Testament, When, and Why

I was sitting on an airplane reading my Bible when the man next to me struck up a conversation. (I've found that reading my Bible on a plane either causes those around me to keep quiet or leads them to want to talk!) He said, "I've always thought it was amazing how God wrote out the entire Bible on tablets of stone!" I replied, gently so as not to embarrass him, "It was only the Ten Commandments that were said to be written on stone tablets by the finger of God." He responded, "Oh, I always wondered how they carried that whole thing around!"

If the entire Old Testament was not inscribed by the finger of God on stone tablets, how, and when, and by whom was it written? Let's start with the foundational books of the Old Testament: the first five books, known variously as the Torah, the Pentateuch, the Law of God, the Books of the Covenant, the Law of Moses, the Books of Moses, or simply Moses.

Moses wrote these first five books—everyone knows that,

right? Well, not so fast. They were traditionally ascribed to Moses, though since at least the 1600s this idea has been questioned. The books don't claim that Moses wrote them. In fact, the books speak of Moses in the third person, as though they were written by someone else. There are other clues that Moses did not write these books. Look at Genesis 12:6, in which the author describes Abraham's journey to the land of Canaan (what would later be the land of Israel): "At that time the Canaanites were in the land." During the entire time that Moses was alive, there were Canaanites in the land. This verse is one of many clues that Genesis and the rest of the Torah was written after the Canaanites had largely been removed from the land, which didn't happen until after Moses's death. Here's another clue: take a look at Numbers 12:3, "Now the man Moses was very humble, more so than anyone else on the face of the earth." If Moses wrote that, he was not the most humble man on the face of the earth! If you turn to the last eight verses of Deuteronomy, you'll find that they describe Moses's death—and it would have been a bit hard for Moses to have written that.

Exodus clearly claims that Moses did write some things down, particularly the Law, or portions of it that were given directly by God (see Deuteronomy 31:24 and Exodus 24:4). This was known as "the Book of the Covenant." So the internal witness of the books points to Moses having written sections, particularly portions of the Law. But they are rightly called the five books of Moses because Moses is, apart from God, the central figure in Exodus, Leviticus, Numbers, and Deuteronomy.

This is a great place to stop and recognize the major dividing lines among biblical scholars and archaeologists. Those on the far left in the field of archaeology are often referred to as "minimalists." They tend to be highly skeptical of the historical value of what's written in the Old Testament. They are likely to believe that Abraham and Moses and perhaps even David are fictional characters. They tend to interpret the archaeological record as showing little or no historical support for the biblical accounts of events in the Old Testament, at least those dating back to Moses and the patriarchs. Maximalist archaeologists, on the other hand, tend to believe that the biblical accounts are entirely accurate and that, given enough time, the archaeological evidence will eventually support this view. There is a tendency among the most ardent maximalists to dismiss any archaeological evidence that counters the biblical accounts.

Among biblical scholars, these same categories exist, though we're more used to calling them "liberal" and "conservative." Liberal biblical scholars, like the minimalist school of archaeologists, tend to minimize the historical reliability or factuality of the events described in the Torah. They often speak of the stories in the Torah as "myths," by which they mean stories that may or may not be grounded in actual facts but which were intended to shape the faith and values of a people. Conservative biblical scholars, like maximalists in archaeology, would be more likely to hold that Moses authored nearly the entire Torah and that it was written very nearly in the form we have it, in the fifteenth century before Christ (conservatives tend to date Moses to the fifteenth century, liberals and many moderates to the late fourteenth or thirteenth century before Christ).

What I'm proposing, and what most moderates on the right and the left believe, is something between these two positions. Portions of the Torah were written by Moses, whom I believe to have been a historical figure. But large sections of the story of Moses and the Exodus, as well as the stories found in Genesis, were passed down orally, told and retold over generations. Individual stories and groups of stories were eventually committed to writing, then collected and edited together into the stories as we have them today.

That final editing process likely was not finalized until the time of the Exile or beyond. The same is true of the books of Leviticus, Numbers and Deuteronomy.

Some believe setting aside Mosaic authorship of the Torah diminishes it, but I don't see how. Jesus didn't write the Gospels; they were written decades after his death, drawing upon, as Luke notes, multiple sources, yet this does not diminish them. Nor does the idea that the Torah had a long history of oral tradition and multiple writers and editors remove the idea that the Holy Spirit was at work in this process.

Thus far I've focused on the Torah, because the stories and Law found in it are the foundation for the rest of the Old Testament. The Torah tells Israel's defining story: the descendants of Abraham, Isaac, and Jacob became slaves in Egypt, but God rescued them and made them his own people, binding himself to them and them to him through a covenant commonly called the Law of Moses.

But while the story of the Exodus is foundational to the Old Testament, there is another story, a historical event not debated by scholars, that looms large in shaping the Old Testament as we have it today: the destruction of Jerusalem, along with its temple, and the exile of the Jewish people to Babylon that occurred in 587 BC. To understand the impact this national catastrophe had on the Jewish people, you would need to put yourself in their shoes. Let me help you do this. Begin with September 11, 2001.

Remember, if you are old enough, what you were feeling that day as you watched the television footage of American Flight 11 and United Flight 175 crashing into the World Trade Center, then shortly afterward, the footage of American Flight 77 crashing into the Pentagon. Then the news that United Flight 93 (which we later learned was targeting the U.S. Capitol) had crashed into a field. I am still moved to tears, more than ten years later, when I think about it or see footage of the World Trade Center collapsing.

It was the summer of 587 BC.[1] After a long siege of Jerusalem, the Babylonian army finally breached its walls. They burned the homes in the city. They captured the Jewish king and his sons. The Babylonian leaders made the king watch as they killed his sons. Then they gouged out his eyes so that the last thing he would see was the death of his sons and heirs to the throne. The Babylonians then plundered the temple of its wealth and holy things before setting it on fire. The people stood and wept as they watched it burn. The temple had stood for nearly four hundred years as a sign of God's presence in their midst. King Zedekiah and many of the other leaders in Jerusalem were bound and led away in shackles, forced to make the long march to Babylon, where they would remain in exile, utterly defeated. You can read this tragic story in 2 Kings 25.

To understand the impact on the Jews, go back to 9/11, but now imagine the entire city of Washington, D.C., destroyed—not just the Pentagon, but the White House, the Congress, and all the homes inside the Beltway. Imagine seeing the president's children killed, then the president blinded and led away in chains. Then imagine many of the leading citizens of America forcibly relocated to a far-off country, while America is overrun with foreign troops with no hope of ever regaining freedom. This was the experience of the Jewish people in the Babylonian Exile.

This event shaped the Old Testament in profound ways. First, many of the prophetic books written before this event warned of something like this. Those written after the destruction of Jerusalem were written to help the people make sense of what had taken place (to cite some examples, Jeremiah writes in the years leading up to the Exile, Lamentations is written while the city still smolders, Ezekiel writes during the Exile, and Haggai after the Exile, encouraging the people to rebuild the temple). Many of the psalms come from this period. The historical books from Joshua to 2 Kings appear to have a common editor or group of editors who wrote Israel's history as if trying to make sense of Jerusalem's destruction by looking back over Israel's history. The two books of Chronicles were written after the end of the Exile, when the Babylonians had been conquered by the Persians and the Persian king had given permission for the Jews to return home to rebuild their city and temple.

During these fifty years in exile (some Jews had been taken to Babylon twenty years earlier, hence the total length of the Exile for some was seventy years), the Jews focused on their story, their history, seeking to understand and make sense of their experience. It was during this time, many biblical scholars believe, that most of the Old Testament took its final form as the Jews reflected upon their story, sought to make sense of their plight, and focused on once more being God's covenant people.

You can hear the influence of the Babylonian Exile on the Torah if you take a moment to read Deuteronomy 31:14–29. Here God warns Moses that the day will come when the people will forsake him and break their covenant with God. He would then hide his face from them, and destruction would come. Some believe these words were added by the priests while in exile, others that they were clarified, and some that they were always there, but regardless, it is clear that even in the Torah the Babylonian destruction of Jerusalem and the subsequent exile were shaping the Old Testament text.

The Old Testament is both Israel's story and the story of the God who chose them to be his people, who loved them as a parent loves a child or a lover loves the beloved, who delivered them from slavery and gave them a land of their own, yet who watched them as they turned from their covenant, worshipped foreign gods, and oppressed their own people. It is the story of God hiding his face from his people, and of the neighboring nations attacking and destroying the Jewish people to control their small but valuable piece of real estate. And in the end it is the story of God restoring them once more, bringing them back from exile, and promising them a new king.

CHAPTER 5

Which Books Made It into the Old Testament and Why

Ask a rabbi how many books are in the Hebrew Bible—what Christians call the Old Testament—and the rab will tell you twenty-four. Ask a Catholic priest how many books are in the Old Testament, and he will tell you forty-six. Ask an Eastern Orthodox priest how many books are in the Old Testament, and he will tell you forty-nine or possibly fifty. Ask a Protestant pastor, and you'll hear that we have thirty-nine books in the Old Testament. This points to the question of what books made it into the Old Testament, for whom, and why?

These questions are summarized by a single word in academic circles: canon. "Canon" comes from the Latin and typically means "rule" or "standard" (or ruler or measuring stick). The process by which certain writings come to be considered "canonical" is called canonization. The fact that various Christian bodies still cannot agree upon what books should be included in the Old Testament points to the complexity of canonization. We'll consider the process for canonization of the New Testament in a few chapters, but for now, let's sort through the question of how many books are in the Old Testament.

First, the easy part. The various Jewish bodies agree that there are twenty-four books in their Bible. But these twenty-four are the same as the thirty-nine in the Protestant Old Testament. Here's how that works. The two books of Samuel were originally one document—the Jewish Bible lists them as one book. The two books of Kings were one book or scroll in Hebrew. The two books of Chronicles were the same, as were Ezra and Nehemiah. In addition, long ago the Jews combined all the shorter prophets, known as the minor prophets (again, due to length, not importance) into one book called "The Twelve." Thus the thirty-nine books of the Protestant Old Testament are twenty-four in the Jewish Bible.

Jews do not call their Bible the "Old Testament." They may use that term to connect with Christians, but they do not consider their Testament to be "old." It has become common for Christians to refer to the Old Testament as the "Hebrew Bible" as a way of demonstrating sensitivity and respect to Judaism. Jews often refer to the twenty-four books simply as the Bible; more often, they refer to these books as the Tanakh. The word "Tanakh" is an acronym for the three major divisions of their Bible (think of this as a library with three sections). The three sections of the Tanakh are

Torah—the Law
Nevi'im—the Prophets
Ketuvim—the Writings.

This is both the order of authority these books have in the Jewish community and the order in which they were canonized or became sacred scripture. Notice the difference in order from the Christian Old Testament. Christians begin with the Law, then come the historical books from Joshua to Ezra/Nehemiah, then the poetry and wisdom literature, and finally the prophets. Jews begin with the Law, move to the prophets, and then finish with all the other writings. Another interesting point: the Jews call the books from Joshua to 2 Kings, which Christians consider historical books, the "Former Prophets." These books include the stories of people God raised up to speak on his behalf and lead the children of Israel, some of whom were traditional prophets (Nahum, Elijah, Elisha), others military leaders, others priests, and still others kings. The "Latter Prophets" are those whose words were written down— those Christians typically think of as the prophets.

Notice that the Writings in the Hebrew Bible include not only the wisdom and poetic literature (Psalms, Proverbs, Job, Song of Songs, and Ecclesiastes) but also short stories of heroes, including Ruth, Esther, and Daniel. The Writings also include Chronicles, Ezra, and Nehemiah (all traditionally believed to have been written by Ezra).

Chronicles, Ezra, and Nehemiah were written after the Jews returned from the Exile. Assuming Ezra wrote these books, he drew upon the previously published accounts in the books of Samuel and Kings, which were compiled and edited while the Jews were in exile. But he reworked the material to serve the needs of the community of Jews as they returned to Jerusalem to rebuild the city, the temple, and their life together in the Promised Land. He left out certain details from the books of Samuel and Kings that did not serve his purposes. He emphasized other things that would be helpful for reestablishing the people.

I want you to notice this because it gives us a more complete picture of how the Bible came to be. We often think of the "historical books" of the Old Testament as simply attempting to tell the story of the kings of Israel and Judah. But what was most important to the writers of scripture was not simply recounting history—such records already existed (the books of Kings and Chronicles regularly refer to other sources with more information about the kings they are writing about). They were writing to *interpret* the history in light of the needs of those to whom they wrote. There was an agenda for their work.

History is told from the perspective of the teller, often to meet the needs of the people in a given time. These books, and all the others we've talked about, were the work of thoughtful scribes who were carefully considering what parts of Israel's story needed to be told and how it needed to be told to address the real needs of the community for whom the story or book was being written. For example, it is interesting to compare the differences between Samuel and 1 Chronicles in the telling of David's story. Samuel includes David's foibles and portrays him as a fallen leader. Chronicles portrays David as an idealized king who is to be a pattern for those who would lead Judah in the future.

We've learned that the Jewish Tanakh and the Protestant Old Testament contain the same books in a bit different order. Before we consider why Catholic and Orthodox Old Testaments have a few more books than the Jewish Tanakh and Protestant Old Testament, let's consider what it means to be in the canon and how the process of selecting certain scrolls or documents as more important than others got started.

If you were to ask a Jewish rabbi what the most authoritative books in the Bible are, there would be no hesitation. The answer would be the Torah—the Law of Moses. Why is this? There are several reasons. First, because it contains God's covenant with his people—his promises and his expectations, the latter coming in the form of the 613 laws found in the Torah. Second, because it tells Israel's defining story of God delivering the Israelite slaves and sending them to the Promised Land. This story is celebrated every year in Passover and every weekend on the Sabbath. Third, this is the oldest part of the Bible. Some Jews, like some Christians, believe God dictated this part of the Bible. Most rabbis don't believe this, but they do believe that these books convey, in a special way, God's will and purposes for his people, and that they reveal God's essence and character to humanity. This points us toward the criteria for canonization of the Old Testament.

By the way, even within the Torah, some scriptures were deemed to be of greater authority than others. First were the Ten Commandments, said to have been written by the very finger of God on the stone tablets; these were given a special place in the Ark of the Covenant (the gilded box that represented God's earthly throne). The fact that the Ten Commandments were all of the Law placed in the Ark of the Covenant would seem to say that the heart of the people's covenant with God was what was listed in the Ten Commandments. Second in authority in the Law were the commands referred to in Exodus 24:7 as the "book of the covenant." Moses read these when he led Israel in entering into a covenant with God. Following this came everything else in the Torah.

The next most authoritative books would be the Prophets. The "Former Prophets" reveal God's will and nature by telling the story of God's interaction with his people. They also teach us about human nature by describing the sinners and saints of old. Through the "Former Prophets," we hear God speaking through his spokespersons: the judges, his servants David and Solomon, and the prophets he raised up throughout the period of the kings. The "Latter Prophets" spoke or wrote as they felt urged by the Spirit. Like the "Former Prophets," they revealed God's will for the people of their day. As we ponder their words and the principles behind them, we begin to understand God's purposes and plans for people in our time.

Last, both in chronological order of when the Jewish community accepted them as authoritative and by how directly they reveal God's will and purposes, are the Writings. Jewish rabbis debated up to the time of Christ whether some of the books in this section should be considered scripture. For example, Esther and the Song of Songs never mention God directly. The Song of Songs was also debated for its eroticism. Ecclesiastes was thought by some to offer too dour a perspective on life with its suggestion that all was folly. For this reason, some thought these should not be included among the authoritative writings—those that should be read aloud in synagogue (you still have to be careful which passages from Song of Songs you read aloud in a synagogue or church!). Some debated whether Proverbs should be read aloud, in part because there were at least two proverbs that contradicted one another. Ezekiel was debated in part because at least two of its visions were questioned by rabbis (the vision of the chariot and that of the future temple). But by the end of the first century after Christ, there seemed to be general agreement that the twenty-four (or thirty-nine) books revealed the character and purposes of God, and were thus helpful for reading aloud in the synagogue and studying in private.

But what of the additional books found in the Catholic and Orthodox Old Testaments? About three hundred years before the birth of Jesus, Jews had spread throughout the Greek-speaking world, including a significant community in Alexandria, Egypt, where one of the great libraries of the ancient world was kept. The king of Egypt in the third century before Christ is said to have commissioned a Greek translation of the Law. Tradition has it that seventy or seventy-two Jewish scribes translated the Law from the Hebrew to the Greek, a translation that became known as the Septuagint (from the Latin word for "seventy"). Following the Law, the rest of the sacred Jewish writings were translated. This work of translating continued to sometime around 100 BC. Together these translated writings became known as the Septuagint. But among those writings were at least ten documents not considered authoritative by Jews back in the Holy Land. Some of these ten were familiar to the Jews back in Judea. Some were important to them. But they were debated and generally not accepted as being of the same level of authority or inspiration as the generally accepted books. So, by the time of Jesus, there were two canons of the Old Testament: what is sometimes called the Palestinian Canon and the Septuagint or Alexandrian Canon. It was not quite as cut and dried as this. As I noted earlier, rabbis in Israel were still debating some of the books in the Palestinian Canon until the end of the first century AD.

As you've no doubt begun to surmise, the extra books in the Alexandrian version of the Jewish Bible are the ones that were accepted by the early church into the Christian scriptures. Why did the church choose the Alexandrian Canon? Paul and the early apostles took the gospel outside of Palestine and to the Roman world. Greek was the universal language of the Roman world. Paul wrote his letters in Greek. The final version of the Gospels was written in Greek. Greek became the language of the early church. So the Christians adopted the Greek translation of the Jewish Bible, including its disputed books. The different order of books in the Christian Old Testament compared to the Jewish Tanakh also came from the Septuagint, where the Jews of Alexandria had ordered the books as we have them in our Old Testament.

In first-century Judaism, there was some debate about these extra books. Some Greek-speaking Jews used them, others did not. Likewise among Christians in the first four centuries of the church, there was debate about them, with some fathers of the church accepting them, others rejecting them.

The early church in the West, which became the Catholic

Church, ultimately accepted seven of these books. The early church in the East accepted at least these seven, and some Eastern Orthodox churches accepted ten or more. The Eastern Orthodox churches continue to debate precisely how many of these third- and second-century BC Jewish writings, translated into Greek, should be considered sacred or inspired.

It wasn't until the time of Martin Luther that these books were demoted by the Protestant reformers, henceforth described as valuable books to read but no longer as inspired. Luther included them in his German translation of the Bible in 1534, but he put them in a section between the Old and New Testaments under the title "Apocrypha: These Books Are Not Held Equal to the Scriptures, but Are Useful and Good to Read."[1] Luther also argued that Esther should not have been included in the canon; it should be in the Apocrypha (the word "Apocrypha" means "hidden"). The books or portions of books found in the Roman Catholic Old Testament that Protestants relegate to the Apocrypha are Tobit, Judith, some additions to Esther, Wisdom of Solomon, Ecclesiasticus, Baruch, Epistle of Jeremiah, Song of the Three Children, Story of Susanna, Bel and the Dragon, 1 Maccabees, and 2 Maccabees. The Eastern Orthodox Canon, in addition to those just listed, also includes 1 Esdras, Prayer of Manasseh, 3 Maccabees, 4 Maccabees, and Psalm 151.

Martin Luther, famous for his conviction that doctrine must be grounded in scripture, was willing to question, nearly 1,500 years after the time of the apostles, which books were or were not inspired, authoritative or canonical. Many have a perception that the Old and New Testament documents were clearly delineated by the Holy Spirit, and the Bible as we have it now is the same as the Bible of the early church. But the truth is a bit more complicated than that.

Today it is common for Roman Catholic and Protestant scholars alike to refer to these debated books as Deuterocanonical. This word means "second canon," signifying that they come later than the rest of the canonical books and have a debated status.

As we conclude this chapter, we've learned a bit about how the Old Testament documents came to be canonized, or thought of as sacred scripture. And we've learned that the process was a bit messy and the question of what belongs in the Old Testament is still, to some degree, being debated by Christians.

Let's turn now to the question of how Jesus and the early church thought about and read the Bible.

CHAPTER 6

Jesus and the Old Testament

As we look at what the Bible is and how we read it, it would be helpful to take a few minutes to consider how Jesus looked at and read the Bible. As we've learned, his Bible was not a book. (Books were just being invented in his time. It would take three hundred years before the book would overtake the scroll as the primary means of sharing information.) His Bible was a collection of scrolls, perhaps twenty-four of them, maybe a few more or less. We know he cited or alluded to at least twenty-three of the thirty-nine Protestant Old Testament books in his teaching found in the Gospels.

Today we carry our Bibles with us and read from them each day. Jesus would not have carried his Bible with him—carrying twenty-four scrolls would have been impossible. The longest of the scrolls would have been the Psalms, at about thirty feet. A first-century copy of the Isaiah scroll was found among the Dead Sea Scrolls. It was eleven inches by twenty-four feet. The scriptures were read in the synagogue and expounded upon by the rabbis. It is possible that his family had some scrolls in their home, though it seems more likely that Joseph and Mary were illiterate. He may have grown up going to the synagogue and studying the scrolls during the week. However he learned the scriptures, one thing is clear in reading his words in the Gospels: Jesus had immersed himself in at least some of the scriptures.

The one childhood story we have concerning Jesus, after his birth and infancy, comes from when he was twelve years old. His family had been in Jerusalem to celebrate Passover, and when it was over, Mary and Joseph separately joined the caravan heading back to Nazareth, each assuming Jesus was with the other. A day later, they discovered Jesus was not with the caravan. "After three days they found him in the temple, sitting among the teachers, listening to them and asking them questions. And all who heard him were amazed at his understanding and his answers" (Luke 2:46–47).

The Jewish Mishnah, the record of the oral tradition and religious practices in Judaism going back to the time of Christ, notes that at the age of five children were to begin studying the scriptures, and by ten they were to begin studying the Mishnah—the oral traditions and commentaries on the scriptures, so that by thirteen they could become men, committed to fulfilling the commandments. Centuries later, this commitment to the commandments would be codified in the practice of bar mitzvah (becoming a son of the commandment). This is also the background for the practice of confirmation in Christian churches.

So Jesus grew up studying the scriptures. We can infer which books might have been his favorites by reading the Gospels to see which he quotes or alludes to most frequently. If you do this, you'll find that the Psalms, Isaiah, and Deuteronomy are the three books

Jesus most often refers to, one from each category of the Tanakh—the Law, the Prophets, and the Writings.

Immediately following his baptism, Jesus fasts for forty days, during which time he is tempted in the wilderness. Three of the temptations are recorded in the Gospels. Jesus responds to each temptation by quoting scripture, and all three of the scriptures he quotes are from Deuteronomy chapter 6, one of the most important passages in Judaism. It is in this same chapter that we find what Jesus calls "the first and greatest commandment": "You shall love the Lord your God with all your heart, and with all your soul, and with all your might" (Deuteronomy 6:5).

It's also important to highlight that in two of the temptations the devil quotes scripture to Jesus—a reminder that *just because someone quotes scripture does not mean what he or she says is from God or God's will*. The devil seems to be proficient at quoting scripture.

As you read the Gospels, you'll find that Jesus routinely challenges the prevailing interpretation of scripture and regularly calls his hearers and the Pharisees to move beyond the letter of the law to the spirit of the law. He frustrates the religious leaders by his refusal to abide by the Sabbath restrictions, noting that it is okay to heal or to pluck grain on the Sabbath because "the Sabbath was made for humankind, and not humankind for the Sabbath" (Mark 2:27). Jesus's teaching on the Sabbath stands in stark contrast to Moses, who taught that if a man picked up sticks on the Sabbath, he was to be stoned to death (Numbers 15:32–36). At the same time, he called upon his followers to see the deeper call of the commandments. He noted that while the commandment prohibits adultery, we're not to even look at another with lust in our hearts. Whereas the Law forbids taking out extraordinary revenge, limiting justice to an eye for an eye or a tooth for a tooth, Jesus said his followers were to love their enemies and to forgive.

At one point, Jesus directly takes issue with something Moses taught in Deuteronomy 24:1–4, when Moses allowed for divorce. Jesus said Moses allowed this because of the hardness of the people's hearts, arguing that God's will was that people not divorce except for marital infidelity. This is an interesting scripture to ponder for what it says about Jesus's understanding of the role Moses played in forming the scriptures. It seems to imply that he believed Moses might have shaped the commands in ways he felt were needed and that at least some of these commands did not fully capture the will of God.

Jesus's ethic was a call to live in radical obedience to God. Yet this was coupled with a radical view of grace and an emphasis on God's love for sinners. Though Jesus clearly called out religious leaders for their hypocrisy, he demonstrated amazing mercy toward tax collectors, prostitutes, adulterers, drunkards, and thieves. He expressed both a prophetic anger toward religious hypocrites and amazing pastoral concern for the broken and lost.

I've often felt that much of Jesus's sense of identity and mission was shaped by his reading of Ezekiel 34. Ezekiel was a prophet of the Exile, trying to help the Jews make sense of the destruction of Jerusalem and its temple, while planting seeds of hope that God would one day restore and heal them. You can hear both God's frustration with the religious leaders (the shepherds of Israel) and his concern for the lost in this passage:

> Thus says the Lord God: Ah, you shepherds of Israel who have been feeding yourselves! Should not shepherds feed the sheep? You eat the fat, you clothe yourselves with the wool, you slaughter the fatlings; but you do not feed the sheep. You have not strengthened the weak, you have not healed the sick, you have not bound up the injured, you have not brought back the strayed, you have not sought the lost, but

with force and harshness you have ruled them. So they were scattered, because there was no shepherd; and scattered, they became food for all the wild animals. My sheep were scattered, they wandered over all the mountains and on every high hill; my sheep were scattered over all the face of the earth, with no one to search or seek for them. (Ezekiel 34:2–6)

Later in the same chapter, God promises to send his servant David to care for the sheep. David, of course, died five hundred years earlier. Ezekiel is promising that God will send a new prince, a leader to search for the strays and bring back the lost.

Such passages seem to have profoundly shaped Jesus's heart and ministry. He embodies and lives them. He never directly quotes this passage, but Matthew notes that Jesus had compassion for the multitudes "because they were like sheep without a shepherd." In response to the Pharisees grumbling because Jesus associated with sinners, Jesus said, "Which one of you, having a hundred sheep and losing one of them, does not leave the ninety-nine in the wilderness and go after the one that is lost until he finds it?" (Luke 15:4). And in John 10:11, Jesus says, "I am the good shepherd. The good shepherd lays down his life for the sheep."

Jesus sees in Isaiah's "suffering servant" (see Isaiah 53) a picture of how God intends to use him to save and redeem the world. He is clearly familiar with Zechariah the prophet and his description of the coming of Israel's messiah "riding on a donkey" (Zechariah 9:9). In fact, Jesus intentionally "fulfills" this prophecy by asking his disciples to fetch a donkey as he prepares to enter Jerusalem.

I'd be remiss if I didn't mention the last time Jesus cites scripture before his death. As he hangs upon the cross, he prays the scriptures. In Matthew and Mark, Jesus's dying words are from

Psalm 22:1: "My God, my God, why have you forsaken me?" The Psalm begins with agony but ends with hope. In Luke, his final words are drawn from Psalm 31:5: "Into your hand I commit my spirit," a passage William Barclay suggests was the bedtime prayer taught by Jewish mothers to their children. As he was dying, Jesus was praying the scriptures.

It is interesting that Jesus never set out a doctrine of the Bible. He never defined which books were in and which were out. He did not offer any clear dogma related to the scriptures. But it is clear that many of the writings of the Old Testament profoundly shaped his heart, life, and ministry. He does not appear to have read it woodenly. He does not quote from all parts equally. He favors those passages that portray God's mercy. He sees the scripture as a fore-shadowing of his mission.

It seems appropriate to conclude our reflections with Jesus's own summary of the scriptures. In Matthew 22, Jesus is asked, "What is the most important commandment?" He gives not one but two: " 'You shall love the Lord your God with all your heart, and with all your soul, and with all your mind.' This is the greatest and first commandment. And a second is like it: 'You shall love your neighbor as yourself.' On these two commandments hang all the law and the prophets" (Matthew 22:37–40). These seem to have been the interpretive lens (scholars might call it Jesus's "defin-ing hermeneutical principle") by which Jesus read the whole of his Bible, a point we'll return to in the chapters ahead.

CHAPTER 7

Prophecy, the Old Testament, and the Early Church

On the first Easter, in the afternoon, the resurrected Jesus appears to two disciples as they travel from Jerusalem to a town called Emmaus. They don't recognize him at first. He seems to be a stranger. They are still grieving, not believing that Christ has been raised from the dead. Luke tells us, "Then beginning with Moses and all the prophets, he interpreted to them the things about himself in all the scriptures" (Luke 24:27). Shortly after this, as he says the blessing over the breaking of bread at mealtime, they recognize that the stranger is none other than the resurrected Christ. The story is a powerful one that points to two ways in which the early Christians encountered Christ: they met him in the Eucharist, and they met him as they read the scriptures.

Just to clarify what you already know, the scriptures they read were not the New Testament. The Gospels would not be written for at least another thirty years. The letters of the New Testament would begin to be written in about twenty years. As the early

Christians read the Old Testament, they did so in the light of Christ's suffering, death, and resurrection, and they saw Jesus on nearly every "page."

As F. F. Bruce notes in *The Canon of Scripture*, the Old Testament became a new book. Every story was reread in the light of the gospel story. When the Old Testament spoke of Adam and Eve turning from God and losing paradise, the believers saw Jesus as a second Adam who had come to restore paradise. When God cursed the serpent in Genesis 3:15, his promise that Eve's offspring would crush the head of the snake was no longer simply about human beings stepping on snakes. It was a prophecy about Jesus, who would come to crush the devil's works. When God asked Abraham to sacrifice his only son, Isaac, this foreshadowed what God himself would do in giving his only son to save the world. When the laws providing for atonement and forgiveness were read through the lens of Jesus's death on the cross, he became the lamb of God who takes away the sins of the world.

There were hundreds of points when the Old Testament seemed to foreshadow, even foretell, the life of Jesus. It seemed to early Christians that the entire story of God's saving work with his people Israel pointed toward this climactic event when Jesus would come as a suffering king, laying down his life for his people. Most contemporary Christians continue to read the Old Testament in this way, and some have suggested that there are as many as 365 biblical prophecies that Jesus fulfilled, thus proving he was the Jewish messiah.

I, too, see Jesus when I read the Old Testament. I see him foreshadowed in many places, and I hear an echo of him in others. There are many places where what God does in the Old Testament points toward what God will do through Jesus Christ. And there are messianic expectations, promises, and hopes that are clearly fulfilled in Jesus. But having said that, it's important to recognize how these "prophecies" actually function, for a Jewish rabbi would be quick to point out that most of these passages are read differently by Jewish scholars than they are by New Testament writers or modern-day Christians. In a college-level course at most state universities, your professor would be quick to point this out as well. Let's consider a couple of examples.

In Matthew's account of the birth of Jesus, Matthew describes the annunciation to Joseph, in which the angel appears to him in a dream and announces that the child Mary has conceived is in fact from the Holy Spirit and not from her union with a man. Then Matthew notes, "All this took place to fulfill what had been spoken by the Lord through the prophet: 'Look, the virgin shall conceive and bear a son, and they shall name him Emmanuel'" (Matthew 1:22–23). Matthew cites this as the fulfillment of a prophecy from Isaiah 7:14. Who could possibly argue that this is not an amazing fulfillment of prophecy?

But grab your Bible and open it to Isaiah 7 and look at the context of this verse about the virgin bearing a child. The year is around 735 BC, and Isaiah is quoting God talking to King Ahaz of the kingdom of Judah. Two kings are preparing to attack Judah. King Ahaz and the people of Judah are terrified. God speaks through Isaiah, offering a prophetic promise that the two kings preparing the attack will fail. Then, in verse 10, God says to King Ahaz, "Ask me for a sign that what I've said is true." But Ahaz says, "I'll not ask for a sign, nor put the LORD to the test." So Isaiah responds, in verse 14,

> The Lord himself will give you a sign. Look, the young woman is with child and shall bear a son, and shall name him Immanuel. He shall eat curds and honey by the time he knows how to refuse the evil and choose

the good. For before the child knows how to refuse the evil and choose the good, the land before whose two kings you are in dread will be deserted. (Isaiah 7:14–16)

Look carefully at this passage and what it is prophesying. Who is the young woman Isaiah describes? By the way, in the Greek Old Testament, the Septuagint, the word for young woman is *parthenos*—virgin. In the Hebrew Old Testament, the word is *almah,* which often means "young woman" but can also mean "virgin." The woman may be Isaiah's wife, or perhaps another young woman. But it is clear that the sign is that she will give birth, and before the child knows how to refuse evil and choose the good— this would be the age at which children are accountable for their deeds, which the Jews believed was thirteen—the land of the two kings Ahaz feared would be deserted.

This prophecy was in fact fulfilled in 722 BC, thirteen years after Isaiah spoke these words, when the kingdoms of Ahaz's foes were destroyed by the Assyrians. Chances are that Matthew knew this. What he saw in this story was a kind of foreshadowing of what God had done in Jesus. God brought a child into the world, through a young woman or virgin, as a sign that God was with King Ahaz. And God brought a child into the world through Mary, as a sign to the human race that God is with us—Immanuel.

This is really unnerving information for many college students who take a course on the Bible as literature. Because their faith in Jesus is in part built upon the fulfillment of prophecies, when they discover that at least some of the Old Testament prophecies appeared to have a different meaning for earlier readers, they find themselves questioning everything they've been taught about Jesus. But if we understand that the early Christians and the New Testament writers described this type of foreshadowing as prophecy and understood that Christ was a greater or deeper fulfillment of things God had done in the past—a kind of climactic fulfillment—we can appreciate the original setting of these prophecies and how they point toward the life and ministry of Jesus.

Let's take another example. Isaiah 53 is one of the passages from the Old Testament most often quoted in the New Testament. It is a powerful piece of scripture about someone who suffers on behalf of the people of Israel. Among its familiar words are these: "He was wounded for our transgressions, crushed for our iniquities; upon him was the punishment that made us whole, and by his bruises we are healed" (Isaiah 53:5). This passage, as read by early Christians, points toward Christ's suffering and death. But ask a Jewish rabbi what it means, and she or he will tell you that the servant, throughout Isaiah, represents the nation of Israel, and that this passage is about the suffering Israel bore in the Babylonian destruction of Jerusalem and the Exile, for the sins of the nation and the nations around her. That rabbi will point to passages like Isaiah 49:3, which clearly describes Israel as the suffering servant: "You are my servant, Israel, in whom I will be glorified."

Isaiah is a fantastic and complex book. It is written in Hebrew poetry—notice that the passages in your Bible are laid out in verse, not prose. Poetry is filled with powerful images that move the soul. The power of poetry is its ability to speak to new situations. Its images can be taken from the original context, retaining that context as a backdrop, and reapplied to new situations. In some ways, when I think of the prophecies of the Old Testament, particularly Isaiah, I think of the powerful words of Abraham Lincoln's Second Inaugural Address and his Gettysburg Address, found on the walls inside the Lincoln Memorial in Washington, D.C. These words were a powerful backdrop when, one hundred years after Lincoln uttered them, Martin Luther King, Jr., stood on those same steps and said, "I have a dream!" Lincoln's words were no longer about the emancipation of slaves and the Civil War, but about the civil rights movement of the 1960s.

To fully appreciate a magnificent book like Isaiah, you must read it at three levels. You should ask first, "What did these words mean when Isaiah first wrote them? How were they understood by the people he was addressing?" Then ask, "How did Jesus and the early Christian community reapply and reinterpret these words? What did they mean to Jesus as he was preparing for the cross? What did they mean to early Christians as they reflected upon the life, death, and resurrection of Jesus?" And finally, you should ask, "What might these words mean for my life today? What would God want me to hear from them now?"

When Matthew quotes an Old Testament passage and concludes, "This was to fulfill what had been spoken through the prophet," it is helpful to know that the Greek word translated as "fulfill" can also mean "complete." Many Old Testament texts quoted in the New Testament had an initial fulfillment nearer the time of the prophet. Others were not predictive texts at all. The New Testament authors saw in these statements a foreshadowing of the life and ministry of Jesus. The words of the Old Testament may have had a fulfillment in the past, but they took on new meaning in the light of Jesus's life and ministry, his death and resurrection. Jesus offered a completion, or a climactic redefinition, of what these ancient words meant because Jesus is the climax of God's saving work in the world.

So, when the young woman Isaiah described to King Ahaz finally gave birth to a child, eight centuries before the birth of Christ, that child was a sign to King Ahaz that God was with him and he need not be afraid of his enemies. In that child's birth, the words of Isaiah 7:14 were fulfilled. But 735 years later, when Mary gave birth to Jesus, these ancient words took on a whole new, deeper and more complete meaning. For *this* child, who was born to Mary, would be a physical reminder to the *entire* human race that God is with us—he is Immanuel. Thus Jesus *completes* a promise given by God some 735 years before he was born.

Am I suggesting that nothing in the Old Testament predicted the coming of Christ? No. I think it is possible that God offered prophecy through the prophets that would be partially fulfilled in one time, but with the full intention of completing it in and through Jesus Christ—in some ways hints of what God had in mind for a future time. But I am suggesting that most of the prophecies could be understood to be pointing to events far closer to the time of the prophets.

One final word: as noted earlier in this book, the prophets were not primarily focused on foretelling but rather on "forth-telling." They were speaking powerfully on behalf of God to the people of their time, offering words of comfort and, more often, words of challenge or critique. They called people to repentance, warned of impending disaster if the people did not repent, and offered words of hope for a future deliverance after the disaster had passed. They described a pattern of straying, suffering, redemption, and hope that has been repeated throughout history—hence the time-less nature of their words. Jesus represents the climactic work of God in redeeming and saving his people from their straying and suffering, and thus in a very real sense he completes all the prom-ises of the prophets for redemption and hope.

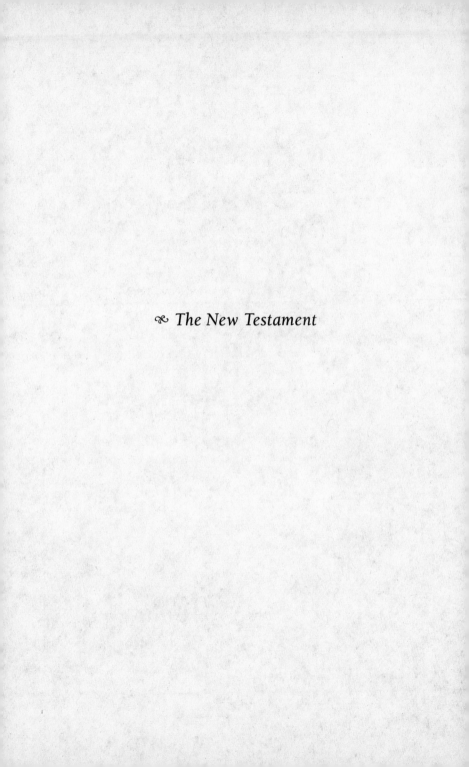

❧ *The New Testament*

CHAPTER 8

The New Testament in Fifteen Minutes

For the next few chapters we're going to turn our attention to the New Testament. Please have a Bible close at hand. In this chapter, we're going to walk through the entire New Testament in fifteen minutes or less.

Start off by putting your finger where the Old Testament ends and the New Testament begins. Now, put another finger at the last chapter of the Book of Revelation. Notice how much of the Bible is the Old Testament and how much is the New Testament. There are approximately 23,145 verses in the Protestant Old Testament, and 7,958 verses in the New Testament.[1] This means that, by verse count, the Old Testament makes up three-fourths of the Bible, and the New Testament one-fourth. As we've learned, for the earliest Christians, their Bible was the Old Testament, and they saw these scriptures as bearing witness to Jesus.

Remember how the Old Testament falls largely into four categories? First are the five books of the Law. They are Israel's defining story of Moses and the giving of the Law. Everything that follows in the Old Testament is a kind of commentary and living out of that story. Next in Protestant Bibles come the historical books—Israel's story from the conquest of Canaan to the destruction of Jerusalem and finally its rebuilding. Then come the Writings—the poetic psalms, the wisdom literature and other reflections upon faith. Finally come the Prophets, who challenge people to remain faithful to God, warn of impending judgment, and offer hope for those who endure.

Now, let's compare the organization of the Old Testament to the New Testament. The New Testament begins with the four Gospels: Matthew, Mark, Luke, and John—the stories of Jesus Christ, the new covenant, and his commands. This parallels the Torah, and just as the Torah tells Israel's defining story, the Gospels tell Christianity's defining story. Next comes the Acts of the Apostles, the story of the early church. It encompasses the period from Christ's ascension to heaven in AD 30 to around AD 65, when Paul is under arrest awaiting the trial in Rome that would lead to his death.[2] This is a much shorter history than the historical books of the Tanakh, but it is similar in its attempt to tell Christianity's early history. Next come the New Testament "writings"—the letters from the apostles reflecting upon the meaning of faith in Christ and the living of that faith. We might think of these as mirroring the wisdom literature in the Writings in the Old Testament. Finally, the New Testament ends with the Book of Revelation—a book that, like the prophets of the Old Testament (and drawing significantly from several of them), challenges the early Christians to remain faithful to God, warns of impending judgment, and offers hope for those who endure to the end. If we laid these out side by side, they would look like this:

OLD TESTAMENT	NEW TESTAMENT
Five Books of Moses	Four Gospels
Historical Books	Acts of the Apostles
Writings (Wisdom Literature)	Letters from the Apostles
Prophets	Revelation

Let's take five minutes for a little more detailed walk through your New Testament.

The New Testament begins with the story of Jesus Christ, who was sent from God to "seek and to save those who are lost" (Luke 19:10). The central theme of Jesus's preaching and teaching, at least in Matthew, Mark, and Luke's Gospels, is the kingdom of God. This phrase and its counterpart, the kingdom of heaven, appear eighty-two times in the first three Gospels. The kingdom of God implies that God is the rightful ruler over the entire cosmos. On our little planet, from Adam and Eve on, humanity has struggled to submit to God's rule. Living in rebellion, humanity has brought suffering and pain to the earth. Violence, warfare, injustice, hate—these are all expressions of the kingdoms of humankind.

Jesus announced the good news that God is still king and invited his hearers to repent. To repent was to turn away from rebellion and once more confess their allegiance to God and his kingdom.

After calling his hearers to repent, Jesus lays out for his hearers what the kingdom of God looks like and how one lives after hailing God as one's king. He came not only to announce and remind his hearers that God is king but as the physical embodiment of the king. He walks on this earth, unleashing the power of the kingdom against the forces of darkness, the liberating power of the kingdom for the oppressed, and the healing power of the gospel for the sick.

Jesus says in the first three Gospels that the kingdom of God is "upon you," and at least once he notes that the kingdom of God is "within you." Each time someone repents and becomes a follower of Christ, the rebellion experiences defeat and the king's rightful rule expands. The impact of each person choosing to follow Christ, living a life in service to God the king, is incalculable. Every relationship, every interaction, every decision across the course of that person's life is different because of this one decision to follow Christ, who comes representing the kingship of God. The world is restored by this preaching of the kingdom and the faith-filled response of those who repent. The message of the kingdom is summarized by two commandments: love God with all your heart, soul, mind, and strength, and love your neighbor as you love yourself.

In John's Gospel, the focus is not so much on the idea of the kingdom of God (the phrase appears only twice in John), though the concept is still present. The emphasis there is on the life Jesus gives us, and that by believing and "abiding" in him, we find life in his name. This relationship with Jesus leads us to a life of love, the same ultimate message we find in Matthew, Mark, and Luke.

In each of the Gospels, Jesus reveals the heart and character of God. He demonstrates God's frustration with religious hypocrisy, God's compassion for those who are poor and oppressed, God's mercy toward those who sin, God's healing power for those who are broken. He calls human beings into right relationship with God, commands them, above all else, to love God and neighbor, and insists that this love includes compassion for the hungry and forgiveness for those who sin against us. He even demands that we apply this love to our enemies.

From a Christian perspective, his trial is an indictment of the human race, his death a judgment upon humanity's sin and a means of revealing God's will, God's grace, and God's love. His resurrection demonstrates God's triumph over sin, evil, hopelessness, despair, and ultimately death. After his resurrection, he sends his disciples into the world to announce his kingdom and to lead a revolution that would put the world aright. That is the gospel story. It is contained in Matthew, Mark, Luke, and John, though, as we will see in the next chapter, the Gospels tell that story in somewhat different ways.

Following the resurrection and ascension of Christ, the early Christians were filled with the Holy Spirit and, through the Spirit's influence and power, continued the ministry of Jesus, healing the sick, casting out demons, and teaching and preaching about Christ and the kingdom he had announced. The disciples took the gospel first to Jerusalem, then to Judea and Samaria, and finally to the "uttermost parts of the earth." A Jewish Pharisee named Paul, who initially sought to suppress the Christian movement, was himself converted to Christ and became its greatest evangelist. He took the gospel across the Roman Empire, establishing churches everywhere he went. This is the story found in the Acts of the Apostles.

Paul started new faith communities, set aside leaders in these fledgling churches, and then would leave to go preach in another town. When those leaders had questions or concerns, they sent messages to Paul, who wrote letters in response. His letters taught, encouraged, and sought to offer practical advice and help to these new Christians. Others also wrote to various communities doing much the same—challenging, encouraging, correcting, and teaching. Twenty-one of the twenty-seven New Testament "books" are letters from the apostles.

The letters of the apostles are organized into three collections. The first two collections are the letters of Paul. The first contains

Paul's letters to churches, arranged from longest to shortest. Next come Paul's letters to individuals, again arranged from longest to shortest. Thirteen of the twenty-one letters of the New Testament are attributed to Paul. The remaining eight letters appear after Paul's collection, which reflects the priority given to Paul's letters in the early church. We'll consider the letters in more detail in chapters 9 and 10.

Finally, the New Testament ends with a book written thirty years after the death of Peter and Paul, one filled with visions of the conflict between good and evil and of evil's final defeat. Various interpretations have been given to this vision. The opening chapters are key to making sense of the Book of Revelation. They tell of seven churches in Asia Minor (modern-day Turkey) and the message of the Lord for each of them. Among them, we find that one group has "lost your first love." Another is "lukewarm." Some have allowed false teachers and seem to have compromised their values, adopting the values of the Roman Empire rather than the kingdom of God. Some practice sexual immorality, eat food sacrificed to idols, or are becoming materialistic. The Book of Revelation is a message to these believers, who had either compromised or were in danger of compromising.

Revelation insists that the kingdom or empire of God will ultimately triumph over the Roman Empire and every other empire that follows in its steps. Those who persevere and remain steadfast in serving Christ regardless of the cost will be accepted into paradise. Interestingly, Revelation ends where Genesis began—in a garden. The paradise that was lost by Adam and Eve in Genesis is restored by Christ in Revelation.

That's the New Testament message in fifteen minutes. Its message of Christ and his kingdom still has the power to change lives. My own was changed as I read its words, put my trust in Christ, and began to follow. Each day as I read from this book, I encounter, once again, God's Son, and I am reminded of his mission for my life and for his world.

With this overview of the New Testament's message in mind, let's take a closer look at the New Testament documents themselves. We'll begin with the earliest documents written in our New Testament, the letters.

CHAPTER 9

Reading Someone Else's Letters

Whereas the Old Testament documents/books were written over a thousand years, the New Testament documents were written over the course of just fifty years. Paul's letters, which represent a significant portion of the New Testament, were written over just a fifteen-year period.[1] The story of how, when, and why they were composed is a fascinating one.

As we learned in the last chapter, the New Testament is less a collection of books and more a collection of letters. Of the New Testament's twenty-seven "books," twenty-one are letters. And while many Christians assume that the Gospels are the oldest parts of the New Testament, it is likely a letter from Paul has that distinction. Paul's letters were written between approximately AD 50 and AD 65. The first of the New Testament Gospels was likely Mark, and scholars tend to date it around AD 65–70. Matthew and Luke are thought to have been written in the 70s or 80s, and John in the 80s or 90s. Revelation is typically dated around AD 95.[2]

Let's recall a bit of the New Testament chronology I mentioned in chapter 3 before we consider the New Testament letters. Jesus was likely born around 4 BC.[3] He was crucified, died, and was buried during Passover around AD 29. His resurrection and ascension occurred shortly after that. Following this, the small church, by this time at least 120 people strong, experienced a powerful outpouring of the Holy Spirit. Soon thousands of people came to believe that a man the religious leaders had condemned to die was the long-awaited Jewish messiah. The religious establishment continued to assert that Jesus was a false messiah.

A young Jewish leader named Saul, zealous for the Law, took on the task of squelching this movement of Jesus followers. He was given authority by the Jewish ruling council to arrest and prosecute the leaders of the movement. Perhaps his first prosecution was a man named Stephen. Saul stood by and gave approval for Stephen to be stoned to death. Acts 8:3 notes, "Saul was ravaging the church by entering house after house; dragging off both men and women, he committed them to prison." Sometime around AD 33, something shocking happened to this young zealot: while on his way to prosecute Christians in Damascus, there was a flashing light, he was blinded, and he heard the voice of Jesus. The experience was so shocking to him that this persecutor of Christians became Christianity's greatest advocate. From this time on, Saul would be known by his Greek name, *Paulos*—Paul.

Somewhere between AD 44 and 48, Paul felt called to take the gospel to the non-Jewish world. He traveled to Cyprus, then on to what is today central Turkey, to preach the good news of Jesus Christ. This is referred to as "the first missionary journey of Paul." Paul's story, including his missionary journeys, is narrated in the Acts of the Apostles.

Here's what Paul did on his missionary journeys: he would

enter a town, preach first to the Jews in the synagogue, and then, when he was inevitably asked to leave the synagogue, he would preach to the Gentiles. He not only had a powerful testimony, having once been a persecutor of Christians, but he also had a powerful message. Paul told the Gentiles of a God who created all things, "in whom we live and move and have our being." This God had revealed himself by sending his son, who suffered and died for the human race but was raised from the dead, offering forgiveness to those who repent.[4] Dozens of people (perhaps hundreds in some places) came to put their trust in Jesus Christ. As noted in the previous chapter, before Paul left each town, he would organize the believers into churches, and then off he'd go to the next town to preach.

These fledgling churches would quickly have questions or encounter challenges; they needed ongoing direction. So they would send messengers from the church to give reports to Paul with their questions or concerns. Paul would write letters in return—letters meant to offer encouragement, instruction, answers to questions, and sometimes correction. These letters became the first documents of our New Testament.

Over the next fifteen years, it is likely that Paul wrote dozens of letters to churches and individuals. Of the twenty-seven documents in our New Testament, thirteen claim to be letters written by Paul. What happened to his other letters? Scholars believe that two or more letters were edited into what we know as 2 Corinthians. It is possible that portions of other letters were used to create those letters thought to have come from a period after Paul's death (I'll mention this in chapter 13). Some were simply lost, as the early Christians would not have seen his letters as scripture at the time they received them.

For purposes of this book, it is important to note that when you read one of Paul's letters, or any other New Testament letter, you are reading someone else's mail. Christians often forget this. They read Paul's letters as though he wrote just for them. This works fine most of the time; Paul's instructions, his theological reflections, and his practical concerns are amazingly timeless. But they become most meaningful, and we are least likely to misapply their teaching, when we seek to understand why he may have written this or that to a given church.

I have a friend whose two adult children could not be less alike. One is driven. She graduated from college in three years. She's working sixty hours a week for a brokerage firm establishing her career. She's a very serious person. Her younger brother dropped out of college. He loves to travel, hang out with his friends, and have new experiences. Imagine if both adult children sent the same note to their dad: "Dad, I value your wisdom. What guidance do you have for my life right now?" Do you think my friend would give the same advice to both children? No, his advice would be specific to each child's character and situation. To one he'd say, "Honey, you need to stop and smell the roses a bit more. You are working too hard, and you've got to remember that life is more than your job." To the other he might say, "I'm so glad you stop and smell the roses, but I think you need to become a bit more serious about your career and your future." The same man would offer nearly opposite advice to his two children based upon their different needs and personalities.

Here's the point: the apostles wrote their letters to address specific needs and situations in communities of the Greco-Roman world of two thousand years ago. What Paul wrote to the Galatians concerning a particular situation may not be what he would say today, two thousand years later, to you or your church. In the category of things Paul speaks to that seem clearly out of sync with the twenty-first century are his instructions regarding slavery and the place and role of women in the church and family.

Having said that, it became clear to early Christians even before Paul's death that what Paul said in a letter to one church offered important teaching and guidance for those in other churches. Churches began to copy and exchange Paul's letters during his lifetime. After his death, many letters were collected and circulated together among the churches, and they became the earliest nucleus of our New Testament—a set of documents written by the great apostle of the faith that continued to be used for guidance in the church.

Today, among the most important and respectful ways to read the New Testament letters is by trying to hear what the apostles were saying to their communities and why, and then to ask, "How does that message speak to my life or our community today?"

We don't have time in this book to go through all twenty-one New Testament letters to consider the circumstances that precipitated their writing. But I'd like to take one, Paul's letter to the Galatians, which many believe is the oldest New Testament document (many believe Paul wrote it around AD 50, though some consider the first letter to be 1 Thessalonians), and consider how we can discern the situation that precipitated these letters and how that might help us make sense of and apply their teachings today.

Grab a Bible and turn to Galatians 1:1. Paul begins his letter, "Paul an apostle—sent neither by human commission nor from human authorities, but through Jesus Christ and God the Father, who raised him from the dead." In his opening to this letter, Paul is establishing that his message and authority came from Jesus Christ and God the Father. This is his only letter to begin with this claim, and as we will see, he begins this way because his authority has been challenged among the churches in Galatia.

Notice to whom he sends this letter in verse 2: "To the churches of Galatia." Galatia was not a city but a geographic region in Asia Minor (modern-day Turkey), which was itself part of the Roman Empire. Paul sends this one letter "to the churches" of Galatia. So he intends this letter to be copied and circulated among several churches some distance apart.

The Eastern Mediterranean in the Time of Paul

Here's some helpful background for unlocking the meaning of the letter to the Galatians: Paul was not the only Jewish rabbi to become a follower of Jesus. Others, including a number of Paul's fellow Pharisees, had also accepted that Jesus was the long-awaited Jewish messiah. But not all Jewish followers of Christ saw the implications of Christ's life, death, and resurrection in the same way that Paul did.

For Paul, Jesus not only revealed God to the human race; he had come to fulfill the requirements of the Law of Moses on behalf of the human race. The covenant God had made with Israel through Moses was now set aside, superseded by a new covenant made with the entire human race through Jesus Christ. The Law was no longer binding. Circumcision and conversion to Judaism was not necessary for Gentiles to receive salvation. All that was needed was faith in Christ.

Many of Paul's fellow Jewish Christians believed the Law was still binding. They believed that when Gentiles put their faith in Christ, they were to be circumcised and were required to follow the Law. They were converting not only to Christ but to Judaism. These Christians have been referred to as Judaizers or, because they believed that obeying the Law was an essential part of salvation, Legalists.

Paul and these Judaizing Christians did not see eye to eye. And the Judaizers had an irritating knack of following behind Paul, shortly after he had started a church, to announce to these new converts that they needed to be circumcised and follow the Law. They came to "correct" Paul's inadequate theology and to lead the fledgling Christians to become Jews. This is the historical situation that lies behind the letter to the Galatians, who had themselves been visited by these Judaizers. The Galatians appeared to have accepted the gospel as proclaimed by the Judaizers and had begun to get circumcised.

With this in mind, look at Galatians 1:6–9:

I am astonished that you are so quickly deserting the one who called you in the grace of Christ and are turning to a different gospel—not that there is another gospel, but there are some who are confusing you and want to pervert the gospel of Christ. But even if we or an angel from heaven should proclaim to you a gospel contrary to what we proclaimed to you, let that one be accursed! As we have said before, so now I repeat, if anyone proclaims to you a gospel contrary to what you received, let that one be accursed!

As you read this, do you feel Paul's indignation? His frustration? Through most of this letter, Paul defends his gospel, confronting this "other gospel" that the Judaizers were preaching. Paul's emphasis in this letter is clear in Galatians 2:15–16: "We know that a person is justified not by the works of the law but through faith in Jesus Christ. And we have come to believe in Christ Jesus, so that we might be justified by faith in Christ, and not by doing the works of the law, because no one will be justified by the works of the law." Paul ends the chapter by saying, "If justification comes through the law, then Christ died for nothing." In Galatians 5:2, he specifically addresses the question of circumcision: "Listen! I, Paul, am telling you that if you let yourselves be circumcised, Christ will be of no benefit to you."

Salvation was a gift from God, made possible by the life, death, and resurrection of Jesus Christ. It is accepted by faith, not earned by our works. This was the centerpiece of Paul's gospel. But, as noted above, some early Christians did not see eye to eye with Paul, including some who had actually known Jesus.

Paul recognized that the challenge of this emphasis on salvation by grace alone is that some might interpret it to mean that so long as you have faith in Christ, you can do whatever comes naturally to you—"whatever feels good, do it." Such people have been called libertines for their emphasis on a Christian's liberty, or sometimes antinomians (*nomos* is the Greek word for Law, hence anti-nomians are those operating lawlessly). In Galatians, Paul devotes four chapters to the problem of legalism, but he then devotes chapter 5 and part of chapter 6 to addressing libertinism.

Look at Galatians 5:13: "For you were called to freedom, brothers and sisters; only do not use your freedom as an opportunity for self-indulgence." And now look at Galatians 5:16: "Live by the Spirit, I say, and do not gratify the desires of the flesh." Then he gets very specific in verses 19–21: "Now the works of the flesh are obvious: fornication, impurity, licentiousness, idolatry, sorcery, enmities, strife, jealousy, anger, quarrels, dissensions, factions, envy, drunkenness, carousing, and things like these. I am warning you, as I warned you before: those who do such things will not inherit the kingdom of God." Paul is pretty clear here that he's not a libertine. But the salvation offered by Christ is still a gift, not earned by our righteousness but simply accepted. And in grateful response, we don't seek to live in obedience to a Law written in another time and place. Instead we are to be led, formed, and shaped by the Holy Spirit. In contrast to the works of the flesh, Paul describes the fruit of the Spirit, which is "love, joy, peace, patience, kindness, generosity, faithfulness, gentleness, and self-control. There is no law against such things" (5:22–23).

These two poles of legalism and libertinism were, and in many ways still are, the proverbial Scylla and Charybdis of the Christian faith. Either side leads to shipwrecking our faith. Christian churches and individuals must carefully navigate between them.

As we read Galatians two thousand years after it was written, there are sections that immediately seem relevant. There are other sections that are a bit confusing. We quickly see that this letter is not simply "the word of God." It is first the words of a frustrated and irritated apostle who is lashing out at those who were seeking to "correct" his theology and leading his converts to be circumcised. It reveals one of the first theological conflicts in the early church and even some tension between Christianity's two leading apostles, Peter and Paul. But in the midst of addressing these contemporary disputes, we find Paul's basic theological convictions and the way he encouraged the Christians of Galatia to carefully navigate between legalism and libertinism. It is precisely here that the letter helps us as we seek to navigate between those same poles today.

To any Christian who has grown up with a guilt-filled, rule-based faith, the epistle to the Galatians offers a powerful answer: salvation, God's love, right standing with God are pure gift. You are saved by grace, not by your works. Yet to any Christian who still "indulges the desires of the flesh," the epistle also offers a powerful warning: "Live by the Spirit, I say, and do not gratify the desires of the flesh. . . . [T]hose who belong to Christ Jesus have crucified the flesh with its passions and desires" (Galatians 5:16, 24).

My aim in walking you through Galatians in this chapter was to invite you to see the New Testament letters for what they are: letters written by first-century Christian leaders to address specific situations, concerns, or questions within the early church.

We often read the New Testament as though the first-century Roman world was little different from our own. But it was a very different world. The assumptions, the culturally accepted practices and norms, the way families functioned, and the cultural practices that Christians rejected were often quite different from our world.

Let's consider just how much America has changed since 1950. In 1950, the Soviet Union was our enemy. The birth control pill was not yet available. Three out of four college graduates were men. Women could not serve as pastors in most mainline denominations. "Separate but equal" was the law of the land, leading to separate rail cars for blacks, separate drinking fountains, and separate schools. African Americans were regularly refused service at restaurants, department stores, and even public pools and parks.

These discriminatory laws and cultural practices were developed in a nation where over 90 percent of the people who made the laws claimed to be followers of Christ, yet they saw no problem with "colored" drinking fountains, pools, and schools.

Our world has changed in dramatic ways in just over sixty years. Think about how technology has affected us in that period of time. We have gone from rotary phones to pocket computers capable of connecting us with more information than anyone could ever imagine. We have gone from record players to iPods, abacuses to iPads. Technological advances have helped us live much longer lives, creating pastoral issues not seriously contemplated in 1950.

Here's the point: The Epistles are amazingly timeless. Most of what they teach we can fairly easily apply to our own lives, but there is room to ask questions about how to apply to our lives instructions found in mail addressed to people two thousand years ago. This task of understanding the original intention of the books, their historical and cultural context, and then seeking to discern how these apply to us today is called interpretation or hermeneutics.

I'll close with an example from Galatians demonstrating how the different contexts (Paul's and ours) may lead to different conclusions. Paul speaks strongly against the practice of circumcision in Galatians. Yet in America over 50 percent of parents have their baby boys circumcised.[5] Health officials continue to debate the merits of circumcision, but few consider Paul's teaching in Galatians to be important in their decision making. Why not? After all, we have in Galatians a clear scriptural mandate not to practice circumcision. We ignore his advice because Paul's teaching in Galatians addressed a different set of circumstances and a different motivation for the practice than are at play today. Christians are not bound to avoid circumcising their baby boys simply because Paul discouraged it in Galatians, unless the parents are doing so in an attempt to fulfill the Law as a way of ensuring their own justification.

When reading the New Testament letters, you'll find a great deal that speaks directly to you and your life situation. But there is also room to question the circumstances and cultural assumptions that led the apostles to write as they did and to ask if the apostles would have written the same thing to you if they were living today.

CHAPTER 10

Who Really Wrote Paul's Letters?

We've been speaking of the New Testament letters, focused largely on Paul's letters, but you may be interested to know that Paul actually wrote very few of the letters sent under his name. Now, that is a bit of an overstatement. Paul dictated the contents of many of his letters to others. Some of these people wrote in a style that indicates word-by-word dictation, while others seem to have taken his ideas and put them in the words that seemed best to them. Scholars believe that in a few cases other people took Paul's teaching and thoughts and composed letters in his name after his death. Let's briefly consider these various ideas for a moment.

My father-in-law, Dick Bandy, had macular degeneration in the years leading up to his death. He had good peripheral vision, but the vision in the center of his eye was severely degraded. It became hard for him to write, and when he did, he wrote slowly. In addition, his letters were larger and not as neat as they had been before he began losing his vision. Some believe that Paul suffered from a similar affliction and that this may have been why he seldom wrote his own letters.

Look at Galatians 6:11, where Paul writes, "See what large letters I make when I am writing in my own hand!" Earlier, in Galatians 4:15, Paul had been speaking of the goodwill of the Galatians toward him when he was with them: "For I testify that, had it been possible, you would have torn out your eyes and given them to me." Some have interpreted this as a reference to Galatian Christians' concern about a problem Paul was having with his eyesight.

Whether Paul was having problems with his eyesight or not, we know that he used an amanuensis at times—a scribe who wrote down his letters as he dictated them—and he often lists a coauthor at the beginning of his epistles. The amanuensis who wrote Romans identifies himself in Romans 16:22: "I Tertius, the writer of this letter, greet you in the Lord." Paul ends 1 Corinthians, Colossians, and 2 Thessalonians saying, "I, Paul, write this greeting with my own hand," which would indicate that the rest of the letter was written by the hand of another, but the mark of authenticity was Paul's greeting or signature at the end. That seems to be the implication of 2 Thessalonians 3:17: "I, Paul, write this greeting with my own hand. This is the mark in every letter of mine; it is the way I write."

My assistant, Sue Thompson, drafts most of my letters for me. When we first began working together, I would dictate to her what I wanted to say. After a while she came to know how I think, my vocabulary and style, and she began writing the first draft of some letters. I might correct this or that thing, and she would bring it back for my signature. Today you could ask Sue a question and she would be able to tell you what I would likely say with 99 percent accuracy. Most of the hundreds of letters I sign every year Sue has drafted for me. I affix a handwritten greeting at the bottom, and then I pause to pray for the person I'm sending the letter to. On rare occasions, I rewrite the letter, or a bit more frequently, I add a paragraph or change a sentence or two.

As noted above, most of Paul's letters were likely written with the help of an assistant, who may have taken down Paul's message word for word, or who may have had a bit more freedom to improvise (which would explain why a handful of letters show a somewhat different style and vocabulary from other letters).

Scholars also believe that 2 Corinthians was a composite made up of at least two letters that Paul wrote to the church at Corinth at different times, edited together likely after Paul's death. Why would someone have done this? It is possible that at least one of the previous letters had been partially damaged or a portion of it lost, hence the need to integrate the existing portion into another letter.

That leads to a discussion of what are sometimes called the Deutero-Pauline or "disputed" letters. Among Paul's letters in the New Testament, five or six are thought by many mainline and Catholic scholars to have been written after Paul's time. These disputed letters are, in the order they appear in the New Testament, Ephesians, Colossians, 2 Thessalonians, 1 and 2 Timothy, and Titus. The last three are referred to as the "pastoral Epistles."

These letters are questioned for various reasons. Some show a vast difference in theology and vocabulary compared to the undisputed letters of Paul. Since Paul used amanuenses, this does not guarantee that the letters were not in fact written by Paul. But the style and ideas seem sufficiently different from Paul's other letters that it is not unreasonable to question the authorship.

A couple of simple analogies will suffice. I never use the word "ain't"—it was sufficiently scrubbed from my vocabulary as a child that I can honestly say it has never been used in any sermon, letter, e-mail, or text I've ever written. If my wife received a letter from me with even one "ain't," she'd be suspicious, but if the word appeared again and again, she'd know the letter was not from me. There are certain words or phrases that show up in the disputed letters but are never found in Paul's undisputed letters.

A second analogy relates to ideas. I have a friend who is a conservative Republican. He's pretty clear that he favors smaller government and lower taxes, and that he opposes government involvement in health care. If I received an e-mail from him asking me to contribute money to the Democratic Party and supporting new government programs, I'd know someone had hacked his e-mail account.

The differences in the disputed letters involve both vocabulary and style, but the letters also contain theological ideas and guidance for the church that not only don't show up in the undisputed letters but seem to come from a time when both the organizational needs of the church and the church's theological convictions had matured beyond what is presumed of the period in which Paul lived.

This idea that several of Paul's letters were written after his time, in his name, is disturbing to some Christians. But here's another way to think about this idea. Tom Shipp was the founding pastor of the Lover's Lane United Methodist Church in Dallas, Texas, back in the 1940s. The church grew rapidly under his leadership. His commitment to ministry with alcoholics was known across the city. Tom had served as the church's pastor for thirty-one years when, one evening, he died of a heart attack while sitting in a church committee meeting. The church grieved his death and never forgot its founding pastor.

Twenty-one years after Shipp's death, my friend Stan Copeland was assigned to pastor Lover's Lane. He learned that Tom Shipp had dictated his sermons into a Dictaphone, and that the week he died he had left a sermon two-thirds finished on the Dictaphone. The tape was still around. Stan had a brilliant idea—he decided to preach Tom Shipp's last sermon. He preached part of it nearly word for word but completed the last third of the sermon, which Shipp had never finished, and adapted it for the church of his time. He connected Shipp's ideas to a new generation. The message was referred to as "A Sermon from the Other Side" by the *Dallas Morning News*. Though Shipp had died twenty-one years earlier, two thousand people showed up to hear the message. Was it Shipp's sermon or Stan's sermon? Well, it was Shipp's ideas and many of his own words, but revised to address a new generation.

This is how I see the letters of Paul that may have been written after his passing. I approach them as if someone took Paul's ideas and themes and prepared a new letter adapting his work for a new generation. That individual may have been Timothy, or Silvanus, or Sosthenes, or Tertius—some follower and associate of Paul who had traveled with him, who knew him so well that he could prepare a letter reflecting Paul's thinking and ideas for a new generation.

Here's the point I want you to see in this chapter—and, really, in the book up to this point: the development of the biblical text is more complex and more intriguing than is usually supposed by most people reading the Bible. It did not simply drop out of heaven. It was not merely a matter of the biblical authors picking up a pen and having their hand moved by the Spirit. The biblical documents were written and edited by persons who were addressing the needs of the people of their time. And these same documents, as complicated as their composition and final editing may have been, are also said to be inspired by God; in and through them, God continues to speak to us today.

CHAPTER 11

How, When, and Why the Gospels Were Written

We've learned that the Epistles were the first documents of the New Testament. Many were written before AD 65, the earliest around 49 or 50. All were written in response to specific circumstances, questions, problems, or challenges related to the intended recipients. When were the Gospels written? Why were they not written before the Epistles? Why do Matthew, Mark, and Luke seem so similar, at times appearing to borrow from one another word for word, while John paints such a different picture of Jesus? These are a few of the questions we'll consider in this chapter and the next.

The consensus among scholars is that the Gospels were written between AD 70 and 90. A precipitating factor was the death of the eyewitnesses—the first generation of Christians who actually knew Christ.

This is not difficult to understand. My great-aunt Celia Belle is ninety-eight years old, and she is as sharp as a tack. She is the family historian. She has old photos going back to the 1800s. She has books containing the family genealogy. For as long as I've known her, every time we were together she would tell me stories about our family. In the last few years, everyone in the family has been cognizant of the fact that Aunt Celia Belle will not be with us forever, and we need to pay attention or we'll lose this history when she's gone.

So it was, we think, with the writing of the Gospels. As long as the disciples were still alive, there was no urgency in writing down the story. The disciples shared it with others, who shared it with others. In fact, oral presentation by an eyewitness was valued far above anything written. But with the death of the apostles, some understood the importance of capturing in writing the story of Jesus's life, teachings, ministry, death, and resurrection as the eyewitnesses had told it.

The Gospels we have were not the first attempts to write down the story of Jesus. Luke tells us in his introduction:

> Since many have undertaken to set down an orderly account of the events that have been fulfilled among us, just as they were handed on to us by those who from the beginning were eyewitnesses and servants of the word, I too decided, after investigating everything carefully from the very first, to write an orderly account for you, most excellent Theophilus, so that you may know the truth concerning the things about which you have been instructed. (Luke 1:1–4)

Luke's introduction tells us that "many" had sought to set down an "orderly account" of the events of Jesus's life. He says that these accounts attempted to do what the eyewitnesses had done in telling the stories of Jesus. He notes that these earlier documents were based upon the accounts of those who "from the beginning were eyewitnesses and servants of the word." Hence these "pre-gospels" would have been written in the 50s and 60s, while many of the apostles were still alive.

Luke's Gospel is typically dated by mainline scholars to the 80s, or to the 70s or earlier by many evangelical scholars. He carefully investigates the story of Jesus from various sources, and then he writes an "orderly account" for Theophilus. Theophilus may be a name or perhaps a title—it means "God-lover" and could represent any Christian reading the Gospel.

As we read the four Gospels, several things quickly become apparent. First, Matthew, Mark, and Luke are very similar in the way they present Jesus. There are key differences, but they share many of the same stories, contain much of the same teaching, and paint a very similar portrait of Jesus. But John's account of Jesus's life is very different. Matthew, Mark, and Luke have come to be known to scholars as the "synoptic Gospels"—*synoptic* is a compound word from the Greek *syn*, meaning "with," and *optikos*, meaning "to see." They "see with" one another. We'll consider John in the next chapter. To study Matthew, Mark, and Luke, I'd like you to have a basic understanding of what scholars call the "synoptic problem."

The synoptic problem is really more like a puzzle. The puzzle is the relationship among the three Gospels. At times, the Gospels agree word for word. For instance, in Matthew 24:15 we read, "So when you see the desolating sacrilege standing in the holy place, as was spoken of by the prophet Daniel (let the reader understand)," and in Mark 13:14 we read, "But when you see the desolating sacrilege set up where it ought not to be (let the reader understand)." What is interesting about these two lines is that both include identical parenthetical statements, "Let the reader understand." So both are quoting Jesus, yet both insert an aside to the reader as a way of saying, "You know what he's talking about here."

What Jesus predicts in this passage is likely the destruction of the temple by the Romans in AD 70 and the subsequent offering of sacrifices to the emperor following its destruction. (Josephus, the first-century Jewish historian, describes these sacrifices in *The War of the Jews*, book 6.) But here's what I want you to notice: both Matthew and Mark include this parenthetical statement urging the reader to understand. The likelihood of their independently including this phrase seems small. More likely, one of them copied the verse from the other or both shared a common source. And this is one of many verses like this in the Synoptics—verses or sections of verses that are repeated virtually word for word. So part of the synoptic question is, who borrowed from whom?

Before we consider the prevailing view of how the synoptic Gospels came to be written and what their relationship is, let's consider some basic information. Matthew has approximately 1,068 verses, Mark has 661 verses, and Luke has 1,149 verses. Approximately 95 percent of the material in Mark's Gospel appears in the Gospel of Matthew. Approximately 80 percent of the material in Mark's Gospel appears in Luke. Approximately 75 percent of the material in Mark appears in both Matthew and Luke. Some of this material agrees nearly word for word. This demonstrates significant sharing of sources or borrowing from one by the other two.

But in addition to the verses that appear in all three Gospels, there are a small number of verses that appear in Luke and Mark but do not appear in Matthew. There are more verses in Mark that appear in Matthew but not in Luke—about 18 percent of Mark's Gospel. This would indicate that for some reason Matthew and Luke chose not to include some of what they found in Mark.

Then there is a significant amount of material that appears in Matthew and Luke but does not appear in Mark. Much of this material is the sayings of Jesus. It would seem that Mark did not have access to this material, and thus Matthew and Luke were drawing upon a common source not known or used by Mark.

Finally, there is material unique to Matthew and other material unique to Luke. Where did this material come from? You begin to see how this is a puzzle, a mystery to be solved. What I've just described looks like this:

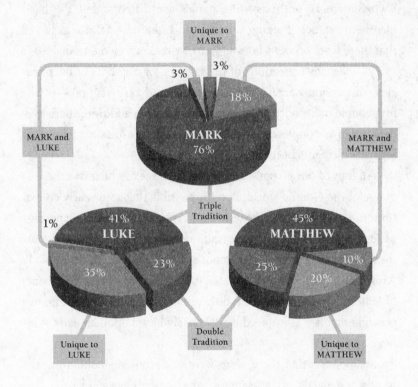

Relationships between the Synoptic Gospels

Some suggest that these relationships are what we would expect if the Holy Spirit were inspiring the text, but the kind of word-for-word agreement seen in the Gospels only appears in certain passages. Further, if the explanation were the Holy Spirit's inspiration down to the exact word order of various verses shared among the Gospels, we would expect the Holy Spirit to have eliminated all conflicts among the texts. Instead, there are places where the Gospels tell conflicting accounts of what Jesus said or did.

The consensus opinion today among biblical scholars is sometimes called the Four-Source Hypothesis (often also called the Two-Source Hypothesis—the names are different but the basic idea is the same). Picking up on what Luke tells us, it is believed that there were others who sought to write down elements of Jesus's story—perhaps collections of his sayings, or accounts of his miracles, or passion narratives of his death and resurrection—in the first couple of decades of the Christian faith. In addition, there may have been a couple of early and brief pre-gospels that brought together elements of these collections.

All four of our Gospels are written in Greek, which was the language of the Gentile world, but it is possible that some early collections of Jesus material were written in Aramaic,[1] the native language of Jesus and the apostles. The tradition of the church was that Matthew the apostle originally composed his Gospel in Hebrew (likely Aramaic) and then later translated it into Greek.[2] While the Gospel of Matthew as we now have it does not bear signs of translation, it is possible that it was inspired by or loosely based upon an early Aramaic tradition.

My point is that there were written documents containing the words and deeds of Jesus before the Gospels we currently have were composed, documents written in the first decades of the Christian faith or at least contemporaneous with the earliest letters of Paul. These documents were the source materials, along with the oral tradition, of the Gospels we have today.

With this in mind, let's consider the Two- (or Four-) Source Hypothesis for how the synoptic Gospels were composed.

It is generally agreed that Mark was the first of our four Gospels. Some date it to the early 60s, others to shortly after Peter's death in AD 65, and a large number of mainline scholars to just after 70. It is seen as one of two primary sources for Matthew and Luke. Fifty-five percent of Matthew's Gospel is found in Mark. Forty-two percent of Luke's Gospel is found in Mark. If this theory is true, Mark was the largest source of material for both Matthew and Luke. But Matthew and Luke share another source. We know this because about 25 percent of the material common to Matthew and Luke is not found in Mark. Again, there is at times virtually word-for-word agreement in some of this material. The material Matthew and Luke share is virtually all sayings of Jesus. This includes the Lord's Prayer, the beatitudes, and Jesus's words during his temptation.

We no longer have this original source. The German scholar Johannes Weiss first came up with the name commonly used for this lost source of so much of Matthew and Luke's Gospels. He called it Q, for the German word *quelle*, which simply means "source." The Two-Source Hypothesis holds that Matthew and Luke took most of their material from Mark and Q but reworked this material in light of other traditions and sources they had at their disposal. The Four-Source Hypothesis provides a way of talking about the other sources and traditions they used to shape and compose their Gospels. One of these sources is called M, for the material that is unique to Matthew, and another is called L, for the material unique to Luke. Thirty percent of Luke's Gospel does not appear in any other Gospel, and 20 percent of Matthew's material is unique to his Gospel. When we speak of M or L, these are simply hypothetical sources and likely represent multiple additional sources drawn upon by Matthew and Luke. This is a typical diagram of the Two- or Four-Source Hypothesis:

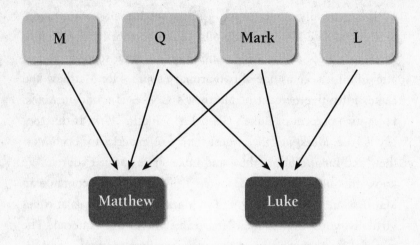

Diagram of the Four-Source Hypothesis

Some Christians find it disconcerting that there were sources behind the Gospels. They prefer to believe that each author simply wrote under the inspiration of the Holy Spirit. I find that the idea of written sources builds my confidence in the Gospels. The Gospel writers were serious about doing their research. They wanted to get the story right. They drew upon sources written in the earliest decades after the death of Christ. The sources we call M, Mark, Q, and L would have included materials from eyewitnesses who had known Christ, as well as materials from those who knew the eyewitnesses. If the Gospel of Matthew was actually written by the disciple by that name, then he also would have drawn upon his own recollections.[3]

So, let's summarize what we've learned so far. The earliest stage of the transmission of the stories of Jesus was simply the preaching of the apostles. The apostles and others bore witness to Jesus through preaching and teaching and telling his story. Soon some sayings of Jesus and stories about Jesus began to be collected and written down. Then some undertook to write more complete accounts of the life of Jesus—forerunners to our Gospels. Next, around AD 70, perhaps a bit later, Mark wrote his Gospel. Mark was Peter's interpreter in Rome before Peter's death, and his Gospel is composed of stories he would have heard Peter tell about Jesus. Mark's writing would have been copied and circulated, likely from Rome.[4] Matthew and Luke both had access to Mark and other sources and likely wrote in the late 70s or perhaps in the 80s.

Some skeptics question the reliability of the Gospels, given that Mark was written forty years after Jesus's death and Matthew and Luke still later. As I've tried to demonstrate, the Gospels drew upon oral and written sources dated much earlier than AD 70. But even if they were not, it is worth considering this question: are documents recording events that occurred forty years earlier reliable?

I have another aunt, Patti Spencer. She just turned eighty, and she is amazing. She doesn't act a day over sixty. In a recent conversation, she described events that happened when she was in her twenties and thirties as if they just happened yesterday. Do you think she is a reasonably reliable source of information about events that happened when she was in her twenties or thirties or forties? Let me ask it another way: if you are in your fifties or sixties, are you a reasonably reliable source of information that happened forty years ago?[5] If so, why would we think the Gospels, written forty to sixty years after the death of Christ, would not be reasonably reliable sources of information about the person these believers called Savior and Lord?

Like the Epistles, the Gospels were written not simply to record the story of Jesus but to record the story of Jesus for a particular community or group of communities. As John notes in the closing words to his Gospel, "There are also many other things that Jesus did; if every one of them were written down, I suppose that the world itself could not contain the books that would be written" (John 21:25). Each Gospel writer had to choose what information to include. That process of deciding what information to include and where to include it in the story related to their objective in writing the Gospel, which in turn had something to do with the needs and perspectives of their intended audience.

As with the Epistles, scholars look for clues in each Gospel that might tell us about the unique concerns or character of the community to which it was first written. These are seen in distinctive emphases and in the different ways that the writers tell the same story or convey the same saying of Jesus. For instance, in the beatitudes, Luke tells us that Jesus said, "Blessed are you who are poor, for yours is the kingdom of God. Blessed are you who are hungry now, for you will be filled" (Luke 6:20–21). But Matthew records the same saying as, "Blessed are the poor in spirit, for theirs is the kingdom of heaven" and "Blessed are those who hunger and thirst for righteousness, for they will be filled" (Matthew 5:3 and 5:6). It is possible that Jesus taught both sayings at different times, but it is also possible that Luke and Matthew interpreted Jesus's words for their community.

We know that Luke's Gospel shows a repeated emphasis on the poor and marginalized. This may reflect Luke's own compassion and concern for such persons, which mirrored Christ's concern. Matthew, in spiritualizing Jesus's words—the poor become the "poor in spirit," and the hungry in Luke's beatitudes become those who "hunger after righteousness"—may give us a clue that the community he was writing to was relatively affluent compared with Luke's community.

This is one example of the way scholars study the Gospels to discern the possible situations of the community to which the Gospel was addressed. It is beyond the scope of this book to go into detail on the unique themes of each and what these may say about the community to which the Gospel was written. You can find this in a good commentary and in some of the bibliographic resources I provide at the end of the book. My point is to help you see that the Gospel writers told the story of Jesus's life and teaching in subtly different ways based both upon their own convictions and upon the needs of the communities to whom they were writing.

We've learned something about the synoptic problem and how it has been resolved, and we've learned about the way scholars think the synoptic Gospels were written and how they reflect the unique perspectives of their authors and the needs of the communities to whom they were writing. In the next chapter we'll consider the Gospel of John.

CHAPTER 12

The Perplexing, Puzzling, and Profound John

If you read Matthew, Mark, and Luke in succession, and then begin reading John, you'll be struck, from the very first verse, by how radically different John is from the Synoptics. John's Gospel begins with these dramatic words, "In the beginning was the Word, and the Word was with God, and the Word was God." This opening statement tells you that John's Gospel is going to offer a different approach to the story of Jesus.

Clement of Alexandria was a Christian leader in the last decades of the second century and the early years of the third century. He famously said of the writing of the fourth Gospel, "John, perceiving that the external facts had been made plain in the gospel, being urged by his friends and inspired by the Spirit, composed a spiritual gospel."[1] Most scholars agree with Clement that John was the last of the Gospels to be written, sometime after AD 90. With Clement, they see John less as an attempt to write a biography of Jesus and instead as a book focused on conveying the spiritual significance of

Jesus's life. When I think of the Gospel, I picture an aged John, at the end of a lifetime of reflections upon Jesus's significance for his life, taking up the pen to compose this Gospel.[2]

With Clement, the earliest Christians recognized that there was something very different about John's account of the life of Jesus. Ninety-two percent of the material in John's Gospel is not found in the Synoptics. The general facts of Jesus's life are the same in all four Gospels: he is from Nazareth, his mother is Mary, he healed the sick, cast out demons, was concerned for the outcast, irritated the religious leaders, was crucified under the governorship of Pontius Pilate at the instigation of the religious leaders, and on the third day was raised from the dead. While most of the stories from Jesus's ministry are different in John, they are consistent with what we find in the Synoptics. To me it is the way Jesus speaks in John that seems so radically different from Matthew, Mark, and Luke.

John is far less focused on telling his readers what Jesus said and did; instead, he focuses on making plain *who Jesus is* and what his life *means*. His "Christology"—his assessment of Jesus's identity and the meaning of his life—is well developed.[3] John repeatedly associates Jesus with God. The multiple "I am" sayings ("I am the bread of life," "I am the resurrection and the life," "I am the good shepherd," and several more) can seem egotistical and grandiose, and many of his other sayings may seem mystical, confusing, and sometimes downright disturbing (for instance, "Unless you eat the flesh of the Son of Man and drink his blood, you have no life in you" in John 6:53—a statement that led many of his disciples to desert him, according to John 6:66). In the Synoptics, Jesus speaks in parables—simple stories that illustrate spiritual truths—but Jesus seldom speaks in parables in John. Instead he uses metaphors.

Was Jesus a mystic who spoke largely in metaphors about himself, or was he a teacher who spoke in parables about the kingdom of God? These are two different pictures of Jesus. But there are also differences in details and chronology.

In the Synoptics, Jesus casts out the moneychangers from the temple at the beginning of the last week of his life, an event that leads to his crucifixion. In John, Jesus casts out the moneychangers at the beginning of his three-year ministry. In the Synoptics, most of Jesus's ministry takes place in the Galilee. In John, most of Jesus's ministry takes place in and around Jerusalem. In the Synoptics, the Last Supper takes place on the evening of the Passover seder, and Jesus transforms the Passover seder into the Christian Eucharist. But in John, the Last Supper happens on the night before the Passover seder, so that Jesus is crucified at the very hour when the Passover lambs are being slaughtered in the temple in preparation for the Passover seder that night.

How do we account for these different portrayals of Jesus? Clement of Alexandria's comments are helpful when he refers to the Gospel as the "spiritual gospel." I believe John does include stories and details from the life of Jesus that are accurate and meant to supplement the synoptic Gospels. But it seems to me that John's primary concern is not to give his readers another account of the life of Jesus but to make clear to his readers Jesus's divine identity and to help them see how faith in and a relationship with Jesus bring life.

If I'm looking for answers to questions of when, what, and how, I look to Matthew, Mark, and Luke. If I'm interested in answers to questions of who and why, I turn to John. Retelling a story while changing the details to make a theological point is John's modus operandi. The very fact that a detail is different from the way the story was told in Matthew, Mark, and Luke should lead the reader to ask, "What does John want me to notice here?" In John, nearly every seemingly extraneous detail is a hint meant to point to the identity and significance of Jesus.

Like the other Gospels, John's primary focus is on Jesus's death and resurrection. It is on the cross that we see Christ's glory. He is God enfleshed, giving his life for the human race. Fully half of John's Gospel is devoted to the events of the last week of Jesus's life, including his death and resurrection.

In my mind, Matthew, Mark, and Luke more accurately portray how Jesus spoke, what he said, and what he did. John's Gospel helps me understand the spiritual significance of Jesus for my life. Matthew, Mark, and Luke offer a more human picture of Jesus, with hints of his divinity. John offers a more divine picture of Jesus, with hints of his humanity. In Matthew, Mark, and Luke, Jesus calls his hearers to be a part of the kingdom of God and to ethical behavior fitting those who hail God as king. The Synoptics, while inviting people to trust in Jesus, are primarily interested in a believer's actions. In John, Jesus calls his hearers to believe in him, to abide in him, to love him, and to be "born again." John, while inviting people to obey Jesus and to love others, is primarily interested in the believer's relationship with Christ.

It struck me recently that the divide between the mainline churches and the conservative and evangelical churches in the last century was largely along the lines of the divide between the synoptic Gospels and John. The mainline churches tend to focus on the Synoptics, teach and preach about the kingdom of God, and call people to repent and to live as though God were king. The parable of the good Samaritan and the parable of the sheep and the goats have been pivotal teachings in shaping their approach to Christian faith. The evangelical, charismatic, and conservative churches have focused on John's Gospel, calling people to a personal relationship with Jesus Christ; for them, John 3:16 and Jesus's call to Nicodemus to be "born again" have been pivotal.

Of course, this is a bit oversimplified, but it captures in some sense the two very different approaches to the Christian faith that are seen in the two sides of Protestant Christianity in America. Yet in God's providence, our New Testament contains all four Gospels. The fact that there are three synoptic Gospels emphasizing life in the kingdom of God may be instructive. We cannot miss Christ's call to be instruments of healing and restoration in this world. But without John's portrayal of Jesus and the call to be born anew, or to be born "from above," we miss the personal power of the Gospel that makes it possible to live as the Synoptics demand.

Once again, as we consider John's Gospel, we see that the biblical documents are more complex than we might have first supposed. John is less a biography of Jesus than a statement of his spiritual significance for our lives. John himself is willing to write less literally, and more figuratively, so that his readers might fully understand the profound significance of Jesus Christ.

Having touched upon how, when, and why the New Testament documents were written and the message they contain, let's turn our attention to the fascinating story of how, when, and why these particular documents were brought together into the New Testament.

CHAPTER 13

Which Books Made It into the New Testament and Why

As we learned in chapter 5, the process by which certain documents came to be considered *ta biblia*—the sacred books or holy scriptures—is called canonization. By way of reminder, the Greek word "canon" was used for a measuring rod; when applied to the Bible, it means those books that were deemed authoritative and by which all other books would be measured.

As we've learned, the sacred books for Jesus and the apostles were the writings of the Old Testament. These writings were not bound together as a book, nor was there complete agreement upon which writings were authoritative at the time of Christ (nor today, which is why the Roman Catholic, Eastern Orthodox, and Protestant Old Testaments have different numbers of books).

Many Christians assume that by the end of the first century, the New Testament as we have it was complete, the documents were bound together, and thus our New Testament had been created. The reality is far more interesting and complex. In this chapter, we'll consider how the New Testament documents were canonized—that is, the process and criteria by which the twenty-seven "books" of our New Testament came to be considered the New Testament.

BEFORE THE NEW TESTAMENT

During the first decades after the resurrection of Jesus, the New Testament was not a book but a person, Jesus Christ. He was God's Messiah, the King, Savior, and Lord. His words, his life, his death and resurrection were God's definitive message to the human race. Jesus never wrote a book; instead, he preached and ministered and then commanded his disciples to do the same. They were to be his witnesses. So, in the earliest decades of the Christian faith, there were no documents; instead there were apostles preaching and teaching and healing in Christ's name.

The preaching of the apostles drew heavily from Old Testament texts that they saw as pointing toward Jesus, but the focus of their preaching, the central "text" from which they drew, was the story of Jesus's death and resurrection. A clear example of the preaching of the early church is Peter's Pentecost sermon, preserved in Acts 2:14–36. Here are just a couple of verses from the sermon:

> You that are Israelites, listen to what I have to say: Jesus of Nazareth, a man attested to you by God with deeds of power, wonders, and signs that God did through him among you, as you yourselves know—this man, handed over to you according to the definite plan and foreknowl-

edge of God, you crucified and killed by the hands of those outside the law. But God raised him up, having freed him from death, because it was impossible for him to be held in its power. (Acts 2:22–24)

We learned that Paul's letters were the earliest documents in our New Testament. Paul's preference was to convey his message in person, but since he could not be everywhere at one time, he was forced to write letters to the churches he founded. These letters had behind them Paul's authority as an apostle, but I don't believe Paul would ever have imagined his words rising to the level of scripture.

Paul recognized that Jesus's sayings had greater authority than his own words, even though Jesus's words were not yet written into Gospels. In 1 Corinthians 7:10, Paul makes a distinction between what he says and what the Lord says: "To the married I give this command—not I but the Lord," which implies that the word he is about to share is of the highest authority, for it was originally spoken by Jesus. Then, two verses later, he qualifies what he is about to say: "To the rest I say—I and not the Lord," as though this statement does not have the authority of Jesus's words but reflects Paul's opinion. In verse 25, he notes, "Now concerning virgins, I have no command of the Lord, but I give my opinion as one who by the Lord's mercy is trustworthy." These passages in 1 Corinthians 7 point to the fact that the sayings of the Lord had authority precisely because he was Lord and Savior and Christ, yet Paul speaks with authority and asserts that his teaching is "trustworthy."

Thus the earliest decades of the first century were a period in which Jesus's words and deeds were taught and preached by those who had heard the Master themselves, and those who heard the disciples share their stories in turn shared them with others.

PAUL'S LETTERS:
A PROTO–NEW TESTAMENT

Paul's letters form the earliest proto–New Testament. They were written documents intended to be read in the church to which he sent them and sometimes intended to be copied and read in other churches as well. These letters were intended to answer questions and to give guidance, instruction, and encouragement to the Christians in the churches he had started (and in the case of Romans, to a church he intended to visit). Shortly after Paul's death, the letters were likely copied, and at least some of them began to circulate as a group.

The earliest quote from a letter of Paul outside of the New Testament is from Clement of Rome, the bishop of the church at Rome. He writes to the Christians in Corinth to correct them. His letter, known as 1 Clement, was written in AD 96. He is clearly familiar with Paul's first letter to the Corinthians and quotes from it as he corrects the Corinthians (see 1 Clement 47:1–4), which tells us that by AD 96, the leaders of the church in Rome and likely many other places knew Paul's letters well. Clement does not quote Paul as scripture, but he does recognize that he wrote "in the Spirit" and as an apostle, and thus that Paul is an important source for instruction.[1]

The fact that Paul's letters were to be read in the churches and were being used years later to instruct Christians set them on a course that would eventually give them the standing of scripture. By the time of 2 Peter, the author,[2] who was himself familiar with Paul's letters, could write, "Our beloved brother Paul wrote to you according to the wisdom given him, speaking of this as he does in all his letters. There are some things in them hard to understand, which the ignorant and unstable twist to their own destruction, as they do the other scriptures" (2 Peter 3:15–16).

There are four things to note from this passage. First, the author is familiar with many of Paul's letters, which tells us that by this time (the late first or early second century), Paul's letters had circulated widely. Second, we learn that even the early church struggled to understand everything in Paul's letters—a source of great encouragement for many of us preachers! Third, we see that Paul's teaching was being distorted by some "ignorant and unstable" people—that his letters were prone to misinterpretation. But finally, when the author writes, "as they do the other scriptures," we see that Paul's letters were being considered scripture. Keep in mind that "scripture" meant "writings," and Christians meant by this authoritative writings. This is nonetheless a clear indication of how quickly after Paul's death his letters began to gain the status of scripture.

THE EMERGENCE OF THE
GOSPELS AS SCRIPTURE

From Paul himself, we learn that the sayings of Jesus carried greater weight in the early church than the apostles' own sayings. This is as we would expect. We also see from Acts that Jesus, not the sayings of the apostles themselves, was the focus of the preaching of the early church.

The first possible quote from one of the synoptic Gospels, or possibly the source behind the Gospel, is found in a book called *The Didache*, where Matthew, or a source from which Matthew drew, is used again and again. *The Didache* is a fascinating document that scholars believe was written in the late first century or early second century. The text, available online, gives an interesting glimpse into the ethical, spiritual, and liturgical practices of the first- or early second-century church. Among the fascinating things found there is a call for Christians to pray the Lord's Prayer (Matthew's version is cited) three times a day.

As Clement of Rome quoted Paul's letters, he also seems to quote material from Matthew's Gospel. This would mean that by the end of the first century, Matthew's Gospel had been copied and was circulated in the Roman capital within ten years or so of its writing.

You may be thinking, "Why do I care about all this?" Here's what I want you to notice. By the end of the first century, there was not yet a New Testament, but particular documents were being quoted by leaders and read in churches, and these were coming to have an authority in the churches. A group of Paul's letters was starting to circulate, and likely four Gospels circulated independent of one another, with Matthew being used and cited most frequently by the early church, though not by name. There was nothing like a list of New Testament books yet, but there was beginning to be a sense that the writings of the apostles concerning Jesus and the letters of the apostles to churches and individuals were important for the church.

THE NEW TESTAMENT EMERGES:
THE SECOND CENTURY

That leads us to the second century. Papias, the bishop of Hieropolis, who lived from AD 60 to 135,[3] mentions the Gospels of Mark and Matthew around 130. From Papias, we learn that Mark was Peter's interpreter and that the Gospel of Mark contains Peter's recollections of the Lord's words. He also describes a Gospel written by Matthew, though he suggests it was written in Hebrew, whereas the

Matthew we know appears to have been originally composed in Greek. Since the Gospels are anonymous documents with no internal claims of authorship, Papias becomes the first to formally associate Mark's Gospel with Mark and Matthew's with Matthew.

Around the year 140, a wealthy man named Marcion arrived in Rome. There is some debate as to whether he himself was a bishop, but his father was a bishop in the region bordering the Black Sea in northern Turkey. Marcion struggled with a question nearly every Christian has struggled with, one we'll consider in the next section of this book. He struggled with how to reconcile Yahweh, the God of the Old Testament, who created all things and at times seems harsh, angry, jealous, even petty, with the God and Father of Jesus Christ, who was loving, compassionate, and kind. It is likely that Marcion was also trying to make sense of the problem of suffering and evil—why bad things happen to good people.

Marcion resolved these two issues by drawing upon a bit of platonic philosophy and borrowing some ideas from emerging philosophical and religious schools of thought that today we call Gnosticism. Marcion suggested that Yahweh, the God of the Old Testament who created the world, was not the God and Father of Jesus Christ. Yahweh was a lesser deity who created the world, claimed the Jews as his people, and was responsible for the ordering of this world and consequently its evil and suffering. The true God was hitherto unknown to the human race, but Jesus had come to reveal him. He was kind, compassionate, and good. He came to set humanity free from the yoke of the Law put in place by Yahweh and to lead people to the God of love. He called his followers to a life of holiness and asceticism. Marcion is best known for seeking to detach Christianity from Judaism.

Marcion was the first person we know of to assemble a book of documents resembling a New Testament. Marcion rejected the Old

Testament on the basis that they were the scriptures of Yahweh. They could be read and learned from, and the prophets even pointed toward the coming of Jesus, but they were not particularly helpful for learning about the God and Father of Jesus. Instead, Marcion assembled a collection that included the Gospel of Luke and ten of Paul's letters (he did not include the pastoral Epistles, 1 and 2 Timothy, or Titus). Even these documents Marcion included he felt free to rework a bit. He cut out anything that did not agree with his theological convictions and anything too closely aligned with the Old Testament.

In response to Marcion's editorial work and his "heretical" beliefs, the church began to take more seriously the importance of determining which books were to be considered authoritative and read and studied in worship.

During this same period, a Christian leader named Justin Martyr, a philosopher and teacher living in Rome, wrote extensively in defense of the Christian faith. Among his writings, there is a description of worship in Rome at the middle of the second century. It mentions the "memoirs of the apostles," which he had, earlier in the document, identified with the Gospels. His description of second-century worship is fascinating:

> On the day called Sunday, all who live in cities or in the country gather together to one place, and the memoirs of the apostles or the writings of the prophets are read, as long as time permits; then, when the reader has ceased, the president verbally instructs, and exhorts to the imitation of these good things. Then we all rise together and pray, and, as we before said, when our prayer is ended, bread and wine and water are brought, and the president in like manner offers prayers and thanksgivings, according to his ability, and the people assent, saying Amen; and there is a distribution to each, and a participation of that over which

thanks have been given, and to those who are absent a portion is sent by the deacons. And they who are well to do, and willing, give what each thinks fit.[4]

Sunday worship in the middle of the second century thus included gathering, reading from the Gospels and the prophets, receiving exhortation through preaching, praying, taking the Eucharist, and giving an offering.[5] But the key thing to note is that by the middle of the second century, the Gospels were read alongside the Old Testament prophets in the churches, and reading from the Gospels was a weekly part of worship.

One of Justin's students was a man named Tatian. Not long after Justin wrote these words, Tatian created a document called the *Diatessaron* (which means "made of four") in which he combined the four Gospels, removing redundant material, fitting the conflicting material together, and creating one continuous story from Jesus's birth to his ascension. Two things to note: First, Tatian's use of the four Gospels indicates that by AD 170 they were considered the authoritative Gospels (there were many other gospels circulating, but none had the general acceptance of these four, and nearly all had been written decades after Matthew, Mark, Luke, and John[6]). Second, it was not viewed by the churches of that time as inappropriate for Tatian to edit the four Gospels into one, cutting things out and smoothing things over to create one account. This points to the fact that in the 170s, though the Gospels were considered important and authoritative texts, their content and status did not put them above a bit of editorial work. Tatian's work was found so helpful by the Syrian churches that it replaced the four Gospels in many of their churches for almost two hundred years!

Iranaeus was a bishop of Lugdunum (now Lyon) writing around 170. He is best known for writings confronting the heretical movements of his time. By this time, a plethora of other gospels were circulating, most written in the second century and many supporting the unique perspectives of the various Gnostic heresies of the time. In that context, he states that there are four Gospels that have been given by God and which are the authoritative witnesses to Jesus Christ: Matthew, Mark, Luke, and John. Irenaeus is also the first to use the term "New Testament."[7]

Here's what we can say at the end of the second century: The four Gospels were seen by most of the church as authoritative and they were freely quoted. Paul's letters, by this time all thirteen of them, were regularly quoted by church leaders. The church fathers quoted 1 Peter, 1 John, and Revelation less frequently but still with some regularity. Hebrews, James, 2 and 3 John, and Jude were generally but not universally known or acknowledged, as certain parts of the church did not accept them. The writings of Christians we have from the second-century church do not mention or quote from 2 Peter.

Also at this time, several books dating back to the first and early second century were read and quoted across the church, sometimes as though they were on a par with the other scriptures. These included *The Shepherd of Hermas*, *The Didache*, *1 Clement*, and the *Letter of Barnabas*.

So by the end of the second century, 170 years after the resurrection of Jesus, we still don't have a book called the New Testament made up of a fixed set of twenty-seven documents. We do have four Gospels that were believed to bear the marks of authenticity. They were used throughout the church. The Acts of the Apostles was valued due to its connection to Luke. All of the letters of Paul we have in our New Testament were used across the church. Some of the other epistles[8] were known and used by many churches. Revelation, despite some hesitancy in parts of the church, was quoted and used in other parts of the church. And there were a handful of other books that did not ultimately become a part of our New Testament but which were thought to be authoritative by many churches and leaders. By the end of the second century there were also many other documents, purporting to be written by apostles, rejected by the churches.

THE THIRD AND FOURTH CENTURIES

The names Tertullian, Clement of Alexandria, and Origen dominate the conversations about the New Testament in the third century. Origen died in 254. Regarding the New Testament books in his day, he listed some as accepted (undisputed) and others as disputed. The four Gospels, Paul's thirteen letters, 1 Peter, 1 John, and Revelation were accepted as authoritative. The disputed books included Hebrews, James, 2 Peter, 2 and 3 John, and Jude. F. F. Bruce points out that Origen is the first of the church fathers to explicitly mention 2 Peter, 220 years after the death and resurrection of Jesus and 155 years after the death of Peter. Such listing of accepted and disputed books becomes common from the third century on.

It was a bishop named Athanasius, writing his Easter letter to the Christians in Alexandria, Egypt, in 367, who first listed the twenty-seven books of the New Testament as we find them today (though in a slightly different order). He felt the need to list these books for his communicants so that they might not be deceived by the many books that purported to be written by apostles but actually supported heretical teachings that had sprung up centuries after the apostles. Of the twenty-seven New Testament books, he wrote, "These are the springs of salvation, in order that he who is thirsty may fully refresh himself with the words contained in them. In them alone is the doctrine of piety proclaimed. Let no one add anything to them or take anything away from them."[9] Athanasius did commend the reading of *The Didache* and *The Shepherd of Hermas*, even though they were not canonical, because they were commended by "the Fathers."

Thirty years later, in 397, a council in Carthage, Africa, pronounced, "Besides the canonical Scriptures, nothing shall be read in church under the name of divine Scriptures," after which it listed the twenty-seven books we have in our New Testament. While individual books would continue to be included or excluded by various parts of the church over the next century, there was now general agreement on the canon of the New Testament scriptures. A full 367 years after the death and resurrection of Jesus, and 330 years after the deaths of Peter and Paul, the final form of the New Testament was fixed.

THE CRITERIA FOR INCLUSION
IN THE NEW TESTAMENT

So what determined if a document was accepted or disputed? Origen simply reports the practice of the churches across the empire, adding his own commentary on this practice. But this question is a good one. The answer is usually called the criteria for canonicity. This is important because it describes the answer to one of the questions we began the chapter with: how was it decided that certain books would be included in the New Testament and others would not?

The process by which our New Testament books came to be seen as authoritative was not neat and tidy, but it does involve identifiable criteria. Typically scholars list these criteria as Apostolicity,

Catholicity, Orthodoxy, and several others. I'd like to offer perhaps a different way of expressing these same basic ideas on how these twenty-seven books came to be a part of our New Testament.

The first and earliest criterion that led documents to have a life beyond the first generation was likely *Usefulness*. Paul's letters were found to be helpful to the churches that read them, so much so that they were copied and shared with other congregations. Their continued usefulness and relevance in the decades following Paul's death ultimately led to inclusion in the canon. The same was true of the four Gospels, which were found to be helpful in understanding and reflecting upon the life, teachings, death, and resurrection of Jesus. They became even more useful as the earliest generations of Christians died. Fewer churches found Revelation to be useful, however—it was difficult to understand, aside from the opening "letters" to the seven churches. Most of the books that ultimately were accepted as scripture had been found useful to large numbers of churches over a period of several hundred years.

The second criterion was *Consistency*. By this I mean that the message of the document was consistent with the faith as it was preached in the churches and as it was thought to have been established by the apostles. Reading the documents of our New Testament and comparing them with some of the other documents written in the late first century and second century, it is easy to see how different the faith is from the earliest teachings of the apostles. This is particularly true when comparing Matthew, Mark, Luke, and John with the gospels associated with the various Gnostic movements. Here's a small example, from the Coptic gospel of Thomas: "Jesus said, 'Blessed is the lion which becomes man when consumed by man; and cursed is the man whom the lion consumes, and the lion becomes man'" (1:7). While you have to think a bit about some of Jesus's sayings in the New Testament Gospels, this saying from Thomas is much more esoteric and inaccessible. Much of the gospel of Thomas is similar. This presentation does not sound like the faith as it was presented in Acts, in Paul, and in the canonical Gospels. This is also why some struggled a bit with John's Gospel. It was generally accepted fairly early, but its portrayal of Jesus sometimes leans toward some of the Gnostic writings (which is why the Gnostics often considered it their gospel of choice). This idea of consistency with the earliest faith was an important criterion in the acceptance or rejection of certain books as authoritative. This criterion is sometimes called orthodoxy.

The third criterion I'll call *Association*. By that I mean that a given book was associated with the first generation of Christian leaders. Many of the books written in the second century that sought a hearing claimed to be written by an apostle, but their date of origin indicated they were not. Conversely, our four Gospels were all written anonymously—they claimed no authorship and did not attempt to deceive others into accepting them by using an apostle's name. It was the early church leaders who associated these Gospels with Matthew, Mark, Luke, and John. Matthew was quickly associated with the disciple by that name. John claims to be written by the "disciple whom Jesus loved," who sat with Jesus at the Last Supper. Early in the second century, Mark was associated with John Mark, who traveled with Paul, was a nephew of Barnabas, and was said to be Peter's companion and interpreter in Rome up to the time of his death. Paul mentioned Luke in his epistles. By the way Luke wrote Acts, he seems to indicate that he was present for some of Paul's travels.[10] Paul was the leading evangelist and apologist for the Christian faith in the first century. His letters were taken seriously because of the prestige of their author. Any documents associated with the apostles or those who knew them carried special authority. This criterion is often referred to as apostolicity.

It also encompasses the criteria of antiquity. By the way, this criterion explains why some considered *1 Clement*, *Barnabas*, *The Didache*, and *The Shepherd of Hermas* to be authoritative, as these were thought to have been connected to early Christian leaders.

A fourth criterion is the product of the first three, and that is *Acceptance*. Long before the church was talking about a fixed canon of scripture called the New Testament, certain books circulated broadly and found widespread acceptance. When it came time to fix the canon—to say, "These books and no more"—the process for deciding which books were authoritative had been going on for three hundred years. If a small handful of churches in the third or fourth century suddenly accepted a book as authoritative, it was unlikely to be considered canonical by the rest of the church because it had not previously been known or accepted. When the vast majority of churches had accepted a book, the church as a whole eventually accepted it. This criterion is often referred to as catholicity. Some books were readily accepted in the East but with hesitation in the West, and vice versa. Some were questioned in the second century but accepted in the fourth. But by the late fourth century, those books included in the New Testament had found broad acceptance among the churches.

Some argued for a fifth criterion: inspiration. Others said this was implicit. The early church fathers believed that the Spirit spoke through them and through the apostles. Clement claims inspiration for his writings, just as he does for Paul's letters. Could inspiration be objectively identified? No. It might be subjectively experienced, but usually the idea was imputed to a text. A letter that was written by Paul, found to be helpful, universally accepted, and seemed to pass on an authentic witness to Christ would come to be viewed as inspired.

One last word about this: the process of canonization is a concept readily hijacked by conspiracy theorists and murder-mystery writers. Some suggest that a council led by the Roman emperor chose which books were in and which were out. Or that a group of church leaders sought to suppress the true Christian faith by weeding out books that disagreed with their views. While it is true that church leaders resisted those who sought to hijack the Christian faith and meld it with the various Gnostic philosophies that were nascent in the Greco-Roman world, the process by which the church ultimately settled on its authoritative books does not really read like a mystery novel filled with conspiracies and intrigue. It was generally a function of what a majority of Christians found helpful, useful, and consistent with the presentation of Jesus and the faith that had been handed down by the apostles.

You've waded through this chapter on the process by which our New Testament documents came to be considered authoritative and the development of the canon, and you know something about the criteria that determined what made it in and what was left out. At the very least, you've seen that the process was more complicated and messy than you might have first supposed. And you've seen that Christians had questions about some books and their content for centuries. This stands in stark contrast to the view of scripture held in many churches today: that the New Testament was essentially complete as we have it today by the end of the first century.

Some might say, "Well, it may have taken several centuries for the church to determine which books were canonical, but by the fourth century the question was settled, and now we're to accept the New Testament books and their contents without question." This was not the view of Martin Luther, the great Protestant reformer. Many Christians are surprised to hear that Luther himself raised questions about Hebrews, James, Jude, and Revelation based upon reservations about their theology. For instance, of the Book of Revelation Martin Luther wrote, "My spirit cannot accommodate itself to this book. For me this is reason enough not to think highly of it: Christ is neither taught nor known in it."[11] John Calvin wrote commentaries on every New Testament book except 2 John, 3 John, and Revelation. Did he simply grow weary of writing after completing commentaries on the other twenty-four New Testament documents? Or is it possible that this was Calvin's way of expressing his less than enthusiastic views of these three books?

Knowing the long process by which our New Testament came to be does not take anything away from my love of the scriptures or my desire to read them each day. I continue to believe that God has spoken through the New Testament's human authors, and I experience God continuing to speak to me through these books, even the disputed ones. But knowing the story of the New Testament's canonization allows me to see its humanity, to see it as the product of human authors, inspired by God, who wrote to meet the needs of the churches of their time. Those writings were found helpful to future generations and gradually came to be seen as being set apart by God for the church.[12]

These last fourteen chapters have laid the groundwork for some questions I want to ask in the next four chapters: Is the Bible inspired? Is the Bible the word of God? How does God speak through the Bible? And is the Bible ever wrong?

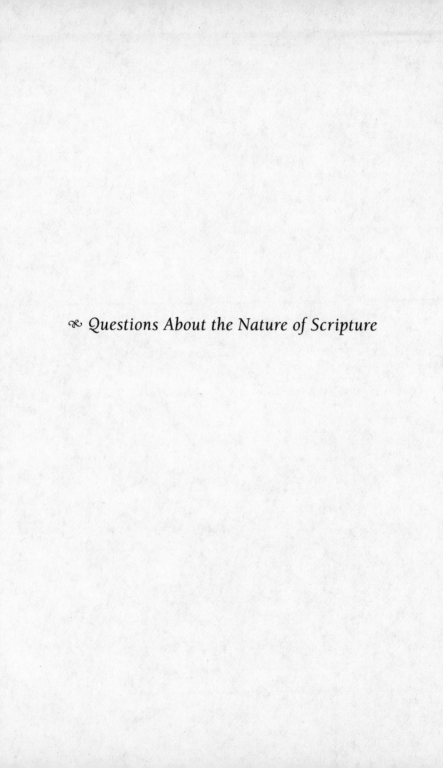

❧ *Questions About the Nature of Scripture*

CHAPTER 14

Is the Bible Inspired?

This week I received an e-mail from a parishioner who said, "Pastor, I need to know—do you believe all scripture is God-breathed? This is what I believe, and I need to know if you and our church believe this. I can't belong to a church that doesn't believe this. If we could meet to talk about this, it shouldn't take more than ten minutes." What I knew in reading her note was that this was not a ten-minute conversation.

This woman wanted to know if I believe the Bible is *God-breathed*. I wanted to know precisely what she meant by that. "God-breathed" is a translation of the Greek word Paul used to describe scripture in 2 Timothy 3:16, a word typically translated as "inspired." In this chapter I'd like us to think carefully about what is, and is not, meant by "God-breathed" or "inspired" as it pertains to the scriptures.

Inspiration is a difficult concept to define precisely, particularly when it comes to the Bible. Many Christians assume that inspiration means that God composed the Bible, word for word. But the word "inspiration," at least in English, is quite different in meaning from the word "composition" or "dictation." Some believe a result of inspiration is that the Bible is completely without error and that its statements are always true and accurate regarding anything it speaks about, not just theological assertions, but science and history as well. But inspiration, at least in English, does not mean perfection. What then does the word "inspired" or "God-breathed" mean when Paul uses it to describe scripture?

Scott Barry Kaufman is a cognitive scientist at New York University. He has spent time studying the concept of inspiration as we experience it in daily life. In an article on the *Harvard Business Review*'s blog, he writes, "Inspiration awakens us to new possibilities by allowing us to transcend our ordinary experiences and limitations. Inspiration propels a person from apathy to possibility, and transforms the way we perceive our own capabilities."[1] That is precisely the impact scripture can have in the life of Christians when they read it, hear it read, or hear it expounded upon in preaching, and it may well describe the inspiration from God that came to biblical authors as they wrote.

I was preaching on forgiveness recently, and a man came to me following the sermon and said, "Hearing what the scriptures said about forgiveness and the way you helped explain it, I am going home to call my Dad. I haven't spoken to him in over twenty years. It's time for me to make amends." That's the power and inspiration of scripture. I think of a woman who gives so much of her time to our work with inner-city schoolchildren. She notes that it all began as she listened to the scriptures and a message on Jesus's parable of the sheep and the goats. The inspiration and power of scripture's message set her on a path to selflessly serving "the least of these." In my own life, while reading Luke's Gospel, I found myself so moved by the story of Jesus that I got on my knees in my bedroom and offered my life to Christ. That is the inspirational power of scripture.

Another way we experience inspiration through scripture is illumination. There are moments when reading scripture, hearing it read, or hearing it preached, that the listener suddenly understands his or her life situation in a new light. Confusion gives way to clarity. These are the kind of "aha" moments that scripture evokes.

Captured in the examples above but often going beyond them, is the way we enter into a conversation with God through scripture. We hear God's voice as we listen to scripture's words. I find I am most likely to hear God in scripture when I approach it anticipating that God will speak. Sometimes, before I read, I pray the prayer that Eli taught young Samuel in 1 Samuel 3:9, "Speak, Lord, for your servant is listening."

Up to this point I've described the way scripture inspires us. But the question we want to consider in this chapter is not simply how we are inspired by the Bible, but in what sense God inspired its human authors or, more to the point, in what sense its words are in fact the message of God.

The phrase "inspired by God" is found only once in the Bible. It appears in 2 Timothy 3:16–17: "All scripture is *inspired by God* and is useful for teaching, for reproof, for correction, and for training in righteousness, so that everyone who belongs to God may be proficient, equipped for every good work" (emphasis added). Before considering what "inspired by God" means, let's begin by asking what "all scripture" refers to.

Though many of the New Testament documents were written before 2 Timothy, it is unlikely that Paul[2] was speaking of any of these documents as he wrote the words "all scripture." I believe it would have been unthinkable to Paul that his letters were on a par with the Law of Moses or the Prophets, even though the church would later consider them so. "All scripture," for Paul, would have referred to those scrolls or documents that were considered authoritative by the Jewish and early Christian community. As we've seen, there was still debate in Paul's day as to which documents were authoritative. Did Paul mean all the documents that were part of the Greek translation of the Old Testament, since he seemed most often to quote from this translation (including those books found in the Orthodox and Roman Catholic Old Testaments and not found in the Protestant Old Testament)? Or did he mean the documents that were accepted by the leaders in Jerusalem, which are only those found in the Protestant Old Testament?

Further, when he said "all scripture is inspired by God," did he literally mean every word of scripture? Or was he referring to its big ideas and key messages? It is not clear, as we read 2 Timothy 3:16, precisely what Paul meant by "all scripture."

Let's consider another question, how precisely does inspiration work? I began the chapter talking about our typical experience of inspiration: We feel moved, provoked, roused, stimulated, influenced, urged to do something. If this is what Paul had in mind, then he may have been saying that each biblical author was moved, provoked, roused, stimulated, influenced, or urged to write.

As I was preparing my sermon this week, I began by praying, "God, please speak to me as I study the scriptures" (I was preaching on the story of Hagar in Genesis 16 and 21). As I read the scriptures, I felt deeply moved by several things in the story. As I studied the stories in more depth, I learned things that I felt urged to share with the congregation. In the end, the story touched me, and I attempted to share what touched me with the congregation in a way that would inspire them. After the sermon, some said that they felt God was speaking to them during the message. I felt *inspired* as I studied and wrote the message. I did not feel God dictated to me what to say, but I did feel a strong compulsion to share the message I did. I prayed that God would use me to speak to the people.

I suspect that we all have experienced this kind of inspiration from time to time—this sense that God wants us to say or do something. Perhaps, in 2 Timothy 3:16, Paul was saying that the biblical authors were inspired like this as they wrote. I would never claim that every word in my sermon was chosen by God. I do pray, however, that the overarching message in some imperfect way communicated God's heart, character, and will to the congregation.

If this is what Paul meant, then the biblical authors were moved, urged, or compelled to write the message yet did so in their own words, with their own cultural assumptions and within the limits of their vocabulary and knowledge. They may not have communicated perfectly, but they were nevertheless used by God as they wrote.

So often those who cite 2 Timothy 3:16 as the basis for their understanding of scripture assume a view of inspiration that Paul never claimed, that scripture nowhere teaches, and which no human being alive today claims to have experienced. One way to understand what Paul meant by "inspired by God" would be to look to our own experience of inspiration from God and posit that the scripture writers were similarly inspired.

Let's take a closer look at the Greek words Paul uses in 2 Timothy 3:16 to see if they can help us understand what he means. This phrase, "inspired by God," is just one word in the Greek: *theopneustos*. It is a compound word, derived from *theo*, meaning "God," and *pneo*, meaning "to breathe out" or "to blow." Paul appears to have created this word himself. It appears nowhere else in the Bible and, to our knowledge, nowhere else in the Greek language until after

Paul's time.[3] That makes it difficult to know precisely what Paul meant by the word. (When you see a new word, you typically learn its meaning by looking at the context and its etymology. To get an even clearer understanding, you look for other uses, but in this case there are no other uses.) It could have meant "God-exhaled" or "God-breathed," or perhaps he was drawing from the Greek word for Spirit, *pneuma,* in which case it might mean something like "God-Spirited."

Let's consider the idea of "God-breathed" or "God-exhaled." What could Paul have meant by this exactly? We don't know. The word seems metaphorical, not offering a precise definition of God's literal involvement with the writing of scripture but clearly associating scripture with God's breathing (an anthropomorphism since we don't believe that God literally breathes).

What if Paul, in using the word "God-breathed," is drawing upon the Genesis story of Creation? Genesis 2:7 says, "Then the Lord God formed man from the dust of the ground, and breathed into his nostrils the breath of life; and the man became a living being." When God first forms man out of clay, he is not yet a living being. God breathes into him and he becomes animated—he is now alive. Paul knew of scripture's human authors. Was he suggesting that God breathes upon the human words of scripture thereby animating them, making them "living and active"?[4] The words come alive in the moment when God, by the Spirit, uses these human words to speak to us.[5]

To clarify this parallel to Genesis 2, we might say that in the view of Genesis 2,

1. God forms the man.

2. God breathes into him.

3. He becomes a living being.

In the case of the scriptures,

1. Authors write scriptures.

2. God breathes on them.

3. The words come to life.

I don't know if this is precisely what Paul meant by the word *theopneustos*. My point is that there are numerous ways of understanding what Paul might have been thinking when he wrote that scripture is "God-breathed."

There are other scriptures that might help us understand how the early church thought of the idea of inspiration. In 2 Peter 1:20–21, we read, "No prophecy of scripture is a matter of one's own interpretation, because no prophecy ever came by human will, but men and women moved by the Holy Spirit spoke from God." Peter[6] is referring here to words he believed foretold the coming of the Messiah. Interestingly, as we learned earlier in the book, many of these prophetic words meant something completely different to generations of Jews before the time of Christ. But when Christians read the prophets, they suddenly heard something that others hadn't heard before. This captures both senses of what *theopnuestos* might mean: the biblical authors were "moved by the Holy Spirit," and the scriptures were breathed upon as Christians read them, so that they saw things that previous generations had not seen in the prophetic words.

In Acts 1:15–26, the disciples are discussing Judas Iscariot, who betrayed Jesus and then took his own life. Concerning Judas's betrayal and subsequent death, Peter says, "Friends, the scripture had to be fulfilled, which the Holy Spirit through David foretold concerning Judas." He goes on to quote Psalm 69:25: "Let his homestead become desolate, and let there be no one to live in it,"

and Psalm 109:8: "Let another take his position of overseer."
Notice once more Peter has made reference to the Holy Spirit's role
in the writing of the scriptures.

Peter seems to say here that the Holy Spirit led David to write
the words of Psalms 69 and 109, and these words were a prophecy
about the betrayal of Christ by Judas Iscariot. Here I'd remind you
of our discussion in chapter 7. The early Christians read the Old
Testament through the lens of Jesus's life. They often gave new
meaning to old scriptures. They saw Jesus on nearly every page of
the Old Testament. But when you go back and read verses like
Psalms 69:25 and 109:8 in their original context, they don't look
like prophecies and they don't sound like things we would expect
the Holy Spirit to inspire.

These two psalms seem to be speaking of events from the time
of David. In Psalm 109, David prays that God will show no pity on
one who has betrayed him. He prays that the man's children will
become wandering beggars.

I love psalms like this because they are brutally and uncomfort-
ably honest in expressing the author's hurt and pain. But here's the
question: Would the Holy Spirit have inspired David to pray such a
prayer? Is it not the opposite of Jesus's command to love our enemies? Though the meaning of David's words seems clear, the New
Testament apostles lifted these words out of their original context
and heard God speak through them a word needed in the light of
Judas's death. This passage points once more to the idea that God
might breathe fresh meaning into the otherwise static written words
of scripture.

Recognizing that we have no clear definition of what Paul meant
by *theopneustos,* we can still say with confidence that the apostles
believed the sacred writings were influenced by the Holy Spirit in
some way, that they not only spoke to the people in the time they

were written, but the Holy Spirit would continue to use these words of scripture and give them new meaning, making them alive and active, and useful for the early church.

So let me ask a question that might make you uncomfortable, one that I've already hinted at in this chapter: do you think the scripture writers Moses, David, Matthew, and Paul were inspired to a greater degree or in a different way than we experience the inspiration and guidance of the Spirit as Christians today? When a pastor prays while preparing his or her messages each week, "Holy Spirit, guide me that I might speak the words you would have me share with the congregation," will the guidance he or she receives from the Spirit be less than or different from that received by the scripture writers?

In the appendix to his excellent book, *A High View of Scripture?*, Craig Allert lists nineteen examples of the church fathers, through the first four hundred years of the Christian faith, using *theopneustos* or similar phrases to describe their own writings or the sermons, decisions, and writings of others.[7] His point is that this term, as used and understood in the early church, apparently did not have the exclusive meaning that many Christians imbue it with today.

As Paul was writing his letters, he no doubt sought to be led by the Spirit, but he does not indicate that he was in any heightened state of inspiration. And Luke, when he describes the process for writing his Gospel, describes doing research, reading what others had written, interviewing eyewitnesses, then intentionally sitting down to write an orderly account of Jesus's life. None of the New Testament authors, with the exception of John in Revelation, claimed an extraordinary inspiration beyond what is available to anyone who is in Christ and led by the Spirit.

What, then, would make Paul's words, or the Gospel accounts of Jesus, of any greater authority than something a contemporary

Christian might write? Isn't that the question the church wrestled with in the process of canonization? Remember, the word "canon" refers to something like a ruler—it is a standard by which other things are measured. The writings of the New Testament are our earliest sources for the Christian faith. The Gospels are the earliest accounts of the life of Jesus—what he said and what he did—that we possess. And the letters of Paul and the other apostles represent the attempts of the earliest leaders of the church to describe both the meaning of the Christian faith and its implications for the lives of believers.

These early Christians may have written under the same kind of inspiration we experience today, but what differentiates their writing from ours is that they were closest to the events described. They had seen Jesus, knew those who had, or had access to the earliest traditions of the Christian church. They are the founding fathers of our faith, just as Washington, Jefferson, and Adams are the founding fathers of our country. Jefferson's words will always have greater authority than any of our nation's leaders today.

Not only that, but during the first four hundred years of church history, the words of the documents in our Bible were found to be useful, helpful, and inspirational for Christians across a wide swath of the ancient Roman world. When the church finally set the "ruler" by which all other words about the faith would be measured and judged, it chose these documents.

Many Christians read the word "inspired" or "God-breathed" in 2 Timothy 3:16 (*theopneustos*) and immediately give a definition that Paul himself did not give. To them, "God-breathed" means something very close to God-dictated. Regardless of what Paul, or Luke, or Peter perceived themselves to be doing, many Christians today believe that God influenced the choice of every word and every idea, so that the words written were literally the words of God. This doctrine is often referred to as verbal, plenary inspiration.

Verbal, plenary inspiration is not taught in the Bible, and it is not the essential meaning of *theopneustos* as it was used by Paul or the early church. It was not a doctrine taught in the creeds of the early church. That's not to say that none in the early church held a similar view. Origen, for example, held such a view, but his belief that each word was chosen by God led to allegorical forms of interpretation that no one finds acceptable today.

The modern adoption of verbal, plenary inspiration was in many ways a response to perceived threats to Christian doctrine and to traditional understandings of the Bible that emerged, particularly in the nineteenth century, as a result of the Enlightenment. When I think of the history of this view of scripture, I'm reminded of Newton's third law of motion, in which he postulated that "for every action there is an equal and opposite reaction." When the Enlightenment thinkers began to critically study the Bible, questioning virtually everything in it, some Christians responded by articulating a doctrine of inspiration which said that every word of the Bible was chosen and inspired by God himself. Why was this important? Because if inspiration means that God chose every word, and God is all-knowing and without error, and thus totally trustworthy, then the book he authored must be without error and totally true and trustworthy. And this means the Bible is above question, and whatever it affirms is true, whether this affirmation is about history or science, geography or theology. Verbal, plenary inspiration was a way of building a fence around the Bible and making it impossible to question it or any doctrine built upon it. Those who held this view knew their doctrines were above question because "God says it (in the Bible), I believe it, that settles it."

Verbal, plenary inspiration and the doctrine of the inerrancy and infallibility of the Bible go hand in hand. If you examine the "faith statement" of many conservative Christian organizations or churches, the very first statement of faith, even before the organization says it believes in God or what it believes about Jesus, is a statement about what it believes about the Bible or a word about verbal, plenary inspiration. This is very different from the ancient creeds of the church, which always began with God, not scripture: "I believe in God the Father Almighty, maker of heaven and earth."

None of the historic creeds of the church, those from the first five hundred years of the Christian faith, mention an infallible or inerrant Bible or the idea of verbal, plenary inspiration, and none begin with an affirmation of faith in the scriptures. But for many, this has become the first and foundational creed of Christendom.

This new foundation for the Christian faith, namely that Christianity is true because the Bible is infallible, inerrant, totally true, and trustworthy, feels to me like a house of cards that can easily be brought down. All that is necessary is for someone to demonstrate even one genuine error or one logical contradiction in the Bible, and the entire Christian faith comes into question. Jesus and the apostles were thoroughly immersed in the scriptures. Yet they never taught this view, and this was certainly not the foundation of their faith. They did not call people to a belief in verbal, plenary inspiration.

Often those who hold this view quote scriptures that they interpret as teaching verbal, plenary inspiration, but if you read these scriptures carefully (the chief of which is 2 Timothy 3:16), none actually teach this. The scriptures are read through the presupposition or filter of verbal, plenary inspiration, leading those who hold this view to interpret scripture in the light of this presupposition.

Verbal, plenary inspiration also claims that every word in scripture is equally inspired. It is interesting, however, that Jesus and the apostles show very clear preferences for certain books of the Old Testament. Psalms is cited sixty-nine times in the New Testament and Isaiah fifty-one times, but Joshua and 1 Samuel are cited only once each, and Ezra, Esther, Song of Songs, Lamentations, Obadiah, Nahum, and Zephaniah are not cited at all. This does not disprove the doctrine, but it does indicate that some books seemed to have been more meaningful to Jesus and the apostles, and hence had a greater impact on the thinking of the early church.

Here's my point: though the tenets of verbal, plenary inspiration have been ingrained in the minds and hearts of many Christians to the point that they are simply assumed to be true, the Bible's own witness about inspiration and the influence of the Holy Spirit on the Biblical text allows for a much broader understanding. Clearly New Testament authors believed that Old Testament scriptures were written under the influence of the Spirit, but the precise nature of that influence is not clearly articulated. Paul's use of *theopnuestos* (God-breathed or inspired) in 2 Timothy 3:16, far from being the precise technical term some conservative Christians have suggested, is a metaphor for God's influence on the Biblical texts that could be understood in a variety of ways.

The various books of the Bible were written by people—people who were shaped by the times in which they lived and the limitations of their knowledge. As we saw concerning Paul in Galatians, their own historical circumstances, their convictions, and even their personalities come through in their writings. They wrote drawing upon the data they had access to and based upon the needs of the communities to whom they were writing. They were devout followers of God, respected and recognized for their spiritual leadership. They sought to love God and neighbor. They wrote to earnestly help their fellow God-followers to know God and to understand God's will and God's ways. Yet they were human beings.

Yes, they were influenced by the Holy Spirit, but God saw fit to leave the exact nature and meaning of this inspiration a bit mysterious. The most important dimension of inspiration may be how God uses the words of scripture to speak to us today.

The Anglican side of the Reformation, and the Methodist views based upon it, held that the Bible contains "all things necessary to salvation" (meaning the teaching or knowledge essential to salvation) and that nothing could be insisted upon by way of doctrine or practice that was not clearly demonstrated in scripture.[8] Neither the Anglican nor Methodist Articles of Religion put forward a particular doctrine of inspiration, but they make clear that scripture is the primary source of faith and practice and that it adequately describes what is essential for salvation. But discovering these truths will require interpreting scripture, making sense of them in the light of the time and circumstances in which they were written. Further, the Jews have understood for millennia the importance of conversation and debate over the meaning of the scriptures as they sought to interpret them.

As we read scripture, we are involved in hearing God speak through it. We may read a passage of scripture and hear nothing at all. Then we read it again prayerfully, and we hear something we did not hear before. We sense God speaking to us. Often it is as we dig deeper into a text, studying the written document's context, background, and the author's intention, that we begin to hear God speak through it. The Spirit also uses the exposition of scripture in sermons and meaningful discussion in small groups studying the Bible to breathe upon us and upon scripture so we hear God speak through it. The church and our own intellect help us discern God's message to us in the midst of the writings of those who lived two and three thousand years ago. Ultimately this understanding of inspiration may sound familiar to some of you: it involves reading and interpreting scripture with the help of the *tradition* of the faith, the *experience* of the Spirit, and the use of our human *reason*.

I've suggested in this chapter that inspiration is not dictation but divine influence, on both the writer and the readers. I've suggested that divine influence on the writers was not qualitatively different from the way God inspires or influences by the Spirit today. The difference between biblical texts and some contemporary writings also influenced by the Spirit is that the biblical authors lived closer to the events of which they wrote, their writings served as instruments through which God spoke to the community of faith over long periods of time, and these writings are the founding documents of our faith. This view allows us to value the Bible, to hear God speaking through it, yet gives us permission to ask questions of the biblical text and to recognize that some things taught in scripture may not represent God's character nor his will for us today, and perhaps never accurately captured God's will. These topics include things like slavery, misogyny, genocide, and other issues we'll consider in section 2 of this book.

Through the words of the Bible, the Holy Spirit has spoken and continues to speak. It is inspired, and it inspires. Its words, coupled with the Spirit's power, are useful "for teaching, for reproof, for correction, and for training in righteousness, so that everyone who belongs to God may be proficient, equipped for every good work." *And* it also reflects at times the limitations, biases, and assumptions of its human authors.

CHAPTER 15

Is the Bible the Word of God?

As children, many of us learned to sing, "The B-I-B-L-E. Yes, that's the book for me. I stand upon the Word of God, the B-I-B-L-E!" As adults, those of us in mainline churches often hear our pastors finish the reading of scripture by saying something like "The word of God for the people of God. Thanks be to God." Those of us in conservative churches are often taught that the Bible is the "inerrant, infallible Word of God." In this chapter, I'd like us to consider the question, "Is the Bible the word of God?"

Maybe we can start by asking, is the Bible *the* word of God, as in the only or even the definitive word of God? To answer this question, let's first consider the words of John 1: "In the beginning was the Word, and the Word was with God, and the Word was God. . . . And the Word became flesh and lived among us, and we have seen his glory, the glory as of a father's only son, full of grace and truth" (John 1:1, 14). I read this passage to say that God's wisdom, God's truth, God's desire to reveal himself and his will became flesh in Jesus Christ. In this sense, Jesus Christ is the *definitive, unmitigated* Word of God. Aside from the Ten Commandments, which Exodus claims were engraved onto stone by the finger of God, Jesus is the only Word from God that does not come to us through the minds, the ears, and the hearts of fallible human authors.[1] When God wanted to speak definitively to the human race, he did not dictate a book; instead, he sent Jesus. And Jesus did not write a book; he preached, ministered, suffered, died, and rose from the grave. Jesus, following his resurrection, did not tell his disciples in the great commission to write a book. He told them to go and make disciples, baptizing and teaching the things he had taught them. Clearly the Bible bears witness to their message and is critically important. My point is that *the* Word of God by which all other words of God are measured must be the Word that was made flesh, Jesus Christ.

If Jesus is the Word of God enfleshed, in what sense should we say that the Bible is the word of God? Let's start with the obvious assertion that some of the words of the Bible do not reflect God's word. For example, much of the Book of Job contains the words of Job's friends who are giving him bad advice and expounding faulty theology. They get far more ink than God does in Job, and God chastises them for their words. Further, the words of liars, cheats, and false prophets are recorded in books of the Bible. Even the devil has a few paragraphs between the opening of Job and the temptation of Jesus. The Psalms are interesting in that most are prayers to God, not words from God. That's not to say that God did not influence any of these prayers to himself, but there are some that seem clearly inconsistent with what God reveals in Jesus. This is seen most clearly in the psalms that cry out for vengeance and retribution against Israel's enemies, which are completely understandable as the cries of human authors but not as inspired words from the God who called us to love our enemies.

As we consider the idea of the word of God, the self-disclosure of God to human beings, it is good to recall for a moment that God speaks to us in a variety of ways. He reveals himself in and through the created world, as the Psalmist notes: "The heavens declare the glory of God." God speaks to us through a whisper in our hearts. When we become quiet and listen, we can often hear the "still, small voice" of God. God speaks through human instruments— prophets and preachers, but also friends and parents. God speaks to us through other written words aside from what is in the Bible: many times I've experienced God speaking to me as I read the words of a theologian, or those of a devotional book, or sometimes a moving novel. God speaks through music, whether it is contemporary Christian music, secular music that speaks to the human condition, or great classical music. I remember sitting in a Broadway musical and feeling God speak to me. I was so moved by something in the musical that, in the darkness, I wrote a page of notes that would become the starting point for a sermon. These are all means by which God speaks to us.

If you look up "the word of God" in scripture, you'll find that it occurs approximately forty-one times in the Bible. ("The word of the Lord" appears far more frequently—about 260 times—and what follows in the next few paragraphs is true of both phrases.) I say approximately because different translations may translate the Greek and Hebrew phrases behind "the word of God" slightly different depending upon the context. The Hebrew phrase is *debar Elohim*, while the Greek is either *rhema theou* or *logon theou* (or slight variations on these phrases). One way to get at the answer to the question, "Is the Bible the word of God?" would be to see how this phrase is used in the Bible itself.

In reading each of the forty-one passages that speak of the "word of God," few seem to refer to something written down in a scroll or book. Most often, the phrase refers to a message about God that is heard—either spoken or preached. In the Gospels, Jesus preaches "the word of God," but that is never an expository sermon on a text of the Old Testament.[2] When the apostles refer to the word of God, they are almost always referring to the proclamation of the good news of Jesus Christ, not something written in the scriptures. Let's take a look at a few of these passages that refer to the word of God.

In Luke 3:2–3, we see a typical use of the phrase: "The word of God came to John son of Zechariah in the wilderness. He went into all the region around the Jordan, proclaiming a baptism of repentance for the forgiveness of sins." The word of God here is dynamic—it comes to John. It is a message, a flash of insight, a prophetic call, an act of God speaking to John, but it does not seem to refer to a book (though John was quite familiar with the writings of our Old Testament).

In Luke 5, Jesus is preaching and teaching on the banks of the Sea of Galilee. Luke tells us that "the crowd was pressing in on him to hear the word of God." Only once in the Gospels does Jesus read a text from the Old Testament and then comment on it. His preaching typically involved telling stories or parables about the kingdom of God, but the Gospel writers considered this to be "the word of God."

In Luke 8, Jesus tells the parable of the sower. He tells his hearers of a farmer who scattered seed. Some was eaten by the birds, and some began to grow but died for lack of deep roots. Some seed fell among the weeds, where it began to grow but was choked out by the weeds. But some seed was sown on good soil, and it grew and produced a harvest, some thirty-, some sixty-, some one hundredfold. Jesus explains the parable by saying, "The seed is the word of God" (Luke 8:11). This seed is the preaching and teaching and sharing of the good news of the kingdom.

In Acts 4:31, we read that the apostles "were all filled with the Holy Spirit and spoke the word of God with boldness." What was the word of God that they were speaking? It was the good news of Jesus. In Acts 8:14, the disciples learned that Samaria had "accepted the word of God." This does not mean they had suddenly accepted the Old Testament (Samaritans viewed the Torah as their sacred scripture, though did not accept the Prophets and Writings as authoritative scripture). Luke (the author of Acts) is telling us that the Samaritans had accepted the "good news of the Kingdom of God and the name of Jesus Christ" (8:12).

In Acts 11:1, Peter reports that the Gentiles had accepted "the word of God." It was not the Hebrew scriptures they had accepted, but rather the good news of Jesus Christ. In Acts 10:38–43, Luke records what the "word of God" was that Peter had shared with the Gentiles:

> God anointed Jesus of Nazareth with the Holy Spirit and with power; . . . he went about doing good and healing all who were oppressed by the devil, for God was with him. We are witnesses to all that he did both in Judea and in Jerusalem. They put him to death by hanging him on a tree; but God raised him on the third day and allowed him to appear, not to all the people but to us who were chosen by God as witnesses, and who ate and drank with him after he rose from the dead. He commanded us to preach to the people and to testify that he is the one ordained by God as judge of the living and the dead. All the prophets testify about him that everyone who believes in him receives forgiveness of sins through his name.

This passage wonderfully preserves the "kerygma," or preaching, of the early church. It is clear in Acts that the "word of God" was not a book—it was a message that was preached, which, when heard, had the power to change lives.

Once more we turn to Peter, who makes the point crystal clear in his first epistle: "You have been born anew, not of perishable but of imperishable seed, through the living and enduring word of God. For 'All flesh is like grass and all its glory like the flower of grass. The grass withers, and the flower falls, but the word of the Lord endures forever.' *That word is the good news that was announced to you*" (1 Peter 1:23–25, emphasis added).

So the phrase "the word of God" as it is used in the Bible is almost always a message from God, disclosed at times through angels, sometimes directly to the heart of the individual, sometimes through dreams and visions, often through preaching and teaching and at times through a whisper. The phrase is used to describe a message conveyed, most often, through human beings, but which is believed to express or reveal God and God's will.

Let's return to the apex of God's self-disclosure of the Word by which all other words must be measured. This act of God's self-disclosure is seen, as we've noted, not in a book but in a person. Again turning to John's prologue, we read, "The Word became flesh and lived among us, and we have seen his glory, the glory as of a father's only son, full of grace and truth" (John 1:14). We find Paul saying something similar in Colossians: "In him all the fullness of God was pleased to dwell." *This* Word of God is inerrant and infallible. He is fully inspired. He did not come mediated by others.

All other words about God are mediated through human beings. But in Jesus, God wrapped his message, his character, heart, and purposes, in human flesh. Jesus is the decisive, definitive, unmitigated word of God.

The Bible is a record of God's self-disclosure to the patriarchs, to Moses, to the prophets and others. But the New Testament records God's most decisive revelation—his coming to the human race in Jesus Christ. The Gospels tell the story of Jesus. Acts tells the story of the Spirit's work as the first generation of Christians spread the good news of Jesus. The Epistles of the New Testament expound the meaning of Jesus Christ for first-century believers and give direction for how to live as his disciples. Revelation ends with the ultimate triumph of Christ over evil. God influenced these New Testament authors as they wrote, but all their writings were reflections upon the definitive Word of God, Jesus Christ. If the apostles' preaching about Jesus was called "the word of God," the writings that contain that message must surely too be called the "word of God." But the word of God preached and written is still a word that testifies to *the* Word of God that is Jesus Christ.

As we bring our discussion of this question to a close, let me offer an analogy. Remember, all analogies break down pretty quickly, but the reason they are used is that there is some way in which they help to clarify something that is difficult to understand. So here's an analogy that might help us think about the question as to whether the Bible is the word of God or only people's words about God.

I have a signed copy of Steve Jobs's biography.[3] Who is it signed by? By the author, of course. But Steve Jobs is not the author—in fact, the book was released just after his death. Walter Isaacson is the author. Isaacson is a pretty impressive guy himself. He was the chairman of CNN and the managing editor of *TIME*, but I didn't buy the book to learn more about Walter Isaacson. I bought the book because I wanted to know more about Steve Jobs, the late founder of Apple Computer. The cover of the book makes it clear what this book is about—it is a black-and-white photo of Steve Jobs.

This is an authorized biography. In this case, that means Jobs actually invited Isaacson to write it. The two men met together and talked by phone, for hours. Jobs shared photographs and stories and insights that no other journalist would have seen or known about. Steve Jobs is often directly quoted. Isaacson tried to carefully and faithfully represent what Jobs had told him. But the book represents *Walter Isaacson's understanding* of who Steve Jobs is. While there are places in the book where Jobs would likely have said, "Walter, you missed it there!" nevertheless the book captures the man Steve Jobs better than any other book ever will.

In a sense, the Bible is the biography of God. It is not an autobiography but an authorized biography. The biblical authors were men who walked with God, experienced God, and had a relationship with God. The Gospel writers were closer to Jesus than any contemporary writers ever will be. They sought to paint his portrait in words, to recall what he said, and to faithfully reproduce it. Paul and the other apostles who wrote Epistles sought to help others make sense of the meaning of gospel and its implication for the individuals and communities.

If you want to know God, there is no other book you can read that will help you know him and his will for your life like the authorized biography. You can read his actual words in many places on its pages. But you'll also hear the human authors' reflections upon God and their attempts to put into words the nature, character, and will of God. The Bible is not an autobiography. And it is precisely in the distinction between autobiography and biography that we might find help in making sense of the difficult passages of scripture that will be the focus of section 2 of this book.

So, is the Bible the word of God? Or is it the words of people about God? I find Karl Barth's way of answering these questions helpful: the Bible contains the word of God found within the words of its human authors.[4]

CHAPTER 16

How Does God Speak to and Through Us?

Has God ever spoken to you? I feel like God has spoken to me on many occasions. But I've never heard an audible voice. I tend to be leery of people who hear voices from God, though I don't doubt that God can speak that way. Some people, like Moses and Jesus and Paul, had moments when they heard the audible voice of God. But even they did not hear God this way most of the time.

As I noted in the last chapter, when I feel God speaking to me, it comes as a flash of insight, or a gentle but persistent nudge, or occasionally as a conversation in my head. These experiences most often come when I'm praying, or when I'm reading scripture, or when I'm listening to a sermon or a song. They sometimes happen when I'm taking a walk, or when I'm sitting with friends talking about matters of faith. Sometimes it's while reading books that have nothing to do with my faith. I once felt God speak to me as I was watching a Broadway play! I often carry a little moleskin journal with me to make note of these moments of inspiration.

When I sense a nudge from the Lord, I then test it against the "rule" of scripture (remember the canon is a rule—the books of the Bible that serve as our standard for teaching, according to the church). Does it line up with the character of God revealed in Jesus? Is it consistent with the ideas of scripture taken as a whole? Are there scripture verses that align with this? This is the process I go through each week while preparing my sermons as I read and study the biblical text. But here's the point I want you to see: I am never completely sure that what I'm sensing is God's word, or whether it is simply something I've felt a strong conviction about based on my study and my own personal ideas.

I will never say to my congregation, "God told me to tell you this!" Instead I say, "I believe this is what God wants me to tell you today." The difference is the recognition that I could be wrong. So I tell my folks, "I've spent twenty hours studying scripture, reading the commentaries, praying, and reflecting upon this message. I have two degrees in theology and biblical studies, a library of great books, and twenty-five years of ministry experience I'm drawing on, but all of that does not guarantee I'm right." I encourage our congregation to take seriously what I've preached for the reasons I've just mentioned, but I also encourage them to ask questions and to engage their intellect and their own study of scripture, whether they are listening to me or to any other preacher. I give them permission to disagree with me. Even with the best of intentions, and spending a lot of time in prayer and reflection, I know I will not always get it right when seeking to convey God's will to others.

Regardless of what your preacher, Bible study leader, or good friend tells you, this is how it is for all of us. We do our best to hear from God, but we are all a bit spiritually hard of hearing. Our own convictions sometimes get intermingled with what we believe God is saying to us. None of us knows everything. We're all shaped by our environment and limited in our understanding. We do our best to hear from God, but we hear God through our individual filters, our preconceived ideas and convictions. This is in part why the God of preachers who are staunch Republicans inevitably sounds like a Republican and why the God of preachers who are staunch Democrats sounds like a Democrat.

In the last chapter I suggested that the biblical authors were inspired by God in ways similar to how we are inspired by God today. When they wrote they did not enter a trancelike state in which God moved their hands. God did not audibly dictate the scriptures to them word for word.[1] Paul, when writing to the Galatians or the Romans, wrote what was in his heart and mind. He did not claim to be speaking directly from God. He clearly identified himself and his co-workers, not God, as the authors of his letters. He didn't often say, "God told me to tell you this." He reflected in his own words what he thought was true and what he believed the people needed to hear.

The same is clear in the Gospels, at least the two where the authors tell us something about why and how they were writing. In Luke 1:3–4, Luke tells Theophilus that he wrote his Gospel after carefully investigating everything, "so that you may know the truth concerning the things about which you have been instructed." If Luke had been simply inspired by the Spirit, he would not have needed to "carefully investigate everything." Luke doesn't say, "God told me to write these things down." Rather he says, "I decided to investigate and to write." Likewise, John tells us that he wrote "that you may come to believe that Jesus is the Messiah, the Son of God, and that through believing you may have life in his name" (John 20:31). He does not say, "The Holy Spirit told me to write these things." In fact, John 21:24 notes of the author (this appears to be an editorial comment by a later editor or the person who assembled John's material into the current Gospel), "This is the disciple who is testifying to these things and has written them, and we know that his testimony is true." He does not claim divine authorship but that the authorship belongs to the "beloved disciple" who wrote what he had personally seen and experienced.

In this and the previous two chapters, I've tried to make the same point in three different ways. Here is the point: We often think of the Bible as a supernatural book whose authors were inspired in a way and to a degree that ordinary Christians are not inspired. We're often not clear how this happened; we simply believe it is true. Yet the biblical authors, with a handful of exceptions, do not claim extraordinary inspiration.

If the biblical authors heard God speak to them as we hear God speak today, then we should expect that their cultural, historical or theological assumptions, presuppositions, and biases will come through in their writings. Being used by God, influenced and inspired by God, did not make them infallible nor did it erase their strongly held personal convictions. The biblical documents are nevertheless those writings that early Christians found to be useful, inspiring and to consistently and accurately convey the charters and rule of the Christian faith.[2]

CHAPTER 17

Is the Bible Inerrant and Infallible?

As we've seen in the last few chapters, ~~many Christians~~ ~~speak of the Bible as~~ "inerrant and infallible." "Inerrant" means simply "~~without error~~," or some would say "incapable of error." "Infallible" is from the Latin *in*, meaning "not," and *fallere*, meaning "deceive." "Infallible" would then mean that the Bible does not deceive or, more commonly, that it is incapable of being wrong. To say that the Bible is inerrant and infallible is to say that it contains no mistakes. Some have replaced "inerrant and infallible" with the phrase "totally true and trustworthy." We've touched on this question of the infallibility and inerrancy of scripture in previous chapters, but because these words have become a kind of litmus test for some Christians regarding the orthodoxy of one's faith, I think it would be good for us to spend a bit more time on this question.

Those who hold to inerrancy and infallibility sometimes point to Christians like Augustine, who noted in the fifth century, "I most firmly believe that the authors [of scripture] were completely free from error. And if in these writings I am perplexed by anything which appears to me opposed to truth, I do not hesitate to suppose that either the [manuscript] is faulty or the translator has not caught the meaning of what was said, or I myself have failed to understand it."[1]

Augustine is strong testimony. This quote points to the fact that even Augustine found things in scripture that perplexed him or appeared opposed to the truth. Yet despite this, he believed that the original documents written by the apostles and the Old Testament authors were "free from error." However, the fact that Augustine and other church fathers may have held to inerrancy does not prove the doctrine is true. Augustine and many other church fathers also believed in transubstantiation—that the bread and wine of the Eucharist actually become the body and blood of Christ—yet conservative Christians reject this understanding of Communion. Augustine and many fathers of the church believed in the perpetual virginity of Mary, yet conservative Christians typically reject this view as well.

As we have seen, the early church had an evolving understanding of exactly what constituted holy writings. But it also had an evolving and inconsistent view of precisely how God inspired or spoke through the scriptures. That they saw certain writings as scripture fairly early in the history of the Christian faith is clear. What exactly they believed about the nature of the scriptures is less so. What we can say for certain is that they believed the scriptures contained accurate testimony concerning what God had done in Jesus Christ and God's will for humanity, and that through them God speaks to human beings.

In this chapter, we'll consider why many mainline Christians and an increasing number of moderate evangelicals have rejected the idea of inerrancy (and verbal, plenary inspiration) that has been championed by conservative Christians, offering instead a view of scripture that takes seriously both the Bible's inspiration from God *and* the humanity of its biblical authors.

Let's begin by considering how those who hold to inerrancy define this doctrine. The definitive statement on inerrancy was drafted in 1978, when three hundred conservative evangelical theologians, biblical scholars, pastors, and laity met in Chicago and produced the "Chicago Statement on Biblical Inerrancy." This statement has been adopted by the Evangelical Theological Society as defining the doctrine of inerrancy. In the document's "short statement," it makes this claim regarding the meaning of biblical inerrancy:

> Being wholly and verbally God-given, Scripture is without error or fault in all its teaching, no less in what it states about God's acts in creation, about the events of world history, and about its own literary origins under God, than in its witness to God's saving grace in individual lives.[2]

Norman Geisler, one of the participants in the Chicago convocation, edited a book with papers written by scholars who drafted the Chicago Statement. The book, entitled simply *Inerrancy*, continues to be a standard for the defense of the doctrine. In the chapter titled "The Meaning of Inerrancy," Dr. Paul Feinberg offers this definition:

> Inerrancy means that when all the facts are known, the Scriptures in their original autographs and properly interpreted will be shown to be wholly true in everything they affirm, whether that has to do with doctrine or morality or with social, physical or life sciences.[3]

Both statements have a ring of truth. If God chose every word of scripture, of course every word must be true, for God does not lie or deceive and God is all-knowing. But there are two things that keep me from adopting this view. The first is that the Bible doesn't actually teach this view. I would encourage you to read every passage of scripture put forward by those who advocate the position. I did that as I was preparing to write this chapter. It seems to me that inerrantists start with a particular view of scripture, then interpret a variety of scriptures in the light of their presuppositions, leading them to read into them a meaning that may not have been held by the original authors. In other words, few if any of the scriptures cited, read in context, actually teach what inerrantists proclaim as the "biblical position" on the Bible.

The second reason I don't accept the doctrine of inerrancy is that the Bible, as we have it, is easily demonstrated to contain errors and inconsistencies. The writers of the Chicago Statement and most informed inerrantists are aware that there are many places where the plain meaning of the biblical text is inconsistent with what we know from modern science, archaeology, or history. They understand that there are inconsistencies within differing accounts of the same story. They acknowledge that there are some teachings in scripture that are no longer binding today, and they typically note that these teachings were shaped by the culture or times in which the scripture was written.

Supporters of inerrancy go to remarkable lengths to smooth over these inconsistencies and apparent errors. In cases where the Bible is inconsistent with history, archaeology, or science, they typically say one of three things: either that science, or archaeology, or history is wrong and the Bible is right regardless of the evidence; or that there is a perfectly logical explanation for the inconsistencies but we simply don't have all the facts at this time; or that this is an error from a copyist of the manuscript, and the error was not in the original "autograph" (an autograph is the original document of a biblical book as drafted by its original author).

The Chicago Statement on Biblical Inerrancy has nineteen articles, each with a statement of what the proponents affirm and deny when they speak of inerrancy. Many of these articles, particularly the denials, serve as caveats to their proposal that the Bible is inerrant. By the time all the caveats have been taken into account, the term *inerrancy* is, for all intents and purposes, devoid of meaning. For many moderate evangelicals and mainline Christians, the affirmations and denials seem like an exercise in mental gymnastics for the sake of preserving the use of the word "inerrant" when it comes to scripture.

For instance, the Chicago Statement and most other statements on inerrancy contain the caveat that inerrancy only applies to the "original autographs," meaning that only Paul's actual handwritten copy of Galatians was without error. Of course, we don't have the original manuscripts of any Biblical documents, so there is no way to prove or disprove this hypothesis. But would we not expect that God, who is said to have provided the grace of infallibility in the writing of the original manuscripts, would also ensure that they were infallibly passed on to us?[4] Otherwise what is the point of infallibility? This idea of the inerrant original manuscripts allows the inerrantist to speculate that any error that cannot otherwise be harmonized or explained did not exist in the original manuscript of the document.

The Chicago Statement goes on to affirm verbal, plenary inspiration. Again, this states in essence that while someone like Paul or Luke thought he was writing the documents that bear his name, God was actually "superintending" them as they wrote, such that God chose every word of scripture down to the exact word order.[5]

Yet supporters of inerrancy say that God did not dictate every word. This seems to defy logic, which is why I think the Chicago statement notes, "The mode of divine inspiration remains largely a mystery to us."

When it comes to the conflict between scientific explanations of the world around us and biblical teaching, the authors of the Chicago Statement deny that "scientific hypotheses about earth history may properly be used to overturn the teaching of Scripture on creation and the flood." In other words, the biblical teachings regarding Creation and the Flood are accurate regardless of what science can discern. (We'll talk more about this in chapters 19–21.)

Article 13 of the Chicago Statement offers this denial:

> We deny that it is proper to evaluate Scripture according to standards of truth and error that are alien to its usage or purpose. We further deny that inerrancy is negated by Biblical phenomena such as a lack of modern technical precision, irregularities of grammar or spelling, observational descriptions of nature, the reporting of falsehoods, the use of hyperbole and round numbers, the topical arrangement of material, variant selections of material in parallel accounts, or the use of free citations.

This is a loophole big enough to drive a truck through. But the next statement should cover any other apparent errors: "We deny that alleged errors and discrepancies that have not yet been resolved vitiate the truth claims of the Bible." So whatever apparent errors are not resolved by all the other denials still do not negate the fact that the Bible is inerrant!

I am grateful for Article 19: "We deny that such confession [of inerrancy] is necessary for salvation." That's a really important statement and greatly appreciated by those of us who reject inerrancy. But the article goes on to say, "However, we further deny that inerrancy can be rejected without grave consequences, both to the individual and to the Church."

The consequences include subtle, and sometimes not so subtle, persecution of those who deny inerrancy. Scholars have been ostracized from theological societies, pastors have lost their pastorates, seminary and college professors have lost their positions, and authors have been blackballed, all for not affirming inerrancy. Many evangelical scholars and pastors who have serious reservations about the doctrine seem to have professed inerrancy with their fingers crossed behind their backs just to keep their jobs or to continue publishing. They found ways to think about the doctrine so they could affirm it. If you can make the definition broad enough and add enough caveats, anyone can accept it.

For instance, if by biblical inerrancy we mean that "those truths that God wants humanity to know are preserved without error in the Bible," I'm ready to sign on. But if by biblical inerrancy we mean that the Bible contains no errors, no logical inconsistencies, no facts that are not historically accurate, I'd have to say, no, the Bible is not inerrant.

Let's consider a couple of errors or inconsistencies in important biblical texts. Genesis 1 states that planet Earth, with its atmosphere, water, dry land, and vegetation, was created on the first three days of Creation. Some conservatives see these days as epochs; others see them as twenty-four-hour days. Genesis then tells us that on day four, God created the sun and the moon.

What we know from modern science is that Earth's distance from the sun makes it possible for the earth to sustain life. It is in the "habitable zone" of our solar system. The gravitational pull of a sun plays a key role in the creation of planets. Day and night result from the rotation of the earth on its axis: as one part of the planet faces the sun, then rotates away from it, it experiences day and night. Modern science tells us that the sun played a critical role in the formation of our atmosphere. And even an elementary school child knows that the sun is essential for plant growth. Yet Genesis says that the planet was formed without the gravitational field of the sun, and it experienced day and night without the sun. It developed an atmosphere without the sun. And plants sprang up and grew without a sun.

It is likely that the biblical author was recounting the order of Creation as understood by the prevailing scientific views of his time. Or perhaps, as some have suggested, he was trying to make a theological statement, not a scientific one, as he told the Creation story. I am not troubled by the scientific inaccuracy because I don't think the story was written to teach science, nor do I expect biblical authors to have a prescient understanding of twenty-first-century cosmology and astrophysics. What troubles me is the fact that some who hold to inerrancy insist that modern scientific theories must conform to the scientific views held by people of the ancient Near East who lived 3,200 years ago.

Let's consider another example. Most inerrantists would agree that the story of Jesus's resurrection is one of the most important stories in all of the Bible. Yet the multiple accounts of the resurrection found in the four Gospels, despite agreeing on the most important fact—that Jesus was raised from the dead—differ in the details.

In Matthew 28, Mary Magdalene and another Mary went to the tomb of Jesus at dawn on Easter morning. An earthquake occurred, and an angel came and rolled back the stone and sat upon it. The guards posted at the tomb, seeing this, shook and fainted. The angel spoke to the women and told them to tell Jesus's disciples that he was raised and to go to Galilee, where Jesus would meet them.

Jesus first appeared to the disciples in Galilee, an eight- or nine-day walk from Jerusalem.[6] After giving the great commission, he ascended to heaven from Galilee.

Now, look at Mark 16. In Mark's version, Mary Magdalene and the other Mary are joined by Salome. No problem—Matthew may simply have forgotten to mention her. But in Mark there are no soldiers and no earthquake, and the stone is already rolled away when the women arrive. Not sitting on top of the stone, as in Matthew, but standing inside the tomb is a young man, who tells the women that Jesus has been raised and to send the disciples to Galilee, where Jesus will appear to them. Mark does not have Jesus appearing to the women. (Either Mark's Gospel originally ended at verse 8 or the original ending has been lost to us; the words that appear after verse 8 appear to have been added later.)

Let's consider Luke 24. Here a whole group of women have come to the tomb (v. 10), including Mary Magdalene, Joanna, Mary the mother of James, and others. They arrive and find the stone rolled away. They go inside, and the body is gone. Then, suddenly, *two* angels appear in their midst and tell them that Jesus has been raised. The women run to tell the disciples. Peter and John come to the tomb and find it empty. Later that day, Jesus appears to two disciples on the road to Emmaus, then to Peter, and finally, to all the disciples. Then Jesus leads them to Bethany, a suburb of Jerusalem, and he ascends to heaven from there.

Do you see how it is getting hard to reconcile these stories? They all agree that Jesus was raised, and this is the important point. But Matthew says Jesus ascends from Galilee, while Luke says he ascends from Bethany. The Galilee region and Bethany were nine days' journey apart. In a host of minor details, the stories disagree. This does not diminish the story for me. It does not make me question its validity. In fact, I would expect the details to differ. If three people who are trustworthy observe the same story and then retell it years later, I expect they will retell the story differently. But I don't think you can pretend that they don't disagree. And either Jesus ascended from Galilee or he ascended from Bethany, but both are not true.

Look at John 20–21. John seems to be trying to reconcile all three previous accounts. He also resolves the question of the location of Jesus's ascension by not mentioning it at all!

Here's the point I'm trying to make: These two stories, Creation and resurrection, are foundational stories in the Bible. Yet, in the Creation story, there is data that cannot be reconciled with what seem to be incontrovertible facts from modern science. And in the resurrection story, there are details from the different accounts that seem irreconcilable.

None of these "errors" or inconsistencies troubles me. Neither do they void the point being made in the stories. But these inconsistencies do, along with a hundred others in the Bible, call into question the dogma of inerrancy and infallibility.

Supporters of inerrancy often ask two questions of those who reject the doctrine: How could God, in his providence, allow biblical authors to make mistakes? And if there is an error anywhere in the Bible, how can we trust anything it says?

The answer to the first question is simple: How could God, in his providence, allow anyone who speaks on his behalf to make mistakes? Every Sunday around the world, hundreds of millions of people show up to hear their pastors and priests speak on behalf of God. Yet God does not guarantee that those who speak on his behalf are infallible. God uses fallible people. Paul did not set out to write the Bible; he set out as a Christian leader to send letters to help small churches scattered across the Roman Empire. We recognize that the Spirit influenced Paul, but those who reject inerrancy do not believe the Spirit guaranteed Paul's infallibility when writing his letters any more than God guarantees the infallibility of the pope or any other pastor or Christian leader when they write. Again, Paul's letters carry a weight of authority, but not because they were given a supernatural grace of infallibility. His earliest readers surely did not believe this about them. They carry a weight of authority because their author was a founding apostle of the Christian faith!

The answer to the second question—if there is an error anywhere in the Bible, how can we trust anything it says?—is also simple. You are constantly trusting the words of people whom you have found trustworthy, even though none of those people are inerrant or infallible. You likely trust your mom and dad, your teachers, your pastor, your professors in college, the people from whom you get your news—yet none of these are given a special grace that makes them free from error or inconsistency. If they occasionally get some detail wrong or misinterpret some fact, does that suddenly mean you can't trust anything they say? Of course not.

Those I trust are not perfect, but they are people of integrity. They are knowledgeable and wise, and they will never willfully mislead. Consider pastors for a moment. Pastors are entrusted with the care of their flock. Most long to hear from God, to rightly interpret and apply scripture to the lives of their congregation. They seek to give wise counsel to their members. Their flock looks to them for spiritual guidance and preaching and teaching through which they may hear God. But no pastor is infallible or inerrant. God knows this and chooses to use fallible people to do his work. God doesn't make them infallible when they step into the pulpit, yet God works through them nonetheless.

Rather than believing in an extra grace of infallibility given to each biblical author as he penned a proverb or a psalm, a part of the historical documents or a letter, I am suggesting once again that

God inspired each writer in the same way that God continues to inspire and speak through his people to this day. God has always chosen to risk using fallible human beings to accomplish his work. The Spirit influenced the authors of scripture and the process of canonization so that today we have a Bible that is trustworthy, but not one that is infallible.

One concern I have for those who hold to inerrancy is that they seem to indicate that their entire faith would collapse if the Bible were found to have one real error. As I noted in a previous chapter, this seems a very weak foundation for one's faith. The early Christians did not see an inerrant Bible as the foundation for their faith. For them, it was Jesus Christ, God's Word enfleshed, that was the foundation of their faith.

I open my Bible each morning, praying for God to speak to me. As I read it, I often feel inspired and moved by its words. I have sought to build my life on its teachings. Its words help me to know, love and follow Jesus Christ. I find it to be true and trustworthy, and I believe it is "useful for teaching, for reproof, for correction, and for training in righteousness, so that everyone who belongs to God may be proficient, equipped for every good work" (2 Timothy 3:16–17). I am also not troubled by occasional inconsistencies or the fact that biblical authors wrote in the light of the scientific knowledge of their time. As we will see in the next section, it is the humanity of the Bible that allows me to make sense of troubling passages of scripture that seem squarely out of sync with the lofty word of God we hear in and through Jesus Christ.

I'd like to end this chapter with another question: if we don't believe in verbal, plenary inspiration and biblical inerrancy, then what should our doctrine of scripture be? I mentioned in an endnote earlier the statement adopted by the Church of England in 1571 as Article 6 of the Articles of Religion (note that unlike many contemporary conservative creeds, the Articles of Religion started with God, not scripture, so that articles 1–5 were all about the Holy Trinity). It was adopted by John Wesley, during the eighteenth-century evangelical revival he led, as the official doctrinal statement of Methodists related to scripture:

> Holy Scripture containeth all things necessary to salvation: so that whatsoever is not read therein, nor may be proved thereby, is not to be required of any man, that it should be believed as an article of the Faith, or be thought requisite or necessary to salvation.

The statement avoids trying to define inspiration. It makes no claim that the Bible is without inconsistency or error, but it implies that whatever God knew we needed to know for salvation is found in the pages of the Bible. It goes on, in the spirit of the Reformation, to state that points of doctrine and moral imperatives that are not clearly found in scripture must not be considered requirements of God nor necessary to our salvation. That seems to me to be a pretty good statement concerning the Bible and one that is broad enough to allow a variety of theories concerning the nature of scripture's inspiration.

CHAPTER 18

A High View of Scripture?

Those who hold to biblical inerrancy and verbal, plenary inspiration often say that they have a "high view of scripture" and suggest that people who hold views other than theirs have a "low view of scripture." I want to end this first section by asking if this is an accurate assessment of what constitutes a high or low view of scripture. I will also summarize the view of scripture I'm proposing and seek to address objections likely to be raised by some Christians regarding this proposal (a proposal that is not original to me but rather how I think many mainline Christians view scripture).

Does a belief in verbal, plenary inspiration and the inerrancy of scripture constitute a "high view of scripture"? Not, I would suggest, if it is a wrong or misleading view of scripture. So we have to establish first whether verbal, plenary inspiration and inerrancy are accurate views of scripture. I've suggested in this book that they are not. Verbal, plenary inspiration and inerrancy constitute a dogma about scripture that is neither high nor low but rather, in my opinion, inflated and inaccurate. Some even suggest that such views are a form of idolatry, ascribing to the Bible attributes or qualities that belong to God alone. I don't doubt the sincerity of those who hold such beliefs. I know that most who hold these views are deeply committed followers of Christ. But I believe they've created a dogma about scripture, in some respects not unlike the Roman Catholic Church's dogma of papal infallibility, that is not substantiated by what we know of how the Bible was written, how it came to be canonized, nor the actual text of the Bible itself. And if, as I've suggested, this dogma about scripture is inaccurate, it does not constitute a high view of scripture.

I would offer a second thought about those who claim to hold a high view of scripture. There are millions of Christians who believe in verbal, plenary inspiration and inerrancy yet who seldom actually read the Bible, who do not engage in serious study of scripture, and who do not live its precepts. I would suggest that such persons, by any definition, do not have a high view of scripture if they neither read it nor seek to live it regardless of their stated belief in verbal plenary inspiration and inerrancy.

To me, someone who holds a high view of scripture approaches the Bible with a deep appreciation for its history and the way God has spoken and continues to speak through it. They recognize both the Bible's humanity and its divine inspiration, and they study it carefully in order to be shaped and guided by it. Someone with a high view of scripture actually reads the Bible, listens for God to speak through it, seeks to be shaped by its words, and seeks to follow its commands. One can long to do these things and not believe in inerrancy, and one can believe in inerrancy and not do these things.

Before moving into the next section of this book, where we'll focus on troubling passages of the Bible and questions thoughtful people raise about it, allow me to summarize once more what I'm proposing.

The Bible was written by human beings who brought to the task of writing their faith, their theological convictions, their experiences of God's presence and God's work in their lives, the needs of the community to whom they were writing, and also their cultural context. The divine inspiration of scripture was not God dictating the scriptures but God working in the hearts of the biblical authors in a way not dissimilar to how God works in the hearts of modern-day preachers and prophets and laity who are moved by the Spirit—through a divine prompting felt in the heart, focused in the mind, and spoken with the lips or the pen. But, as Paul noted in 1 Corinthians 13:9, "we know only in part, and we prophesy only in part." We are all spiritually a bit hard of hearing. And no preacher perfectly hears and communicates God's will all the time.

I am suggesting that the Spirit's inspiration of the biblical authors was consistent with the way the Spirit inspires human beings today. As the Spirit does not preclude error or inconsistency in those the Spirit uses today, the Spirit did not preclude error or inconsistency on the part of the biblical authors. As the Spirit uses people today to speak God's words to his people, the Spirit spoke through the biblical authors.

I'll ask once again, how are the scriptures of any greater authority than something written by C. S. Lewis or any other popular Christian of the last hundred years? What gives the biblical writings greater authority than contemporary writings? I've suggested that it is not a greater degree of inspiration but closer proximity to the events described in the Bible. Just as importantly, the scriptures are the foundational documents of the Christian faith and have been found faithful, helpful, inspirational, and useful to the community of faith over the nearly two-thousand-year history of the church. (These are the same qualities that led them to be included in the canon to begin with.)

No contemporary authors, regardless of how devout they may be or how clearly led by the Spirit, knew Jesus or the apostles personally; they were not a part of the conversations that helped shape the foundations of our faith; their work has not received the imprimatur of the councils of the early church; nor have their writings been found to have the universal impact the scriptures have. The biblical documents are "the writings" par excellence. They serve as the foundational documents of the Christian faith.

An analogy, though it quickly breaks down, is the Declaration of Independence and the Constitution, which are among the foundational documents of the form of government we have in the United States. No modern document, regardless of how brilliant the author, will ever match their authority in shaping our nation, because these two documents were the foundational documents, written by the founding fathers of our country. They have a different level of authority than any documents written since.

Finally, there are times when biblical authors express things in one place that seem to contradict what we learn of God's character and will expressed somewhere else. There are statements in the Bible that must be interpreted to make sense. And there are, on rare occasions, things that we rightly question, of which we may ultimately say, "I don't know precisely what to make of that passage, but the plain meaning of the text seems out of character for God based upon what Jesus has shown us about his Father."

The inerrantist will undoubtedly raise another question, and it is a good one: if you allow people to wrestle with and question the Bible, even at times setting aside something because it does not seem consistent with the nature and will of God revealed by Jesus, what keeps us from "picking and choosing" among the scriptures, setting aside those passages that we find inconvenient or not to our liking?

First, I would suggest that both conservatives and liberals regularly "pick and choose" scriptures to emphasize or deemphasize, whether or not they believe in inerrancy. Conservatives have at times deemphasized or spiritualized the Bible's teachings on justice and the poor. Some routinely set aside passages that do not support their political convictions. Liberals have at times deemphasized passages concerning God's judgment, and at times have deemphasized scriptures related to personal piety. Both conservatives and liberals have ways of reinterpreting certain passages that do not support their biases and political or theological convictions.

Be that as it may, it is important to ask by what criteria or hermeneutical principal we decide which scriptures may no longer be binding or which may not capture the will of God for us today. I agree with conservatives' concerns that our human sinfulness will lead us to set aside passages that are inconvenient. We might choose to set aside passages on justice, or mercy, or self-discipline, or loving our enemies. We cannot merely decide that we like or don't like this or that scripture. What I'm proposing is that we hear, examine, and interpret all scripture through the lens and filter of the *definitive* and *unmitigated* Word of God, Jesus Christ.

Jesus stated that there were three commands that summarize "the law and the prophets." In Matthew 7:12, Jesus says, "In everything do to others as you would have them do to you; for this is the law and the prophets." We know this as the Golden Rule. We might say that anything that violates this statement in scripture or calls us to violate this statement would be open to question. In Matthew 22:35–40, he offers two more commandments that act as summaries of the rest of the scriptures:

A lawyer asked him a question to test him. "Teacher, which commandment in the law is the greatest?" He said to him, "'You shall love the
Lord your God with all your heart, and with all your soul, and with all
your mind.' This is the greatest and first commandment. And a second
is like it: 'You shall love your neighbor as yourself.' On these two commandments hang all the law and the prophets."

A friend and fellow preacher noted that these two commands
function like a kitchen colander or strainer, holding the important
things while the less desirable are rinsed off. He proposed that anything in the Bible that is inconsistent with these great commands,
which Jesus said summarized the law and the prophets, could be
open to question.[1]

Perhaps a broader and more important colander would be Jesus
himself. What is the heart, character, and will of God that Jesus
reveals? For example, Leviticus 21:9 says, "When the daughter of a
priest profanes herself through prostitution, she profanes her father;
she shall be burned to death." Yet Jesus befriends prostitutes and
shows them mercy. These are two very different pictures of God
and how God looks at the prostitute. When we see this kind of dis-
parity between Jesus and anything else in scripture, it is the witness
of Jesus that we hold on to. We may see the conflicting passage as
reflecting a cultural context or the biases and assumptions of the
human author, or perhaps the passage served a purpose we don't
understand. But if Jesus is our colander, we may question whether
the passage from Leviticus ever actually reflected God's timeless
will for humanity.

As we seek to interpret scripture faithfully, we must not set aside
what is inconvenient or challenging to us simply because it is difficult. We will, however, read scripture in the light of the life, ministry, teaching, death, and resurrection of Jesus. When we find

something that is inconsistent with the way God reveals himself and his will through Jesus Christ, we may legitimately ask questions. In those situations, it is Jesus who serves as the final Word by which other words of scripture are to be judged.

There are also other important tools at our disposal as we seek to make sense of difficult passages of scripture, particularly tradition—the work of biblical scholars and theologians, and the reflection of the church's leaders through the ages as captured by creeds, catechisms, and doctrinal statements. Drawing upon these resources invites other Christians across the course of two thousand years to help us make sense of the Bible. We also bring our intellect and the power of reason to bear on our work of interpreting scripture. This includes our study of history, geography, archaeology, and a variety of other fields that help us understand the historical context of scripture. We are meant to engage our intellect in the study of scripture. Finally, we reflect upon scripture and interpret it in the light of our experience and the witness of the Spirit in our lives and in the lives of others.

Scripture, interpreted with the help of tradition, reason, and experience, helps us to know and understand God and God's will for our lives. Scripture is the primary source document for understanding God's heart, character, and will. We interpret it with the help of tradition, reason, and experience.

If what I'm suggesting still seems unsettling—that Christians may legitimately set aside clear teachings of scripture as no longer binding, seeing them as written primarily for another time and not reflecting God's timeless will—consider the dramatic scene in Acts 15. Paul and Barnabas had been preaching to the Gentiles, and they had seen many come to faith in Christ. But Paul and Barnabas did not insist that these new converts be circumcised as the Law of Moses required, nor did they insist that they obey many of its other

613 laws. This was scandalous to some Jewish Christians. What right did Paul and Barnabas have to determine, on their own, that parts of the Law were not binding upon Gentiles?

This question of what right Paul and Barnabas had to make such a sweeping determination is an interesting one. Remember, the only scripture that Paul had which he might describe as "inspired" was what we call the Old Testament (the New Testament not having been written yet). In the Old Testament, the Law of Moses was considered the most important and authoritative part by the Jewish people. Yet Paul and Barnabas made a determination that circumcision and other commands in the Law were no longer binding upon those who would follow God.

How did they arrive at such a dramatic and far-reaching conclusion? Jesus never personally taught that he was setting aside circumcision or any Law of Moses. We have no evidence of a vision directly from God to Paul and Barnabas. No, they seem to have reflected upon the significance of the "new covenant" that Jesus mentioned at the Last Supper. They reasoned, theologically and biblically, that Jesus had fulfilled the old covenant and instituted a new covenant by his death and resurrection. You can read their theological rationale in Galatians and Romans.

Yet not every Christian accepted their conclusions. In fact, they were fiercely opposed by some believers. Ultimately, Paul and Barnabas and those who opposed them traveled to Jerusalem and appeared before the apostles. Acts 15:5 notes, "Some believers who belonged to the sect of the Pharisees stood up and said, 'It is necessary for them [the Gentiles] to be circumcised and ordered to keep the law of Moses.' " Much debate ensued. Finally James[2] spoke up:

I have reached the decision that we should not trouble those Gentiles who are turning to God, but we should write to them to abstain only

from things polluted by idols and from fornication and from whatever
has been strangled and from blood. (Acts 15:19–20)

This is astounding! A council of disciples, upon hearing the testimony of Paul and Barnabas concerning the faith of the Gentiles,
set aside much of the Law of Moses as no longer binding upon the
church.

What just happened? And how was it determined that this was
the correct course of action? What happened was the recognition
that parts of the Bible no longer reflected God's will for his people.
This determination was made based on a theme of the Old Testament (that God would draw the Gentiles to himself), theological
reflection upon the nature of the new covenant Jesus had instituted,
conversation among the disciples, and the observation that the Holy
Spirit had already been poured out upon the Gentiles even without
circumcision.

The council prepared a letter to be sent with Silas and Judas,
two believers who also had prophetic gifts, and they read the letter
to the churches in Syria, including Antioch and Cilicia. This would
nonetheless continue to be, as we saw in Galatians, a source of conflict in the fledgling church, particularly for those associated with
the Pharisees, who did not accept the council's decision.

Here's the point I want you to see: Even the apostles did not
read the Bible from the perspective of "God (or the Bible) says it, I
believe it, that settles it." They were willing to debate how their
Bible applied to new situations. They recognized that parts of the
Bible needed to be reinterpreted. They concluded that some things
which had been very important within Judaism did not express
God's timeless will for humanity. Whatever view of the inspiration
of scripture they held, it allowed such conclusions.

Are there things clearly taught in scripture about which we

might say today, "That really doesn't capture God's will"? Yes. Both conservatives and liberals agree on some of them. With the apostles, we agree that we are not required to be circumcised. We recognize that the death penalty is not appropriate for most crimes for which the Law commanded it. Most agree that women are not required to pray with their heads covered, even though Paul commands it. The New Testament commands slaves to return to their masters and to live in submission to them, but Christians working in human trafficking today do not believe this passage relates to those caught in the web of modern human slavery.

It is this ability to ask questions of and wrestle with the Bible that makes it a living document in much the same way as the U.S. Constitution is said to be a living document. (I am not claiming the Constitution and the Bible are similar in content, and certainly not that the Constitution is inspired by God, but rather that the Constitution might help us to think about the Bible.) The framers of the Constitution were brilliant men. They had the foresight to draft a document that has stood the test of time. It was found by the people of the thirteen states to be useful and helpful, accurately capturing their hopes and ideals. But it was not perfect. And the framers of the Constitution knew that. They believed it was the best thing they could come up with at the time. But they also knew that circumstances would change, and there needed to be a way to amend the Constitution.

This was another sign of their genius. They made the bar very high to amend the constitution, yet they made it possible. Twenty-seven times the Constitution has been amended since 1789. In 1791, the Bill of Rights was added. Later slavery was abolished, and former slaves were made full citizens and guaranteed the right to vote. Still later, women were guaranteed the right to vote. The Constitution is said to be a "living" document precisely because it can be modified and reinterpreted in light of the changing world in which we live.

I believe God's wisdom far outshines that of the Constitution's framers. God knew that the problem with the Law and laying down moral absolutes is that situations change. While most of the absolutes might remain intact forever, at least some of them would need to be changed or dropped in the light of a changing world.

As with the Constitution, the bar should be very high for laying aside any clear command, practice, or teaching of scripture. It should be so high that we seldom do it. But there should be some way to bring reason, experience, and the theological reflections of the church to bear upon the scriptures, such that we can from time to time confess, "This is no longer binding upon us. It does not reflect God's timeless will." This is precisely what Jesus did at times in reinterpreting the Law. It was what Paul did in laying aside the requirements for circumcision of Gentile converts to the faith. It is what the apostles did in Acts 15, when they no longer required the Gentiles to fulfill much of the rest of the Law. I believe there must be a way for the church to continue to recognize that though God does not change, the needs of communities sometimes do.

We began the chapter by asking what constitutes a high view of scripture. I don't believe a high view of scripture is defined by inerrancy or verbal, plenary inspiration. I don't believe it is defined by an unwillingness to wrestle with the Bible or even to say that this or that text may no longer capture the will of God for our lives. If this were the case, then the apostles in Acts 15 did not have a high view of scripture. Yet Jesus and the apostles clearly demonstrated a love of scripture and a willingness to wrestle with the Bible and the prevailing interpretations of it.

As we close this chapter, and this section of the book, let me reiterate my own understanding of what constitutes a high view of scripture: Someone who holds a high view of scripture approaches scripture with a deep appreciation for its history and the way God has spoken and continues to speak through it. That person recognizes both the Bible's humanity and its divine inspiration, and seeks to study it carefully in order to be shaped and guided by it. Someone with a high view of scripture actually reads the Bible, listens for God to speak through it, seeks to be shaped by its words, and tries to follow its commands.

We've come to the conclusion of section 1 of this book. It's time to stretch your legs and refill your glass of tea. In the next section, we're going to take on the questions people often ask of the Bible, questions that trouble many when they read scripture. In these discussions, we'll touch on some errors, inconsistencies, or challenges that were resolved for me only when I let go of verbal, plenary inspiration and the inerrancy of the scripture and began instead to recognize and appreciate the Bible's humanity.

Section Two:

Making Sense of the Bible's Challenging Passages

CHAPTER 19

Science, the Bible, and the Creation Stories

L et's begin our exploration of the questions people ask about the Bible with the biblical story that is at the center of the conflict between science and religion: the Creation story. We've already touched on this story a bit in chapter 18, but here I'd like to address a question I was asked not long ago by a biology student: "In biology I'm learning that the earth is billions of years old, that life evolved from the most primitive elements to what it is today. How can I reconcile that with what I read in Genesis chapters 1 and 2?"

Several years ago, I showed up as a visitor to a gathering of Young Earth Creationists (YEC for short). I came just to listen and to better understand what motivated this group of Christians to insist that the earth is less than ten thousand years old, and that it was created in six literal days, pretty much as Genesis 1 describes it. The participants were sincere and passionate about their beliefs regarding Creation. They described the reasons they rejected carbon-14 dating, offered explanations for scientific data typically used to demonstrate that Earth is much, much older than what they accept, and described the underlying convictions that led them to believe in a young earth.

They believe that God created the earth in a day, then the atmosphere on a second day. Dry land and plant life were created on the third day, the sun and the moon on the fourth day, fish and birds on the fifth day. All other animals and, finally, the first two human beings were created on the sixth day.

They believe Creation happened in this way because this is what Genesis 1 teaches. And they believe it happened roughly six thousand years ago because they added up the lifespans of the descendants of Adam as they are listed in Genesis and found, using this math, that Adam and Eve were created around six thousand years ago.[1]

These sincere Christians believe this because, as several of them said at the gathering, Genesis is the "eyewitness account" of Creation. Asked what they meant by this, they said, "God was the only one present at Creation. Only he truly knows what happened. The Bible is his word. He inspired Moses to write these things. They are a trustworthy and reliable account of what happened, for God does not lie." The view they articulated about the Bible was verbal, plenary inspiration. And the implication of this is inerrancy—the biblical account is "totally true and trustworthy," regardless of what it is teaching about, including science.

A further implication of this view is that, if modern science conflicts with the Genesis account of Creation, modern science must be wrong. Now, not all inerrantists believe the earth is only six thousand years old. Some suppose the six days of creation were not twenty-four-hour days but rather epochs or periods. But many would accept the order of Creation and the idea that God created human beings, and largely everything else that exists on earth, just as we observe them today, as the Genesis account teaches.

As I noted in chapter 2, most scientists believe the earth was formed 4.57 billion years ago out of the stellar dust left from the formation of our sun. Water came to our planet with the help of comets and asteroids and chemical reactions over the next billion years. After that, simple single-cell life-forms began to develop. About 500 million years ago, an explosion of multicell life-forms developed, called the Cambrian Explosion. Dinosaurs roamed the earth from 230 million years ago to about 65 million years ago, when a major event, perhaps a giant asteroid striking our planet, led to a mass extinction. Sometime around 2 million years ago, prehuman hominids evolved, and over the next 1,900,000 years they evolved through a process of genetic mutation and natural selection. Nature favored those with larger brain cavities and more advanced brain function, and somewhere around 100,000 to 200,000 years ago, anatomically modern humans emerged. Yet even then it would be a long time before what we think of as fully modern humans with developed language would emerge.

The scientific consensus and the YEC views are irreconcilable, as are the ways these views are derived. The YEC view starts with a conclusion, and then forces all observable data from science to support this conclusion. Modern science, on the other hand, is built upon a scientific method that starts with a question and follows with observation and reflection, leading to a hypothesis that is then tested, disproven, clarified, or substantiated. Conclusions come at the end of a process of observation of the physical world. Further, the scientific method generally seeks to explain the observable universe in terms of natural processes, without asserting or denying the existence of God.

Based upon the latest polls, it is clear that many Americans have been strongly influenced by the creationist view of scripture. In a recent Gallup poll, 46 percent of Americans indicated a belief that God created human beings, fully formed, not evolved, less than ten thousand years ago. Another 32 percent believed that human beings evolved over millions of years but with the guiding hand of God. Fifteen percent believed that human beings evolved over millions of years without the guiding hand of God. Thus nearly half of Americans surveyed believed that a somewhat literal reading of Genesis was to be preferred, at least regarding human beings, to the prevailing view of modern science.[2]

The tragedy of a literal or creationist reading of the Bible is that it sets up a false dichotomy: one must choose between science and God. But this dichotomy only exists when one insists upon a literal approach to scripture or believes that the Bible's account of Creation (as well as the Flood, as we will see, and the genealogies in Genesis) is God's account of precisely how, and how long ago, he created the world and everything in it.

Let's return to the Genesis account of Creation for a moment, revisiting an idea we first considered in the chapter on inerrancy. As we read this account we'll see why viewing Genesis 1 as a literal account of creation seems like a losing proposition to many Christians and the vast majority of scientists. Open your Bible to Genesis 1, and take a few minutes to read this chapter, through chapter 2 verse 3.

Let's notice the details of what you just read. Note the order of Creation described in Genesis 1:

On day *one* God created *light and darkness*. (vv. 3–5)

On day *two* God created an *atmosphere*. (vv. 6–8)

On day *three* God created *dry land* and *plant life*. (vv. 9–13)

On day *four* God created the *sun, moon, and stars*. (vv. 14–19)

On day *five* God created the *fish* in the sea and the *birds* of the air. (vv. 20–23)

On day *six* God created all other *animals* and, lastly, *human beings*. (vv. 24–31)

On day *seven* God rested from his labor. (2:1–3)

It is possible that this order of Creation reflected the accepted scientific consensus of three thousand years ago. It recognizes that light and dark and the atmosphere were necessary for life on our planet. It recognizes that more primitive life-forms were created first, and then more complex (plant, fish, birds, other animals, and finally human beings). But this account, if it is seen as God's account of how things were created, also raises some questions.

Genesis teaches that our planet formed, its atmosphere developed, and even trees and plants grew *before* the sun was created. While this made sense to ancients, today we know that it was the sun's gravitational field that made possible the formation of our planet. The sun was pivotal in the formation of our atmosphere. And even elementary school children learn that sunlight is essential for plants to grow.

Is science wrong here? Or did God mislead us in giving us this account? In a moment I'll suggest that neither of these is the case. But first let's consider the second Creation account in Genesis.

Genesis contains two accounts of Creation. We usually read them as one, glossing over the inconsistencies, but they appear to be two different stories, drawn from two different traditions or sources, each making a distinct theological point. They agree at points, but they are irreconcilable at other points. (Inerrantists have a way of reconciling them, though I'm not convinced that their attempts at harmonizing them do justice to either.)

Turn to Genesis 2:4–10 and read it carefully. You might want to lay this account side by side with the one you just read in Genesis 1 to compare them. We are so familiar with these stories that we have merged them in our minds without noticing how different these creation accounts are.

One obvious discrepancy is that in Genesis 2, God created man before he created vegetation, while in Genesis 1, God created man three days after he created vegetation. Notice also that Genesis 2 speaks of Creation occurring in one day. Genesis 1 tells us that it occurred over six days. In Genesis 1, man and woman are both created in the image of God, simultaneously (Genesis 1:27), but in Genesis 2, God creates man out of the dust of the earth (no mention is made of him being created in God's image); only later does God create woman, from man (in Genesis 1, there is equality between the sexes, whereas in Genesis 2, woman is clearly subordinate). Genesis 1 is a positive and optimistic account of Creation. Genesis 2 takes a more pessimistic (realistic?) view of human nature. Genesis 1 ends by noting that the Creation and human beings are good. Genesis 2 and 3 teach us of the loss of innocence and describe the universal struggle we humans have with temptation and sin.

There are more differences in these two accounts, but I'll leave you to discover them. Here's the point I want you to notice: neither of these two accounts of Creation is meant to provide a science lesson.

Genesis 1 is majestic, beautiful, and poetic. It is not a lesson in cosmology; it is a creed. It is not a science lecture; it is poetry. Each day in Genesis 1 begins with, "And God said," after which he decrees that another part of Creation come into existence. And it ends, "And it was so, and God saw that it was good. And there was evening, and there was morning, the first day . . . the second day . . . the third day." It makes a claim not about scientific knowledge but about truth and theology. There is a God. This God is good and glorious. Creation is good. We, both men and women, were made in God's image. Life is a gift. God is the rightful ruler of all things. As a creed, a hymn of praise to God, and a theological lesson about the ultimate nature of existence, YES! But as a scientific text, no.

Why not? Why can't it also be a scientific text? Because, being a document written by and at least initially to prescientific people, it tells me what late Bronze and Iron Age people of the ancient Near East believed about the order of Creation. When we treat this text as a scientific account, we miss the point and end up with bad science.

Genesis 2 and 3 offer a different lesson. Here the focus turns from Elohim (the generic name for God used throughout Genesis 1) to Yahweh (the personal name by which the Israelites addressed God, sometimes translated as Jehovah. This is the name used for God throughout Genesis 2 and 3). In Genesis 2:4 and following, Yahweh lovingly forms the first two humans and places them in the Garden of Eden, where he blesses them with the most wonderful of things. God even walks with them in the cool of the afternoon (3:8). This story is the kind you would tell children to teach them important truths. In fact, it was likely told generation after generation around campfires long before it was written down by a master storyteller. It is, like Genesis 1, meant to be one of the defining stories of our lives, if we understand it properly.

Yahweh, who loves these humans dearly and who has compassion and concern for them, gives them one rule: you can eat anything in the garden, except the fruit from the Tree of the Knowledge of Good and Evil. Once the rule is given, how do Adam and Eve feel about the fruit of the Tree of the Knowledge of Good and Evil? You know the answer intuitively. They suddenly want the one fruit they are not supposed to have. They hear a talking serpent whisper to them all the reasons why they should disobey Yahweh's command. This is not ancient history. This is *your* story. It is *my* story.

Which of us has not heard the serpent's whisper in our ears, beckoning us to do what we know is wrong? And which of us has not been Adam and Eve, eating the forbidden fruit, feeling ashamed, and blaming someone else for our sin?

The story ends with Adam and Eve being banished from paradise. Paradise is lost, yet Yahweh still shows mercy and compassion for them. This story, along with the Creation story of chapter 1, teaches us profound existential, theological, psychological, and sociological truths. But when we take these stories and force them to be scientific accounts of Creation we miss the point and discredit the texts in the eyes of many.

I appreciate Darwin's theory of evolution. There are many Christians who hold to a view called theistic evolution, which sees evolution as an accurate picture of how life on our planet adapts and changes over time, yet also believe that God guides this process in various ways. Jimmy Cochran, a young man in my congregation, noted concerning his belief in both God and evolution, "Any craftsman can build a chair, but how many can design a chair that builds itself and improves over time?" Evolution doesn't diminish God's glory, as some Christians seem to believe. To me, it magnifies God's glory, as Jimmy captured so well in this analogy.

As important as evolutionary theory may be, it has little effect upon how I think about life on a daily basis. But the truth that there is a God of beauty, love, and grace who created the cosmos; that Creation is good; that we're meant to reflect the image of God in our lives; that like moths to a flame, we're drawn to do what harms us and others; and that despite our failures, there is grace—this is a message I think about, experience, and need every day. This is an important point to me. Science teaches one kind of truth, and it is really important and wonderful. The Bible teaches another kind of truth—about the meaning of our existence, the nature of God, and what it means to be human. The latter, in my experience, is the kind of truth that I draw upon every day.

Here's an attempt to summarize what I'm inviting you to consider: The first Creation story is something like a hymn, a creed, or a liturgy declaring that God exists, that God is the Creator of the world, that Creation is a good and beautiful gift from him, and that human beings are created in his image. The order of Creation likely represented the best thinking of the Israelites at the time. But Genesis 1 is not meant to teach science; it is meant to make a powerful theological statement about God and a terribly important affirmation about God's will for humanity.

Genesis chapter 2 is a Creation story that any child could understand. It was intended to teach something important about God and about humanity. It was more than a parable but, I suspect, not intended to be a biography. I think of it as an archetypal story. What is an archetype? Think of the word "typical," meaning that whatever is being described is normative. Think of the word "prototype"—a prototype is a pattern that all others will follow. An archetype is the original pattern for all that follows. Thus the Genesis 2 story of Creation and Adam and Eve's turning from God (the Fall) is the first pattern, which all humanity ultimately repeats. Adam and Eve are prototypes—they represent or symbolize all of humanity.

It is interesting that elements of the story clearly point in the direction of an archetypal understanding of the story. The names Adam and Eve, not mentioned in the Creation story in Genesis 1, are representational. In Hebrew, Adam simply means "man" or "human" (though it appears to have originated from a word meaning "of the ground," thus pointing to God creating Adam from the dust of the earth). Eve means "life" or "bearer of life." Both names are symbolic. As for the Tree of the Knowledge of Good and Evil, the name itself points to a deeper meaning than simply a tree with toxic fruit. The tree is the archetype of a test, its forbidden fruit an archetype for doing those things that we know are wrong, which seem so alluring yet which, when acted upon or consumed, bring shame and pain and separation from God and others. The talking snake represents temptation, the voice we hear in our heads that woos us to do what we know is wrong. Even Adam and Eve's response when confronted by God after eating the forbidden fruit is archetypal: they blame others for the sin they've committed, a typical human response.

This is why we can look at this story and see ourselves in it. It is, as I've said, *our* story. Yet it is also God's story, for in this story and God's care for and response to Adam and Eve, we find God's care for and response to us when we turn from him. God wishes to walk with us in the cool of the afternoon. God looks at us with compassion and love. God warns us against things that will bring us pain and shame. When we inevitably succumb to temptation, there are consequences. Yet despite the alienation and pain that results from sin, God continues to care for us just as God did for Adam and Eve. They continued to be his children.

So Genesis 1 is a magnificent and powerful creed laying out the foundational theological claims of the Bible. And Genesis 2 and 3 tell an archetypal story meant to teach foundational truths about the human condition and the nature, character, and will of God. It is this, not a science lesson, that we find in the opening chapters of the Bible. These lessons are not in conflict with science. They are the deeper truths about the nature of the universe and our place in it.

CHAPTER 20

Were Adam and Eve Real People?

An old friend called one day. She was in an in-depth Bible study that suggested the story of Adam and Eve was not a historian's account of the first two humans, but instead an archetypal story about the human condition. She was unsettled by this. She felt her faith was being challenged and stretched too far. She told me she had always taken these stories at face value, as describing historical events, and had not considered they might be something else. She asked, "Does this mean that Adam and Eve were not real people?"

This is a great question. As we've learned, their names are symbolic. Adam and Eve represent humanity; in this sense, they are archetypal—the first of a kind. We've noted that their story is our story. Understanding this, my friend said, "Yes, but were there two original human beings named Adam and Eve? Did they really eat from the forbidden tree?"

We'll come back to her questions in a moment. But first, let's consider another set of questions raised by the discoveries of paleo-anthropologists. For instance, what are people of faith to make of the fossil record where humanlike creatures start to appear about two million years ago? Or the discovery of even more humanlike creatures cooking with fire and making and throwing javelins to hunt 400,000 years ago? Or Neanderthals and Cro-Magnon humans, living tens of thousands of years ago, producing art, developing advanced tools, and with brain capacities rivaling modern humans? Where does the story of Adam and Eve fit into this long line of human development? Let's start with this last question about early humans, and that will lead to the answer I gave my friend regarding Adam and Eve.

I've always loved fossils. As a kid, I searched for them in a creek bed not far from my house. Recently, on a mission trip to South Africa, I stopped to tour caves where some of the oldest hominid fossils have been found. (By the way, "hominid" and "hominim," if the words are unfamiliar to you, typically refer to creatures that walked upright, had larger brain capacity than apes, and were more like humans than apes.) Most paleoanthropologists date anatomically modern humans to around 200,000 years ago. We have fossils of *Homo sapiens* from this time period—creatures who looked very much like you. But they weren't exactly like you. They likely lacked anything similar to modern language. They did not yet think abstractly in the ways you do. They looked human but likely could not have reasoned the way you reason.

Sometime between 45,000 and 35,000 years ago, *Homo sapiens* began creating musical instruments, more complex artwork, delicate jewelry, and even more complex tools, like sewing needles for preparing clothing. They developed more elaborate burials in which they prepared the dead for an afterlife. Language developed sometime during this period, if not before. These attributes mark a significant change in hominids. Though the humans that came before looked like us, they did not reason or communicate or act like us. There were subtle and significant advances in behavior that happened over the 200,000-year history of anatomically modern humans, but there seems to have been a burst of advances in symbolic thinking in a relatively short period of time. No one knows precisely why, but many believe it is tied to the advent of complex language.[1]

My own thinking is that this period of critical advancement in human *being* is tied to God's intervention and involvement in human development. The biblical language for what was taking place is that God breathed into these hominids the "breath of life," and they became "living beings" created in the image of God. I picture Michelangelo's ceiling in the Sistine Chapel where Adam is shown, fully formed, but not yet fully human until God touches him.

Sometime 35,000 to 45,000 years ago there was a hominid that began to think in ways other hominids did not. Perhaps God said, "It is not good for the man to be alone" and then there were two who shared this capacity, long latent, for higher level reasoning, for love, for creating, for faith. Did they, in their interaction with others, unlock this capacity in them? Or did God directly intervene to "flip the switch"? I don't know, but it appears that these new capabilities began to spread fairly rapidly among hominids. And might we not use the names, Adam (man of the earth) and Eve (life bearer)—names that we've already recognized were symbolic—to describe these early modern humans? And is it not likely that once humans began to reason, love, speak, they also began to wrestle with temptation, eating "forbidden fruit" and that this resulted in alienation, pain and shame for them just as the biblical story describes?

Paleoanthropologists tell us of the archaeological data that shows that human beings took a major leap forward 35,000 to 45,000 years ago that included the attributes that we consider essential elements of being human today. It also notes, as we'll see in the next chapter, that human beings quickly began to turn violent. The biblical narrative speaks of God breathing into humanity a soul. With the soul came the capacity for reason, love and faith. And temptation, sin, and death entered the world shortly after this. Aren't these two different ways of telling us about the human race?

So, to my friend who asked if Adam and Eve were real people my answer was, "The Genesis 2 and 3 story of Adam and Eve and how they succumbed to temptation was not written to be a journalist's or biographer's eyewitness account of the first two humans. Adam and Eve represent all of us. Nevertheless, it seems to me that their story is, in a very real way, the story of the earliest modern humans and how God gave them a soul and of their tragic decision to turn from God's will, a decision that brought with it pain, shame, alienation and death."

CHAPTER 21

Were There Dinosaurs on the Ark?

Children often ask questions about the Bible, forcing their parents to think. A woman wrote me recently with a question put to her by her daughter: "Mommy," her daughter asked, "were there dinosaurs on Noah's ark?"

Now, this child was reading the Bible, as we would expect. There was the Creation story, and then, a few chapters later, was the Flood. Though Genesis doesn't mention dinosaurs, science does, and we can visit their fossilized remains at any museum of natural history. Noah takes two of every kind of animal on the ark. The child reasons that this must have included dinosaurs. But the five-year-old continues to think about this: "How did they fit on the ark?" "Wouldn't the dinosaurs have eaten all the other animals, and even the people, who were on the ark?"

As someone who accepts the scientific consensus on the age of the earth and the timeline of various life-forms on our planet, the answer is simple: Dinosaurs became extinct 65 million years ago.

Homo sapiens did not come on the scene until around 200,000 years ago. No, there were no dinosaurs on the ark.

But let's consider the story of Noah's ark for a moment more, because other questions have been raised, not by children but by thoughtful adults, that might lead us to reconsider how the story should be read. Here are a few of those questions: Is the story historical? Was there a Noah? Did flood waters really cover the whole earth and destroy every living thing except what was on the ark? How do we reckon with the morality of God sending universal destruction such that every terrestrial creature, including every human being, was destroyed? This story seems harsh and unjust to many who read it. And what do we make of the connection between the story of Noah and flood stories that appear in other ancient cultures, including one in the Epic of Gilgamesh (a story found among many groups in the ancient Near East that is very similar to the Noah story, though dating possibly to several hundred years before Moses)?

Before answering these questions, let's take a look at the story of Noah and the ark found in Genesis 6–9. Grab a Bible and turn to Genesis 6:5–6, where a foundation is laid for the story of the flood. God looks upon the earth and sees that humanity has become evil, their hearts filled with evil thoughts. Verse 11 expands upon this indictment: "The earth was corrupt in God's sight, and the earth was filled with violence."

There is a moving statement in verse 6 that captures God's response to the violence human beings were committing on the earth: "And the LORD was sorry that he had made humankind on the earth, and it grieved him to his heart." This verse is a profound statement about God and the way our behavior and thoughts affect God. In the New International Version, verse 6b says God's "heart was filled with pain."

I'm reminded of the comments of Susan Klebold, whose son Dylan, along with Eric Harris, took the lives of twelve students and one teacher at Columbine High School in April 1999. Ten years after the crime, she wrote a powerful essay titled, "I Will Never Know Why," in which she said, "In the weeks and months that followed the killings, I was nearly insane with sorrow for the suffering my son had caused. . . . It was impossible to believe that someone I had raised could cause so much suffering."[1]

This is the backdrop for the story of God's sending a deluge to destroy the earth: human beings doing horribly violent things to one another—horribly evil things—and God being grieved that he had created the race at all.

This story leads me to think about what paleoanthropologists believe happened after the advent of the human spirit, with its expansion of language, culture, higher-level reasoning, music, and more complex tools. With these advances came more sophisticated weapons. It was not long after this time that the Neanderthals, a close but less advanced cousin of modern humans, began the long road toward extinction. There are various theories about why the Neanderthals became extinct—from climate change to interbreeding with modern humans. But many believe it was the result of violence committed by the more intelligent and better armed modern humans.

I don't think the story of Noah and the Flood was written to teach us ancient history. It was intended to teach us something about God and about ourselves. But I do think this story is anchored in history, that its occurrence across multiple ancient cultures testifies to a period of massive flooding, and that it is possible these floods came at the end of the last Ice Age.

At the close of the last Ice Age, geologists tell us that major flooding occurred across the Northern Hemisphere. Ice sheets melted, creating shallow inland seas. In certain places, ice dams created massive bodies of water. When the dams eventually broke, the force of the water destroyed everything in its path. An example in the United States is the Columbia River Gorge in Washington and Oregon. There were as many as forty, perhaps more, massive floods during a two-thousand-year period, which released massive amounts of water, as much as three hundred feet deep, with a force that carved out major gorges, created the Scablands of Washington, and destroyed all life in their path. These floodwaters did not cover all the earth as the Noah story suggests, but the magnitude of the flooding was so great and destructive that it was remembered as a flood that covered the entire earth.

Similar phenomena happened in various parts of the world at the end of the last Ice Age. It seems likely that these events were remembered and passed on by humans living during these times but only written down long afterward, with the advent of written language around 3200 BC in the ancient Near East and 600 BC in the Americas. The flooding from the last Ice Age seems mostly to have occurred during the period from around 15,000 BC to 10,000 BC. This would explain why people around the world seem to share a common story about a massive flood. Hence, to answer one of the questions posed at the beginning of this chapter, the Epic of Gilgamesh and Noah's ark reflect the same common story, retold in the light of differing theologies.

Many Christians would ask, "Why not simply accept that the story of Noah was literally true, rather than deferring to the geologist's account of flooding from the last Ice Age?" If you research Noah's ark and geology online, you'll find hundreds of websites sponsored by Young Earth Creationists who seek to make the geological evidence support their view of a literal worldwide flood that covered all the earth for a short period of time. If you don't read the arguments on the other side of the issue, it is easy to find the YEC explanations compelling. But in my opinion, the evidence in favor of an old earth and against complete flooding of our earth in recent history seems overwhelming.[2]

So, is the Noah story true or not? Great question. As many ask it—meaning, did it happen exactly as recorded in the Bible?—the answer is "sort of." Did Noah bring two of each of the millions of species of animals that otherwise would not have survived a global flood onto an ark? No, I don't believe so. Did water cover the earth to twenty feet above the highest mountains? Again, I don't think so. But were there localized floods that humans remembered and which were survived by some? Could there have been a Noah who built a boat and brought his family and some animals on the boat as an ice dam was preparing to break? Maybe. Did God destroy every animal and every human being on the planet except Noah and those on his boat 4,300 years ago, or ever? I don't think so. The story seems to me to be anchored in historical events that happened at the end of the last Ice Age but is not entirely historically accurate.

That's one way to answer the question, "Is the story of Noah's ark true?" But in a more important sense the answer is "Yes, the story is absolutely true!" Like the Creation story, this story teaches profound truths. The point of its being recorded in the Bible wasn't to give us an account of ancient history. Earlier in this book, I mentioned Paul's words concerning the point of what was written in scripture. He notes in 1 Corinthians 10:11, speaking of other Old Testament stories, "These things happened to them to serve as an example, and they were written down to instruct us, on whom the ends of the ages have come." And in Romans 15:4, he writes regarding a passage from the Psalms, "For whatever was written in former days was written for our instruction, so that by steadfastness and by the encouragement of the scriptures we might have hope."

Paul's words substantiate the idea that the point of Noah's story was not to teach history, or geology, but to teach us about God and God's will for our lives.

So, what truths does this story intend to teach us? I'll mention a few, and then encourage you to reread it for yourself and see what you think. As I noted earlier, I am touched by Genesis 6:6, where we read that God's "heart was filled with pain" as he looked at the violence human beings committed against one another. "The Lord was sorry that he had made humankind on the earth" as a result of their violence and corruption. How this story still speaks of God's grief over the violence we human beings commit against one another, sometimes in God's name! When I read Genesis 6, I can't help but think about the fact that in the last century, when humanity reached the apex of technological development (to that point), over 100 million people died by war and genocide.[3]

I'm reminded of President Eisenhower's famous speech to the American Society of Newspaper Editors in April 1953, shortly after the death of Joseph Stalin. It was a gutsy speech calling for reining in the Cold War:

Every gun that is made, every warship launched, every rocket fired signifies, in the final sense, a theft from those who hunger and are not fed, those who are cold and are not clothed. This world in arms is not spending money alone. It is spending the sweat of its laborers, the genius of its scientists, the hopes of its children. The cost of one modern heavy bomber is this: a modern brick school in more than 30 cities. It is two electric power plants, each serving a town of 60,000 population. It is two fine, fully equipped hospitals. It is some 50 miles of concrete highway. We pay for a single fighter plane with a half million bushels of wheat. We pay for a single destroyer with new homes that could have housed more than 8,000 people. This, I repeat, is the best way of life to be found on the road the world has been taking. This is not a way of life at all, in any true sense. Under the cloud of threatening war, it is humanity hanging from a cross of iron.[4]

Perhaps the author of the story of Noah and the Flood was trying to make a similar point about violence and war in his time.

In addition to seeing ourselves and our society in Noah's story, we might also see in Noah an exemplar of how we are meant to live, for as the writer of Genesis notes in chapter 6 verse 9, "Noah was a righteous man, blameless in his generation; Noah walked with God." The story goes on to illustrate Noah's righteousness with these words: "Noah did all that the Lord had commanded him" (6:22, 7:5, and 7:9). Many a preacher and Sunday School teacher has noted that Noah teaches us to listen for God's commands and follow them.

The element of this story that children love speaks to God's character and God's concern for the animals. The ark was not only meant to save humanity; it was meant to save the animals as well. God cares about saving the animals and not just the people on this ark of salvation. In a day and time when so many nonreligious people care so deeply about their animals, the story might be an interesting way to connect with them, demonstrating God's love and concern for their animals.

My point is that this story is filled with truth that is relevant for us today, but the important truth found in this story has little to do with the size of Noah's ship, the number of animals it could contain, or whether the floodwaters literally covered the entire earth. Once more we find in Genesis an archetypal story that reveals who God is and who God calls us to be.

There's one final word I'd leave you with related to the stories in Genesis: The stories in the first eleven chapters of Genesis are typically seen by mainline scholars as the foundational stories of the scripture. They are told less to inform us of ancient history than to teach us about the human condition and about God who created us. As we read them, we are meant to worry less about whether they really happened in exactly the way they are described, and more about the truths God intends us to see in them. Am I suggesting that none of the Old Testament stories are historically accurate? Of course not. There is much in the Old Testament that describes Israel's story and God's dealings with his people. But the point of the ancient stories preserved in Genesis is less about offering history than about teaching us about God, about ourselves, and about God's will for our lives. As Paul wrote, "For whatever was written in former days was written for our instruction, so that by steadfastness and by the encouragement of the scriptures we might have hope" (Romans 15:4).

CHAPTER 22

God's Violence in the Old Testament

Among the questions I'm most often asked about the Bible is this one: "Why does God seem so loving in the New Testament but angry, harsh, and vengeful in the Old Testament?" The question is not new. In chapter 13, we discussed Marcion, the second-century Christian who was so troubled by this question that he suggested Yahweh, the God of the Old Testament, was not really God but a lesser being. The Heavenly Father of Jesus was, according to Marcion, a different God—the true God—who sent Jesus to proclaim forgiveness and salvation. The church quickly rejected Marcion's solution, but the question remained.

In the last chapter, we saw that God was grieved by human violence. Yet Old Testament passages where God commands violence and even genocide stand in stark contrast to the Noah story and to Jesus's call to love our enemies. These violent passages not only trouble thoughtful Christians but they give fodder to the new atheists who assert, sometimes rightly, that religion is the source of much of the violence in the world.

Let's consider three categories of Old Testament texts that are morally problematic: the "crimes" for which God prescribes the death penalty, God's anger and wrath in punishing his people, and God's command to the Israelites to commit genocide.

The death penalty. There are numerous "crimes" for which God, through the Law of Moses, requires the death penalty. It may not surprise us that the death penalty is prescribed for premeditated murder and human sacrifice. Rape and kidnapping also are punishable by death according to the Law. But consider some of the other "crimes" for which God requires the death penalty in the Law of Moses:

1. Sacrificing to a god other than Yahweh (Exodus 22:20)
2. Persistent rebelliousness on the part of a child (Deuteronomy 21:18–21)
3. A child who hits or curses his or her parents (Exodus 21:15 and 17)
4. Working on the Sabbath (Exodus 35:2)[1]
5. Sexual intimacy when one partner is married to someone else (Leviticus 20:10)
6. Premarital sexual intercourse (Deuteronomy 22:13–21)
7. Male homosexual sexual intimacy (Leviticus 20:13)

This is not a comprehensive list of scriptures and commands. For instance, a priest was to burn his daughter alive if she became a prostitute (Leviticus 21:9). Deuteronomy 13:6–10 notes, "If your very own brother, or your son or daughter, or the wife you love, or your closest friend entices you, saying, 'Let us go and worship other gods' . . . show them no pity. You must certainly put them to death. Your hand must be the first in putting them to death. . . . Stone them to death" (NIV). From time to time, we hear stories coming out of Islamic communities where people are put to death for such crimes and we recoil. Yet here, in our own scriptures, the Law of Moses asserts that God commanded people to be put to death for such things, often at the hands of their own parents, spouses, or loved ones. We rightly ask, how do we reconcile God's mercy and grace with God assigning the death penalty for such things?

God's anger and wrath. In the Old Testament, God's anger repeatedly burns against his people for their disobedience. At times, the punishment he dispenses seems particularly harsh, unjust, and disproportionate. Let's consider a couple of examples.

Exodus 32 tells the well-known story of Moses's brother Aaron crafting a golden calf that was to represent Yahweh. At the time Aaron made the idol, Moses was on Mount Sinai meeting with God. Moses makes his way down the mountain and, seeing the people carousing, shouts, "Who is on the Lord's side? Come to me!" The sons of Levi run to Moses's side. Here's what happens next:

> Then [Moses] said to them, "Thus says the Lord, the God of Israel, 'Put your sword on your side, each of you! Go back and forth from gate to gate throughout the camp, and each of you kill your brother, your friend, and your neighbor.'" The sons of Levi did as Moses commanded, and about three thousand of the people fell on that day. Moses said, "Today you have ordained yourselves for the service of the Lord, each one at the cost of a son or a brother, and so have brought a blessing on yourselves this day."[2] (Exodus 32:27–29)

Can you imagine God asking you to strap on a sword and kill your friends, neighbors, and family members because they had offended him?

Or consider 2 Samuel 24, where we find that King David decided to take a census of the men of fighting age. The prophet Gad was sent to David to announce God's displeasure with the taking of the census. The punishment for David's sin: "The Lord sent a pestilence on Israel from that morning until the appointed time; and seventy thousand of the people died" (2 Samuel 24:15).

David makes a decision that does not please God, and God kills 70,000 Israelites for it? How could this action ever be reconciled with a God of mercy, compassion, justice, and love? It is easy to understand why Marcion was troubled by the portrayal of God in the Old Testament.

Genocide in the name of God. I'll mention one last category of scriptures related to the violence of God: those that describe the conquest of Canaan.[3] At the time the Israelites entered the land to conquer it, Canaan was populated with small city-states or kingdoms made up of various ethnic groups speaking similar languages. God promised Israel that he would give them this land, but to do so these people had to be displaced. This is problematic enough, but God wasn't asking the Israelites to forcibly relocate them to other lands. God instructed the Israelites to kill every man, woman, and child among these Canaanites.

Turn in your Bible to Deuteronomy 20:16–18. Moses gives these instructions: "As for the towns of these peoples that the Lord your God is giving you as an inheritance, you must not let anything that breathes remain alive. You shall annihilate them—the Hittites and the Amorites, the Canaanites and the Perizzites, the Hivites and the Jebusites—just as the Lord your God has commanded."

The Hebrew word for "annihilate" has as its root *herem* (also transliterated as *cherem* or sometimes *charam*). The classic *Brown-Driver-Briggs Hebrew and English Lexicon* notes the meaning of the word in English is "to exterminate." It also has the sense of devoting something to God by completely destroying it.[4] This is sometimes translated as "ban"—a word that in this context means "given to God by complete destruction."

In Joshua 6:20b–21, you can read about what this looked like as the Israelite army entered the town of Jericho: the Israelites "charged straight ahead into the city and captured it. Then they devoted to destruction by the edge of the sword all in the city, both men and women, young and old, oxen, sheep, and donkeys." After the destruction of Jericho, next would come the people of Ai, then the people of Makkedah and Libnah and Lachish and Eglon and Debir—every man, woman, and child slaughtered and dedicated to God. In the end, the entire population of thirty-one city-states was utterly destroyed.

In the last chapter, we learned that God was "grieved to his heart" by the violence human beings were committing against one another, and for this reason he decided to bring an end to the human race. Now God is commanding the Israelites to slaughter entire towns, tribes, and nations, showing them no mercy and providing them with no escape. How can this be?

I suspect that most people who read the Bible either don't think about this, gloss over these sections, or skip them altogether. I was fourteen years old when I first read the Book of Joshua. The stories didn't trouble me at that time. They were epic battles with great story lines and heroic figures. Who doesn't enjoy reading about how the walls of Jericho "came tumbling down"? Behind each story was the idea that God was fighting on behalf of his people. I suspect that's how most people read these stories today.

But when I grew up, I reread these stories and began to think about the humanity of the Canaanites. These were human beings who lived, loved, and had families. Among them were babies and toddlers, mothers and fathers. Yet they were all put to the sword by "the LORD's army." Thirty-one cities slaughtered with no terms of surrender offered and no chance to relocate to another land. I came to see the moral and theological dilemmas posed by these stories.

POSSIBLE SOLUTIONS TO THE
MORAL AND THEOLOGICAL DILEMMAS

How do we resolve the moral and theological dilemmas that confront us in these Old Testament texts? As I see it, there are two broad paths forward.

The first—and the only option as I see it, for those who hold to verbal, plenary inspiration—is to accept that these commands and stories accurately capture what God said, what God did, and what God commanded his people to do. Then the task is to explain how the character of God revealed in these seemingly harsh and violent texts is consistent with the character of God revealed by Jesus Christ.

To make this case, advocates usually speak of God's authority to give and take life at will, and of the need for God to demonstrate a firm hand to the Israelites in order to lead them to walk in his path. In the process, they downplay God's attributes of love, kindness, mercy, compassion, and justice.

To explain the total and merciless destruction of the Canaanites, they point out the Canaanites' wickedness, surmising that they were more wicked than other peoples in the ancient Near East. They argue that the Canaanites deserved their extermination. One author describes it as a form of collective capital punishment for the evil every Canaanite had committed.[5] In response, it's been pointed out that this is the same argument that has often been made throughout history to justify genocide. Think back to the arguments Hitler made concerning the Jews.[6]

Many of us read these conservative justifications for why God prescribed horrible and seemingly immoral acts of violence but find it impossible to reconcile these acts with the character of God Christianity proclaims. Jesus breaks bread with sinners. He ministers to prostitutes and adulterers. He hangs on the cross and prays for his accusers and executors, "Father, forgive them for they know not what they do." "God so loved the world that he gave his only begotten Son . . ." This is far from the God who, with little compunction, destroys tens of thousands of people.

So what is the alternative? The Bible *says* these things. If the Bible says it, are we not required to accept it? The point of the first half of this book was to recognize the complexity of the Bible and to help you see its humanity. If we understand the Bible as having been essentially dictated by God, then yes, we have no choice but to accept what is written as accurately describing God's actions and God's will. But if we recognize the Bible's humanity—that it was written by human beings whose understanding and experience of God was shaped by their culture, their theological assumptions, and the time in which they lived—then we might be able to say, "In this case, the biblical authors were representing what they believed about God rather than what God actually inspired them to say." If we use Jesus's words, and his great commandments, as a colander, we'll see that these violent passages in the Hebrew Bible contradict not only these great commands, but the very life and ministry of Jesus who was God's unmitigated Word.

The impulse to kill, to destroy the enemy, and to put to death those who violate social norms is a continuing part of our world today. For those who believe in God, this violence is often perpetrated while asking for God's blessing and help, and at times it is even committed in the name of God. But violence is an equal-opportunity illness in the human condition. Atheist regimes have sought to impose their view of utopia by slaughtering millions of people in the last century. It is the human story that, throughout history, we have tragically supported the use of violence to enforce the will of dictators, kings, and even the majority in democratic societies. What is true today was true in the ancient Near East, only without the terrifying weaponry that can destroy entire cities with a single bomb.

In August 1868, a stone was found in a field in Jordan, commonly called the Moabite Stone or the Mesha Stele. It dates to around 840 BC, and it describes the victory of King Mesha of Moab over Israel. Mesha and the people of Moab worshipped the Canaanite god Chemosh. Listen to King Mesha's account in this selection from the Moabite Stone: "And Chemosh said to me, 'Go, take Nebo from Israel!' so I went by night and fought against it from the break of dawn until noon, taking it and slaying all, seven thousand men, boys, women, girls and maid-servants, for I had devoted them to destruction for (the god) Ashtar-Chemosh."[7]

What we see in this text is that Mesha believed his god had urged him to go to war, and as an expression of devotion (or possibly as a means of justifying genocide), the people of the town were "devoted to destruction" (others translate this as "put to the ban"). The mention that a god had directed the king to go to war, and that the king was leading his people in battle on behalf of, at the will of, and with the help of a god seems to have been a common way of justifying war and rallying the people to fight.

So one possible resolution to the moral and theological dilemma raised by the texts we've been studying is that Moses, Joshua, and David were warriors living in times when violence was seen as part of God's way of accomplishing his purposes. They attributed to God words, commands, and deeds that they believed God would have authorized or done. What I am suggesting is that Old Testament passages about violence and war thus tell us more about the people who wrote them and the times they were living in than about the God in whose name they claimed authority to do these things.

A second possible way of making sense of the violence of the

Old Testament, particularly related to war, is to recognize that Moses, Joshua, and David were Israel's heroes. They were warrior-saints. These stories were written down long after their time to inspire others to courage and absolute commitment to God.

An analogy would be the story of William Wallace of Scotland. Wallace died in 1305, but to this day he is a legendary hero in Scotland. He fought against the English in the wars for Scottish independence. Every Scottish child is taught about William Wallace. Memorials to him are found throughout the country. Sir Walter Scott expanded the legend with his writings. And Wallace's story was told in the 1995 Oscar-winning film *Braveheart*, with Mel Gibson playing the part of Wallace. Only the English criticized Wallace's methods in war, accusing him of killing civilians. In Scotland he's remembered for his heroism.

Here's what I'm suggesting: Perhaps the stories of the conquest of Canaan were to ancient Israelites what the stories of William Wallace are to the Scots. Written long after the time of these heroes, they were meant to demonstrate courage, resolve, and faith and to inspire later generations still struggling against their own enemies. These stories were written from the theological perspective of the ancient Near East, where gods sent heroes into battle and fought alongside them. No one reads Sir Walter Scott's book on William Wallace to find a model of ethics of war. They read it to be inspired by a national hero. The same was true of the Book of Joshua.

There's a lot more about this topic that should be said; entire books have been devoted to addressing the issue of violence in the Bible. My goal is to point you toward some possible ways of making sense of this violence without justifying it. The answers that make the most sense to me require that we recognize the humanity of the Bible's authors, their intent in writing, and the culture that shaped them. This approach also invites us to question those parts of scripture where God is portrayed in a way inconsistent with Jesus's life and message. Where a particular teaching in scripture is at odds with what Jesus said, we are right to consider that the passage may reflect the culture, the worldview, or the perspectives of the human author of scripture rather than the timeless heart, character, and will of God.

It would be easy to decide never to read difficult sections of scripture like Joshua, but that would be a tragic mistake. There are a great many ways in which God speaks through these biblical texts. There are a handful of passages in Joshua that are moving and powerful, including its dramatic conclusion, when Joshua calls the Israelites to "choose this day whom you will serve, whether the gods your ancestors served in the region beyond the River or the gods of the Amorites in whose land you are living; but as for me and my household, we will serve the Lord" (Joshua 24:15).

But perhaps the most important reason for reading Joshua is to remind us of how easy it is for people of faith to invoke God's name in pursuit of violence, bloodshed, and war. The Crusaders marched into battle in Jerusalem in the name of Christ. Colonists from the Old World arrived in the New World, Bibles and weapons in hand, to claim America for Christ. Nazi belt buckles proclaimed, "Gott Mit Uns"—God is with us—as they sought the extermination of Jews and other "undesirables." "Christian" nations have often gone to war invoking God in their efforts. When America marches to war, patriotism and faith are quickly melded so that to be a good Christian is to support the war effort. At times those war efforts might have been morally justified (if one holds to the theory of just war), but at times they were "pre-emptive wars" that did not meet the criteria of the just war. Regardless of whether the war effort was morally justified or not, our troops marched off to battle to the tune of "God Bless America."[8] If this is the case today, it should not surprise us that people who lived 3,500 years ago also invoked God as they marched off to war.

If every word of the Bible was chosen by God, then our conclusion must be that, at least in the Old Testament period, God was a violent God, burning people alive, stoning them to death for anything that brought him offense, killing tens of thousands for the sin of their king, and commanding his own people to wipe out entire cities and peoples.

But if we take the Bible's humanity seriously, we find the possibility that the violence of scripture is a reflection of the values and the theological and moral vision of some of its human authors, not of the God they sought to serve. I've repeatedly suggested that we judge all other words of scripture in the light of God's definitive Word, Jesus Christ. He taught that his followers were to love their neighbors, turn the other cheek, forgive those who wrong them, and pray for those who persecute them. This Word stands in direct opposition to the encouragement of slaughter in the name of God.

Ultimately the violence-affirming passages of the Old Testament serve as a reminder of how easily we might still be led to invoke God's name as a justification of violence in our world. To the degree that we see Jesus as the definitive Word of God and that we listen carefully to his words, we are able to free ourselves from this tragic dimension of our human condition.

CHAPTER 23

Suffering, Divine Providence, and the Bible

Several days before I sat down to write this chapter, I was sitting next to the bed of a twenty-one-year-old man dying of a rare form of cancer. I had baptized him just after his birth. I had given him his third-grade Bible when he was eight and confirmed him upon his profession of faith when he was twelve. Now I was sitting with him talking about what heaven might be like. I read a couple of scriptures to him and then prayed and gave him to God, not knowing if this would be the last visit I would have with him.

Twenty-five years of visits like this force you to think long and hard about God, the Bible, and suffering. The Bible can be a source of wonderful and comforting words for those grieving or suffering. At the same time, its words, "promises," and teaching regarding God's providence can at times be confusing and lead to profound disappointment with God, and for some, a loss of faith. This confusion has plagued people all the way back to biblical times.

Let's begin with the idea of divine providence. Providence refers to God's involvement in superintending, governing, guiding, directing, and caring for the universe and, more specifically, the affairs of this world and the people who live in it.

From cover to cover, the Bible teaches that God cares for, sustains, and governs our world, but there are vast differences in how the biblical authors, or contemporary Christians for that matter, understand the mechanism and extent of God's governance.

Some Christians believe everything that happens in this world happens according to God's will and governance. You only thought you were deciding what to have for breakfast this morning; it was really God's plan. I think of this as the "God the micro-manager" model of providence (others call it hyper-Calvinism or determinism). You can certainly find some support for this view in the Bible. On the opposite end of the spectrum are those who believe that God created the world and the natural laws, then stepped back, leaving us to our own devices and offering no help or guidance whatsoever. I call this the "God the absentee landlord" model of providence (others call it deism).

Somewhere between these two extremes is a place that likely accurately describes God's ways of superintending what happens here on earth. There's a lot more to be said about the various ways God might be involved in our world, but the point of this book is to make sense of what the Bible says. So let's begin by recognizing that at one point in history, nearly everything that could not otherwise be explained was attributed to God's providence. The biblical authors lived in a time when much of what we know today was not yet known.

For instance, today we understand the forces that shape the weather, and a meteorologist can tell us that tomorrow's forecast includes a 70 percent chance of rain in the morning hours but a sunny, hot, and humid afternoon. Experts can even give us a five-day forecast that is reasonably accurate. But in ancient times, people believed it was God who opened the heavens, blessing the earth with rain. Or that God shut the heavens and brought drought. Sacrifices were made around planting season to procure God's blessings. And when there was a drought, the people repented and made special appeals to God for relief. The biblical authors presumed that God controlled the rain.

And though ancient people understood that childbirth resulted from intercourse and had something to do with semen, the rest remained a mystery. They did, however, believe that God "opened up" wombs and that he "shut up" wombs. Today we know some of the causes of infertility. We can treat some of them. But the biblical language of God shutting and opening wombs is still there, offering an often unhelpful or hurtful explanation for something that usually has medical causes.

Here's my point: The biblical view of God's providence was shaped by what the biblical authors could know in their time. And this should lead us to read critically at least some of what they say about God's intervention in matters of the weather or childbirth, as well as a host of other areas.

In addition, some biblical authors had theological convictions that later ones would struggle with. A really important example is that many biblical authors assumed if you were faithful to God and sought to do his will, God would reward you with blessings. And if you were unfaithful to God and rejected his will, you would be cursed or punished. This was true on an individual level, and it was true for the nation. This view of providence is simple and undoubtedly has some truth to it.

In Deuteronomy 7:12–15, we read, "If you heed these ordinances, by diligently observing them, the LORD your God will . . .

love you, bless you, and multiply you; he will bless the fruit of your womb and the fruit of your ground, your grain and your wine and your oil, the increase of your cattle and the issue of your flock, in the land that he swore to your ancestors to give you. You shall be the most blessed of peoples, with neither sterility nor barrenness among you or your livestock. The Lord will turn away from you every illness." The converse was also promised: "But if your heart turns away and you do not hear, but are led astray to bow down to other gods and serve them, I declare to you today that you shall perish" (Deuteronomy 30:17–18).

Likewise, Psalm 1 promises that those whose "delight is in the law of the Lord" are like "trees planted by streams of water. . . . In all that they do, they prosper." But "the wicked are not so, but are like chaff that the wind drives away." This was how many understood God's providence—he gives and takes away, he blesses those who are good and he curses those who are bad. This was the theologically orthodox position on divine providence in ancient Israel.

But over time this prevailing orthodoxy found in scripture began to be questioned by other scripture writers. Their life experience did not line up with what the scriptures taught. So Jeremiah the prophet wrote, "You will be in the right, O Lord, when I lay charges against you; but let me put my case to you. Why does the way of the guilty prosper? Why do all who are treacherous thrive?" (Jeremiah 12:1). Some of the psalmists raise similar complaints (a moving example of the struggle to understand why the wicked seem to prosper and the righteous suffer is found in Psalm 73). And when we come to the New Testament, Jesus promises just the opposite of Deuteronomy and Psalm 1. He tells his disciples, "In this world you will have trouble," and he outlines the kind of suffering they may experience. He himself was tortured and then crucified;

ten of his disciples were put to death for their faith. Once again the righteous suffered while the wicked prospered.

In the Old Testament, the greatest challenge to the view that the righteous are blessed and the unrighteous suffer is to be found in that epic work of Hebrew poetry, Job. The author of Job was a master storyteller and poet who sought to confront the prevailing theological view that suffering is God's just punishment for sin.

The Book of Job begins in the heavenly courts, where a figure called "the accuser" (this is the meaning of the name Satan) approaches God. His role appears to be something akin to a prosecutor. The accuser is unable to find anyone to bring accusations against. God says, "Have you considered my servant Job? There is no one like him on the earth, a blameless and upright man who fears God and turns away from evil" (Job 1:8). The accuser tells God that Job is only faithful and righteous because God has blessed and protected him. But if bad things happened to Job, the accuser says, he would curse God to his face. God then gives the accuser permission to test Job. Job's livestock are stolen or killed, his servants too. A strong wind destroys his house and kills his children. Finally the accuser afflicts Job with terrible sores on his skin.[1]

Much of the rest of Job is a conversation between Job and four friends (the fourth only speaks up near the end). His friends reflect the prevailing view that if bad things happen to you, it's because you have done something wrong. They tell Job that he must repent. But Job repeatedly defends himself.

Two things are happening in the story. The first is that the orthodox view of divine providence is challenged at the opening of the book, through Job's speeches, as well as in God's concluding remarks. God sees Job as righteous and blameless, yet Job still experiences great suffering. God has not sent this evil to Job. It is not a punishment or curse for doing wrong.

The second is that Job demonstrates faith and trust in God in the face of adversity. Thus he becomes a model for all who face adversity. Two passages capture this remarkable faith in the face of adversity. The first is Job 13:15, where Job says, "Though he slay me, yet will I trust in him" (KJV).[2] The second passage is Job 19:25–27, where we hear Job say, "I know that my Redeemer lives, and that at the last he will stand upon the earth; and after my skin has been thus destroyed, then in my flesh I shall see God."

In the end, God speaks to Job. Though he reveals how much higher God's ways are than those of mortals, God never really answers Job's question as to why the righteous suffer. The book closes with blessings returning to Job.

So Job doesn't solve the problem of suffering, but the book does make clear that the then prevailing biblical view of divine providence was not entirely accurate. Sometimes the righteous do suffer. Job expands the understanding of why God inflicts or allows suffering: suffering may be punishment, or it may be a test of one's faith.

But are these are only two options? Is suffering either a punishment or a test? The challenge of viewing suffering as punishment is twofold: it places God in the position of dispensing suffering, and it leaves the victim constantly wondering what he or she did to merit punishment. Similarly, when suffering is seen as a test, it is still being dispensed by God (or the devil with God's permission), thus again placing God as the source of suffering, and it leaves the person wondering, "What am I supposed to learn from this?"

I remember a man whose teenage daughter had just died in a terrible accident. He asked me, "Adam, what did I do that was so bad that God would kill my daughter?" In his shock all he could think was that God had done this thing to his daughter in order to punish him. This lines up with a number of passages in the Old Testament (and a few in the New Testament could be read in this way as well). Likewise I once spoke with a woman who had lost her job, her house was being foreclosed upon, and her mother died, all in a one-year period of time. She said to me, "I know God is testing me. I just don't know how much more I can take of his testing." But did God really get her fired from her job, send the bankers to foreclose on her house, and take the life of her mother to test her?

Whatever we might say of God's punishment for sin in the Old Testament, in the New Testament the apostles believed and taught that Jesus bore the punishment for humanity's sins. In 1 Peter 2:24, it says, "He himself bore our sins in his body on the cross." Paul teaches in Romans 5:10, "While we were enemies, we were reconciled to God through the death of his Son." The writer of Hebrews notes, "He has appeared once for all at the end of the age to remove sin by the sacrifice of himself" (Hebrews 9:26b).

Many progressive Christians struggle with this idea of Christ atoning for sin by his suffering and death on the cross, but I wonder if this language doesn't free us from the burden of thinking that our suffering, when it inevitably comes, is punishment for some sin we've committed. Whatever punishment we think we deserve from God has been borne by Christ on the cross.

That's not to say that our actions have no consequences. In fact, I believe that much of what is described as punishment in the Old Testament would actually be better described as consequences. What's the difference between consequences and punishment? A man I have loved for much of my life recently died. He was a good man, but he struggled with alcoholism. His serious and chronic alcohol abuse led to multiple physical maladies, an early forced retirement, and the absence of close friends or family. His life was cut short by at least a decade. I never saw these as the judgment of God upon his sin, but rather as the consequences of abusing alcohol for most of his life. Punishment is the direct and intentional intervention of God bringing suffering to us, while consequences are the natural results of our actions.

I'd suggest that God does not inflict cruelty and suffering to teach us, any more than you would do something cruel and hurtful to those you love to teach them something. But when suffering comes, God forces good to come from it if we allow it. Every experience of hardship or suffering is, by its very nature, an opportunity to learn something. Paul notes in Romans 5, "We also boast in our sufferings, knowing that suffering produces endurance, and endurance produces character, and character produces hope." But he doesn't say that God sent the sufferings for this purpose. Instead, when suffering came, it was not wasted by God but instead put to good use.

A pastor friend, now deceased, once gave me this clipping from a local newspaper from the 1950s. I can find no source for it, but I believe it is helpful in making sense of suffering.

> Suffering is not God's desire for us, but it occurs in the process of life. Suffering is not given to teach us something, but through it we may learn. Suffering is not given to teach others something, but through it they may learn. Suffering is not given to punish us, but sometimes it is the consequence of our sin or poor judgment. Suffering does not occur because our faith is weak, but through it our faith may be strengthened. God does not depend on human suffering to achieve his purposes, but sometimes through suffering his purposes are achieved. Suffering can either destroy us, or it can add meaning to our life.[3]

I was in Haiti shortly after the earthquake of 2010. Over 100,000 died in the quake. We were making plans to start sending teams down when we came across the wreckage of a three- or four-story school with children still unrecovered under the rubble. A noted

TV evangelist said this was God's punishment upon the people of Haiti for sins committed generations earlier.

That God causes earthquakes may have been a biblical perspective in the days before we came to understand plate tectonics. Today we understand that the earth's tectonic plates are constantly moving as an essential part of our planet's cooling system. This mechanism is what makes our planet habitable. But it is also what causes earthquakes.

The biblical perspective on how God governs and works in our world was shaped both by the theological assumptions of the Bible's human authors and by the state of science two and three millennia ago. Of course, earthquakes, tornadoes, floods, and famines, as well as infertility, diseases, and untimely deaths, must have been the will of God. How else could they have been explained at that time? But standing outside a collapsed school where dozens of little children died, their bodies still under the rubble, their toys and books strewn all over the ground, I found the explanation of plate tectonics more comforting than thinking that God had intentionally crushed these children for some supposed sin committed by their ancestors.

Allow me to offer a word of caution when speaking with those who are suffering. Be careful about saying things like "Everything happens for a reason," or "It must have been the will of God." These are phrases we say when we don't know what else to say. They sound pious at first, but if you stop to think about them, they are the kinds of things that turn people away from God.

When we say, "Everything happens for a reason" or "It must have been the will of God," we typically are not talking about cause and effect. Usually we mean that God must have a plan we cannot yet see. Some find this comforting. Often it has just the opposite effect. A woman once told me how, after the death of her six-year-old son, her church friends sought to comfort her by telling her that "everything happens for a reason." That was the last time she went to church. She asked herself, "If everything happens for a reason, then God must have wanted my son to die. What kind of God decides that, in order to accomplish his purposes, he will take the life of a six-year-old boy?"

I don't believe that it was God who decided to make this little boy ill. He became ill with a disease for which researchers are working hard to find a cure. If it was God's will that the boy become sick, then his doctors must have been actually fighting against God's purposes as they sought to heal him. And if sickness comes from God, and healing too, then what is the point of doctors, or medicine, or medical research?

So we return to divine providence. Some believe that everything happens according to the will of God. These often speak of God's "sovereignty"—that is, God's authority, power, and dominion, as if believing that everything happens according to God's will is an essential part of believing that God is sovereign. But the overarching biblical story doesn't seem to be that God's will is always done. In fact, starting with Genesis chapter 2 and continuing until the final battle in Revelation 19, the Bible appears to be, in part, the story of human beings rejecting God's will, doing the very things God has commanded them not to do, and in the process harming one another and alienating themselves from God. No, everything does not happen according to the will of God.

The idea of God's sovereignty does not mean that everything happens according to the will of God, but that human evil, natural disasters, illness, and even death *will not have the final word*. God will ultimately force good from evil, and his love and goodness will finally prevail. This truth is seen in the rebuilding that takes place in our lives and in our world after tragedy strikes, and in the hope of the resurrection when we see God face-to-face.

We live in bodies that are fearfully and wonderfully made, yet they are not immune to illness and pain. We have hearts that are capable of experiencing great love, but sometimes they get broken. We live on a planet that is amazing, beautiful, and full of wonder but not protected from powerful destructive forces of nature. We are capable of doing wonderful and selfless things but also self-absorbed and harmful things. This is the world we live in.

God's role in superintending our world, and our lives is neither absentee landlord nor micromanager. God created the world and the laws of nature that govern it. God created human beings in his image. Through Jesus, he has shown us the way, the truth, and the life. By means of the Spirit, the scriptures, and the church, he continues to reveal his will to us. He has given each of us a heart, a mind, and a conscience as tools to help us find our way. And he gives us freedom to accept his guiding hand or reject it. God's primary instrument in caring for his planet and the people on it is other people and collectively the church. We are our brother and sister's keepers. God works through doctors and nurses, friends and family, and even strangers. This is God's ordinary way of working in the world. Our task is to pay attention and see who might need us.

And when this life draws to a close, whether through some untimely tragedy, a terminal illness, or simply old age, I trust in the words of Jesus, and the witness of his resurrection, that there is something more. I've been with hundreds of people as they approached their own death, and with hundreds more as they approached the death of their loved ones. And while I believe the Christian life is meant to be lived here and now, and not primarily for heaven, I also believe that "death has been swallowed up in victory" (First Corinthians 15:54, NIV). I believe that Jesus has gone "to prepare a place for you" (John 14:2, NIV). I don't spend a lot of time thinking about this, but the belief that I have in the resurrection, both Christ's and ours, changes how I face death.

As I am finishing the final edits on this chapter the young man I described in the beginning of the chapter has passed away. Just before he passed he told his dad, "I want to go home." His death was not a punishment for some sin he or his parents had committed. If we're inclined to believe that, we do well to remember the gospel assertion that Christ bore our sins on the cross. His death was not a test, nor a way for God to accomplish some greater good. He had a rare form of cancer researchers haven't yet learned how to effectively treat. His absence is felt deeply and profoundly by his parents every day. They don't believe God "took" their son. But they do believe God welcomed their son with open arms, and that one day they will see him again.

Some biblical authors believed that God controls everything, and that bad things happen as punishment for sin and good things are a reward for righteousness. Others asked why, if this is true, the wicked prosper and the innocent sometimes suffer. The New Testament authors said that Jesus himself bore the punishment for humanity's sin, as if to put an end, once and for all, to the idea that God was in the business of inflicting us with suffering for the bad things we've done.

There are consequences to our actions. There are natural disasters that bring devastation. There is illness that doctors have yet to find cures for. God's sovereignty does not mean that God causes these things, but instead that none of them will ultimately have the final word. God will bring good from evil, and not even death can separate us from his love.

CHAPTER 24

Can We Trust the
Gospel Accounts of Jesus?

I mentioned in the introduction to this book an attorney who said to me, "In a courtroom, when witnesses disagree . . . I know there is a problem with their testimony." He then said, "As I read the Gospels, they disagree at many points regarding exactly what Jesus said and what he did. The general testimony is consistent, but they differ in details. Can I trust their witness concerning Jesus?" This is an important question, particularly because the Christian faith in part depends upon their reliability. Are the Gospels trustworthy records of the life, teachings, death, and resurrection of Jesus?

We've learned already that the likely period in which the Gospels were written was sometime between AD 65 and 90. This means the Gospels were written thirty-five to sixty years after the time of Jesus. This is plenty of time for details to get confused, facts to be misconstrued or exaggerated, and legends to be born. It is also easy to understand how certain details in the life of Jesus could have been remembered differently even by those who knew Jesus personally.

In addition, we know the Gospel writers were not simply writing biographies of Jesus. They were writing gospels—proclamations of good news. They wrote not as historians but as Christians who were committed followers of Jesus Christ. In other words, they were biased—they were telling the story of one they had come to believe was the Messiah. As we learned in section 1, the Gospel writers brought their unique perspectives to the task of writing—what they found compelling about Jesus—and they wrote with the needs of their readers in mind.

It is easy to understand how a secular historian (or a religious skeptic) would read the Gospels and discount their historical reliability. After all, they record the story of a man who was born of a virgin, changed water into wine, opened the eyes of the blind, walked on water, healed the lame, raised the dead, and was himself raised from the dead. If you read such a story about anyone other than Jesus, what would you think?

Some liberal scholars discount the historical veracity of much of what the Gospels say about Jesus, particularly anything that points to the miraculous, or to his identity as anything other than a first-century Jewish rabbi and reformer. They believe the miraculous elements in the Gospels reflect the faith of the early church and not the actual Jesus of history.

So, are they right?

I understand their skepticism, and I think it is appropriate to question the historical reliability of the Gospels. We must do this, as their testimony about Jesus is the foundation upon which the Christian faith is built. But in the end, it is impossible to prove that the Gospel accounts are either reliable or not reliable.

Let me interject one thing here before considering the reliability of the Gospel accounts of Jesus. A young man I know and care deeply about was once actively involved in church, but now, as a grown man, he's got lots of questions. Whereas once he had an unexamined and uncritical faith in everything he was told, today he is a skeptic who has no room at all for faith. He said to me, "You know, there is actually no evidence from the first century that Jesus even existed. Historians of the time do not mention him. There is no documentation of his existence. He could have been fabricated by early Christians."

We actually have twenty-seven first-century documents (twenty-six, if you place 2 Peter in the second century) that speak about Jesus, written by at least nine different authors over a period of fifty years. They make up the New Testament. These documents are generally independent of one another, but all bear witness to the fact that Jesus lived in the Holy Land during the first half of the first century. They consistently bear witness to the fact that a man who was tortured and killed by the Romans was actually the long-awaited Jewish messiah. They tell of his resurrection from the grave and their continuing experience of him in their lives. They describe two foci of his message: the kingdom of God and the call to "love your neighbor as you love yourself."

These documents, though written in various parts of the Roman Empire, include details that root Jesus's story in actual places, connecting with real people, some of whom were known among Christian communities throughout the empire. Only the most skeptical of historians question whether Jesus actually existed.

Whether we dismiss these New Testament accounts of and witnesses to Jesus as pious myths held by gullible believers or reasonably reliable[1] accounts of the life of Jesus the Christ comes down to a decision we each must make.

For those looking for a detailed argument on the historical reliability of the Gospels, I'd recommend F. F. Bruce's *The New Testament Documents: Are They Reliable?*[2] I'll offer just a few comments about why an intelligent person would find it reasonable to trust in the historical reliability of the Gospels. But then I'd like to share a few words about my own decision to trust in the reliability of the Gospel accounts of Jesus, which had little to do with these reasons.

First, a word about anything being "historically reliable." If you've removed the idea of verbal, plenary inspiration, as I've sought to do with you, then we recognize that the Gospels are the accounts of four men whom tradition has called Matthew, Mark, Luke, and John.[3] As we've learned already, each drew upon a combination of sources for his Gospel—eyewitness accounts, early gospels, the preaching and teaching of the disciples, and likely other written sources. The earliest wrote thirty-five to forty years after the death of Jesus.

My wife and I first met thirty-five years ago. In some ways, we remember events from that time better than what happened yesterday. We remember most of the big events from those early years pretty much the same way. But sometimes we tell the same story in slightly different ways. There are some events she describes that I don't recall at all, and likewise, there are events that I remember which she has totally forgotten. Thankfully, there are two of us, and between the two of us, I think we're a pretty reliable source for what happened thirty-five years ago.

In the case of the Gospels, we have four written documents telling the same story. Is their historical reliability compromised if they remember this or that detail differently, even though the main details of the story are the same? Are we to discount their credibility because one remembers this and another remembers that? Or if one says an event took place at this point in Jesus's ministry, while another says the same event took place at a different point? These should only trouble us if we hold that God has chosen each word of each Gospel, in which case God's memory is a bit faulty. But if Matthew, Mark, Luke, and John were writing using their own faculties (albeit moved by the Spirit in ways we cannot fully define), then we should expect these differences. In a court of law, if four witnesses were called upon to testify about a crime they'd seen committed thirty-five or forty-five or fifty-five years earlier, and they had the level of agreement the Gospel writers have, their testimony would be considered remarkable and compelling.

We've noted earlier in the book the differences between John's Gospel and the Synoptics. I love preaching through John. It is a rich theological Gospel. I believe it is grounded in actual events in the life of Jesus. But John seemed far less concerned with getting the exact details correct than with making sure the details pointed to the theological message he was trying to convey. If I'm interested in the meaning of Jesus's life, I might first turn to John. If I'm interested in knowing what happened, I turn to the Synoptics.

So, with that caveat about historical reliability, why is it reasonable for an intelligent person to believe the Gospels are reasonably accurate? Here are a few answers I find compelling.

We have multiple letters from the apostle Paul, the earliest written just twenty years after the death of Jesus, which corroborate the basic convictions of the Gospels. Paul's testimony is particularly compelling because he was an opponent of Christianity before experiencing his own vision of the risen Christ. He had gone from persecuting and even presiding at the death of Christians to become Christianity's first-century champion. Perhaps even more compelling is the fact that Paul would suffer on many occasions for this Gospel, and ultimately die for his testimony concerning Jesus. The willingness to suffer and die for one's convictions does not prove that these convictions are true. Terrorists are willing to die for their convictions. But at the very least, Paul's willingness to suffer and die for his convictions is testimony to the depth of his faith in Christ, which I find compelling. Said another way, I think it is unreasonable to think that Paul, a well-educated Jewish Pharisee, would have devoted his life, suffering beatings, imprisonment, and ultimately death, to something he knew to be a myth.

At one point in Paul's first letter to the Corinthians, he offers a comment in passing that points to something important. He writes that the resurrected Jesus "appeared to more than five hundred brothers and sisters at one time, most of whom are still alive, though some have died" (1 Corinthians 15:6). In other words, hundreds of people in Judea could corroborate the events of Jesus's life, perhaps thousands (when we consider all who had seen or heard Jesus during his public ministry). To imagine that the Gospel writers could fabricate significant events from the life of Jesus while so many who were still alive had heard or seen Jesus seems unreasonable to me.

Luke, in his Acts of the Apostles, describes the early conflicts between the apostles and the Jewish leadership in Jerusalem after Christ's resurrection and ascension. Paul's story in Galatians seems to corroborate these stories. What this means is that within weeks of Jesus's death and resurrection, the disciples were proclaiming him to be the Jewish messianic king, crucified and resurrected. So though the Gospels were finally written sometime in the period between AD 65 and AD 90, the proclamation of Jesus as the crucified and resurrected Messiah was the church's message from the beginning.

The willingness of the disciples to proclaim this message in the face of certain opposition and the threat of death (two of the early leaders in the church, James and Stephen, were put to death by AD 45) testifies to the depth of the conviction regarding the truthfulness of the gospel. Tradition holds that ultimately ten of the twelve original disciples would be put to death for their faith. Again, I find this compelling testimony and consider it unreasonable to believe that these ordinary, uneducated men would face persecution, imprisonment, and death to proclaim a crucified Messiah if they did not actually believe he was raised and was in fact the Messiah.

It is one thing to be willing to die for a story you've heard secondhand yet believed. I would like to believe I would give my life to testify to Christ. But in the case of the earliest apostles, they personally knew Jesus. They testified to his death and resurrection with their lives. I would find it hard to die for something I knew to be a falsehood. Again, this does not prove that Jesus was more than a first-century itinerant preacher. But it does lead me to say that it is reasonable to believe that they believed Jesus was the resurrected messianic king.

Many have found Luke's testimony about how he wrote his Gospel and the subsequent historical reliability of details he includes in Luke and particularly his Acts of the Apostles as lending credence to the view that it is historically reliable. You'll recall Luke begins his Gospel with these words:

> Since many have undertaken to set down an orderly account of the events that have been fulfilled among us, just as they were handed on to us by those who from the beginning were eyewitnesses and servants of the word, I too decided, after investigating everything carefully from the very first, to write an orderly account for you, most excellent Theophilus, so that you may know the truth concerning the things about which you have been instructed.

Luke identifies his intention in writing the Gospel and the process he went through to research his material. He is claiming to have created a historically reliable account and not simply a recounting of hearsay and myths believed about Jesus. My own conclusion, and that of many others, is that Luke took seriously the recording of this story, seeking to record it accurately, and that he is a trusted source for the earliest traditions concerning Jesus.[4]

Ultimately, for many, the question of the reliability of the New Testament witness concerning Jesus boils down to whether we can accept the idea that Jesus did things that other human beings are unable to—miraculous healing, for example—and whether he did in fact rise from the dead. The four Gospels, Paul's letters, and the other writings of the New Testament provide twenty-seven first-century documents testifying that Jesus did these things. Those who became followers of Jesus Christ based on the disciples' testimony to the resurrection found their witness compelling. The birth of the church, fifty days after Jesus had been crucified, is itself testimony that "something happened" which would lead thousands to believe that Jesus, who had been crucified by the Romans seven weeks earlier, was in fact the Messiah.

None of these things proves that the Gospels are reliable or that Jesus performed miracles or was raised from the dead. Yet they are all pieces of information that we draw upon to determine whether we deem the Gospels to be trustworthy first-century accounts of the life of Jesus.

As I noted, these are just a few of the things I think about when I ask myself why it is reasonable to trust in the Gospel accounts of Jesus. In addition to this line of reasoning—and admittedly, this is highly subjective—is the personal experience of persons who claim to have had an encounter with Christ or whose lives have been positively affected by their faith in him. I count myself as one of these. So, while this is not proof of the historical reliability of the Gospels, I offer it as my own story of how I came to believe that the Gospels give us a reliable account of what Jesus said and did.

As a teenager, I had come to believe that religion was a crutch for people who were weak. I'd heard this idea from someone else, and I suppose it made me feel a bit superior to say it. At the same time as I professed to be an atheist (I suppose I was really more of an agnostic), I also felt compelled to actually read the Bible at least once. I had never read it before. I did not go to Sunday School or Vacation Bible School as a child. But I did have a large Bible my Roman Catholic grandmother had given our family when I was just a boy. I decided to read it cover to cover. I started reading five chapters a night before going to bed.

After a couple of months of reading stories about people's experience of God, I began to wonder if there might not actually be a God after all. I kept reading and kept wondering. Eventually I came to the Gospel of Matthew. I immediately found myself taken by Jesus. I was skeptical of the virgin birth and the miracles, but when I read the Sermon on the Mount, I found it spoke to me.

Jesus's parables, his images of the kingdom of God, his compassion for the sick, and ultimately his willingness to stand up to religious leaders who had clearly missed the point of their religion drew me to him. When I came to the end of the Gospel of Matthew, I was moved by Jesus's tragic death at the hands of the religious leaders and the Romans. Then came the story of the resurrection. It was just too much for me to believe. I suppose at some level I wanted it to be true, but I did not believe it.

Then I read Mark's Gospel. It is similar to Matthew's Gospel but lacks much of Jesus's teaching and preaching that is found in Matthew. I was once more drawn to Jesus and moved by his crucifixion. Once again I read that the tomb was empty on Easter, and I found myself thinking that this ending changed the story for the better. No longer would evil, hate, jealousy, and death have the final word; if Christ were resurrected, then hope and love and life would have the final word. But though I saw the logic of the story, I still did not believe.

Then I read Luke's Gospel. Many Christians love John. But Luke is my favorite Gospel. In Luke, Jesus is clearly portrayed as born into poverty and concerned for the poor. Throughout the Gospel, he is a friend of sinners. This picture of Jesus demonstrating mercy to those considered sinners and enemies of God was deeply moving to me.

In Luke 2, Jesus is born in a stable and sleeps in the animals' feeding trough on the night he's born. The night-shift shepherds, the lowest rung in first-century society, are invited to celebrate his birth. In Luke 7, Jesus eats at the home of a religious leader, but to the horror of the religious leader, Jesus shows grace and mercy to the town prostitute who barges into the dinner party. In Luke 15, the religious people grumble because Jesus eats with sinners and tax collectors. To eat with someone in that time was to proclaim them your companion and friend. Jesus is a friend to sinners. Finally in Luke 19, Jesus eats supper with a chief sinner, a man named Zacchaeus, and then, after others grumble once more that he is eating with sinners, Jesus says, "The Son of Man came to seek and to save those who are lost" (Luke 19:10). I came to love Jesus as I read Luke's Gospel.

Once more, the Gospel reaches its climax with the crucifixion of Jesus. Here, only in this Gospel, Jesus prays from the cross, "Father forgive them, they know not what they do." What kind of man prays from the cross for mercy for those who have subjected him to such a horrible death? The same kind of man who draws sinners and tax collectors to God.

This time, when I came to the resurrection story, something changed in me. I found myself thinking, "If Jesus did in fact come from God, the resurrection is entirely logical. How else could this story end? If Jesus remains in the tomb, the story is over—darkness has overcome light, hate has overcome love, and death has overcome life." It seemed illogical to me that Jesus would have remained dead and buried. At that moment it hit me: if Jesus was in fact who the New Testament claimed, the miracles, too, made sense. If God had come in human flesh, would he not open the eyes of the blind? Would he not heal illnesses no doctor could heal?

That night, when I closed Luke's Gospel, I put my faith in Christ. Putting my faith in him started with trusting that the Gospels were reasonably reliable testimonies concerning Jesus. I came to believe what Luke had written about Jesus. Was it all exactly right, happening in just this way? I didn't know—even then I could see there were places where Matthew, Mark, and Luke differed in details. But the overall story, the picture of Jesus they conveyed, was consistent and compelling.

I got down on my knees next to my bed, and I spoke to this crucified and resurrected Jesus and said, "I wish to follow you. I pledge my life to you and to your service. I would like to be your disciple." From that time until the present, thirty-five years later, I have sought, albeit imperfectly, to live as his follower.

The best parts of my life have all been somehow connected to that decision to believe the witness of the Gospels and entrust my life to Jesus Christ. I am a better husband, father, and boss because of this. Does this prove the reliability of the Gospels? Of course not. People of other faiths also report how their own deeply held convictions shape their lives in positive ways. I can only say that the gospel Jesus preached, the life he lived, his death on the cross, and his resurrection from the grave form the story that I hope defines my life. The Gospels are his story, and as we read them and listen to him and trust them, they become our story.

In the end, no one can prove (or disprove) that the Gospels are reasonably reliable accounts of the life of Jesus. You have to decide this for yourself. I don't expect them to be inerrant or infallible. I don't expect them to be completely consistent in every detail (in fact, I value their differences). But I do trust that these first-century documents, the Gospels and Letters of the New Testament, provide a reliable account both of the life and ministry of Jesus and of how his life affected the lives of his first-century followers. It is by believing this and following him that I've found, in the words of John, "life in his name."

CHAPTER 25

Did Jesus Really Say That?

Forty-six-year-old Aldo Bianchini was sitting in mass at Sant'Andrea Catholic Church in Viareggio, Italy, in October 2011. Just as the priest began his sermon, Bianchini, a native of Great Britain, stood up and began gouging out both his eyes before the congregation of three hundred people. He survived the experience, but doctors were not able to restore his eyes. Aldo said a voice told him to do this.

Clearly Aldo was suffering from some kind of mental illness, but he was also literally fulfilling the words of Jesus in Matthew 5:27–30: "Everyone who looks at a woman with lust has already committed adultery with her in his heart. If your right eye causes you to sin, tear it out and throw it away; it is better for you to lose one of your members than for your whole body to be thrown into hell. And if your right hand causes you to sin, cut it off and throw it away; it is better for you to lose one of your members than for your whole body to go into hell" (Matthew 5:28–30).

Unlike Mr. Bianchini, most of us recognize that Jesus did not intend for us to take all his words literally. Jesus often used a form of speech that we might call prophetic hyperbole. Prophets spoke in absolute, black-and-white (and sometimes harsh) terms. Hyperbole is an intentionally over-the-top exaggeration designed to make a point. In the case of Jesus's words regarding plucking out our eyes, Jesus is telling us that lust for those who are not our mates is serious. It can lead to infidelity or sexual addiction. It can destroy our relationships and harm our souls. I don't believe he intends, however, that we literally pluck out our eyes.

I sat with a man recently who told me that he'd been struggling with pornography. What started as an occasional release had become an addiction. What began with online pornography had turned into paying for sex. Now he'd discovered that he had contracted a sexually transmitted disease which threatened his own life, and which he might have passed on to his wife. He now had to tell his wife about this so that she could be tested. He was devastated by the thought that he might have given a life-threatening illness to his wife through his infidelity. He also knew his wife might leave him when she found out what he had done.

Jesus did not intend that people pluck out their eyes or cut off their hands. These hyperbolic words were meant to shake his hearers into taking sin seriously. Take Jesus's words seriously, but don't always take them literally.

Are there other places where Jesus uses hyperbole to make a point? What about this one: "I tell you, it is easier for a camel to go through the eye of a needle than for someone who is rich to enter the kingdom of God" (Matthew 19:24). What's his message? Riches can be toxic to your soul. Don't let them enslave you!

Any other examples in the Gospels? I knew a man who did not believe in either life insurance or saving for retirement. Why not?

Because Jesus said, "Do not store up for yourselves treasures on earth, where moth and rust consume and where thieves break in and steal" (Matthew 6:19). Was Jesus really telling us not to set money aside for retirement? Or save for college, or have an emergency fund for when your car breaks down?

Sometimes Jesus makes confusing promises, like this one: "Truly I tell you, if you have faith and do not doubt . . . even if you say to this mountain, 'Be lifted up and thrown into the sea,' it will be done. Whatever you ask for in prayer with faith, you will receive" (Matthew 21:21–22). We read this and wonder why our prayer for the healing of someone we love did not occur. Did we lack faith? Did they lack faith? Or was Jesus deploying hyperbole to teach us to trust God with our lives or to be bold in prayer?

Here's my point: Jesus often speaks using hyperbole. You do too. When someone says, "I'm so hungry I could eat a horse," do you believe they actually could? A friend has told me she would die if I asked her to pray aloud before a group. Would she really? I know a guy they say snores louder than a freight train. Does he really?

It's also helpful to interpret the words of Jesus in the light of his deeds. For instance, Jesus said, "I say to you, whoever divorces his wife, except for unchastity, and marries another commits adultery" (Matthew 19:9). In Catholicism, this is the basis for refusing the Eucharist to persons who were married in the church, then divorce and remarry without their first marriage being annulled. Catholics take this scripture literally.

Regarding the issue of divorce, we might ask how Jesus's response in John 4 to the woman at the well, a woman who had been divorced and remarried five times, might inform our understanding of how Jesus actually viewed those who divorced. Far from forbidding her from receiving the Eucharist, Jesus offers her living water and calls her to be a witness among the Samaritan people. He does so knowing that she, at the time, lived with a man who was not her husband. Jesus's grace toward the divorced woman does not diminish his strong words about divorce, but they do demonstrate his greater concern for drawing those who've been pushed away from God back into the fold.

I once met a woman who was afraid she had committed the "unpardonable sin" of Matthew 12:32, blasphemy against the Holy Spirit. She was truly worried she had done something that made it impossible to receive God's forgiveness. I assured her that, whatever that passage means, if she was worried that she might have committed this sin, then she had not committed it. Anyone who had committed an unpardonable sin would have turned so far from God that he or she would no longer care about God's pardon. But I also reminded her that we read passages like this recognizing that Jesus spoke in hyperbole, and we have to read them in the light of what Jesus actually did. I reminded her that Jesus hung on the cross, looking down upon those who nailed him there, and prayed, "Father forgive them, for they know not what they do." It seems likely that Jesus's mention of an unpardonable sin was another example of prophetic hyperbole. He was likely warning against a hardness of heart that persistently refused to acknowledge the Spirit's work, cursing it instead.

Here's the point: take Jesus's words very seriously but not always literally. He's trying to lead you away from things that can harm you. But by his actions he's regularly demonstrating the grace he offers sinners, including those whose eyes cause them to sin, who find themselves with riches, who have been divorced, or who have offended the Spirit.

CHAPTER 26

"No One Comes to the Father Except Through Me"?

I was sitting at a funeral led by another pastor. He was reading from John 14:1–6, a favorite Gospel passage for many and a scripture often read at funerals. The passage, in which Jesus is preparing his disciples for his own death, begins, "Do not let your hearts be troubled. Trust in God; trust also in me. In my Father's house are many rooms; if it were not so I would have told you" (NIV). Jesus goes on to say, "I am going there to prepare a place for you. And if I go and prepare a place for you, I will come back and take you to be with me that you also may be where I am." I love this passage and the image of Jesus preparing a place for us in his Father's house.

Many pastors stop there, with the beautiful promise. But many continue with verses 4–6, as this pastor did: "You know the way to the place where I am going." Then Thomas, later known as "the Doubter," speaks up: "Lord, we don't know where you are going, so how can we know the way?" Then comes the majestic verse 6:

"I am the way and the truth and the life!" But as the pastor began to read it, I wondered, is he going to read the second half of verse 6? The pastor continued, quoting from Jesus, "No one comes to the Father except through me."

The guy sitting next to me at this particular service leaned over and said, "Did Jesus just say that everyone who is not a Christian is going to hell? Why would the preacher read that *now*, at a time like this?"

I've been asked about these words by many people over the years. For many Christians, these words are clear: unless an individual personally accepts Jesus Christ as his or her Lord and Savior, he or she will not enter heaven. I wonder if this is really what Jesus was trying to teach in this passage? Once again, this is a huge topic. Entire books have been written about God's final judgment and the fate of the faithful of other religions.[1] My intent here is to have the conversation with you that I've had with a host of others over a cup of coffee and hope it spurs you on to further reading.

We don't have time to unpack the marvelous creedal and Christological statement in John 14:6a, "I am the way and the truth and the life." But let's devote one paragraph to it. As you may know, every part of that statement links Jesus to God, and every part makes clear who Jesus is and how his life connects with our lives. This is one of the famous "I am" statements in John, in which Jesus hints at the divine personal name for God in the Old Testament, Yahweh, which means something like "I am who I am." I read that divine name to be God stating, "I am life, or being, or existence itself!" By beginning his statement with "I am," John may intend his readers to hear this connection to God. Then Jesus makes three statements, each of which apply to God. Jesus does not say, I am one way, part of the truth, or one among many sources of life. No, John 14:6a is a dramatic, definitive, and sweeping statement identifying Jesus with the very things, at an existential level, we long for—to know the way, to understand and apprehend the truth, and to find full, authentic life. This passage asserts that Jesus is the very essence and source of these things.

But let's return to the second half of that verse, "No one comes to the Father except through me." Let's consider two ways we might understand this statement.

The first is to believe that Jesus intended to make a statement about the eternal fate of all non-Christians, as if to say, "No one who has not accepted me as their personal Lord and Savior will come to my Father. They will be eternally separated from him." This is how many Christians understand John 14:6b. It is certainly how my friend heard the line as we sat there listening to the young pastor read these words at the funeral.

A second way of understanding Jesus's words in this verse is "No one comes to my Father except through my saving work." Notice the difference. In the first case, above, the emphasis is on what an individual does—their decision to receive Christ ("No one comes to the Father unless they accept me"). In the second way of interpreting the text, the emphasis is on what Jesus does to save the world ("No one comes to the Father except by my saving work").

Remember, Jesus speaks these words just hours before being arrested and tried. The next day, he will be crucified. John is clear that on the cross Jesus brings about the salvation of the world. In this context, it seems likely to me that Jesus is referring to what *he* does to save the world (the second interpretation of John 14:6b) rather than what *humans* do to receive salvation.

If 6b is about what Jesus does to bring about human salvation, not what we do to respond to it, then this passage is saying that everyone who comes to the Father (the implication is, to the Father's house—that is, heaven) will do so as a result of what Jesus has done. If we use the old metaphor often deployed to describe the work of Christ, he is the bridge over which everyone who finds salvation will cross.

This takes us back to the question of the eternal fate of non-Christian people. There are three broad categories of views on this question:

Pluralism or universalism says that everyone will ultimately go to heaven. God will not allow any to be lost. I find this view attractive until I think of those who are truly evil, or those who earnestly and persistently reject God's grace. It seems to me that salvation is a gift that can be refused and that God will not force salvation upon anyone. I appreciate C. S. Lewis's quote concerning this. In *The Problem of Pain* he wrote, "I willingly believe that the damned are, in one sense, successful, rebels to the end; that the doors of hell are locked on the inside."[2] For both these reasons—truly evil people and the value God places on allowing us to choose to accept or reject his love and not forcing us to do his will—I reject the idea that everyone ultimately goes to heaven.

Exclusivism or particularism says that only those who have personally accepted Christ will go to heaven. Human beings are affected by sin. God offers salvation as a gift, but it must be accepted. Only by personally receiving this gift can one be saved. There are some who hold this view yet who believe there may be exceptions—children below the "age of accountability," for instance, or, for the more gracious expressions of this view, those who did not have the opportunity in this life to hear the good news of Christ, but who, had they heard, would have responded. Otherwise all others will be consigned to hell, including all the faithful of other religions.

Christian inclusivism affirms that Jesus is the way, the truth, and the life. He is the source of salvation. His death was for the sins of the world. But God can give the gift of salvation to anyone he chooses based upon the criteria he chooses. It is possible, according to this view, for God to give the gift of salvation to those who have sought to love and serve God even if they had never heard the gospel or had not fully understood or accepted it. He can give it to people who had heard the gospel but for whom it did not make sense, or who heard it presented poorly, or who were raised in another faith and simply could not imagine that the faith their parents had taught them was not true. This view is clear that Christ is the Savior of the world. But his salvation is given by God as God chooses.

Christian inclusivism allows that God might look at the heart and earnest faith of those who are of other faiths, and he might see in them a desire to know the way, the truth, and the life, and an earnest desire to love God and love their neighbors. Seeing this, God could, if he chose, apply the saving work of Christ to these persons.

The inclusivist would remind us that the Christian gospel makes plain that salvation is a gift from God. Paul makes clear that we are saved only by God's grace: "For by grace you have been saved through faith, and this is not your own doing; it is the gift of God—not the result of works, so that no one may boast" (Ephesians 2:8–9). "Grace" in the New Testament refers to God's kindness, his love, his care, his work on our behalf, his blessings, his gifts, his goodness, his salvation. But it is more than that—it is these things when they are *undeserved*. It is pure gift.

Jesus makes clear that the evidence of this faith is the fruit produced in our lives. He notes that there are many at the last day who will say, "Lord, Lord!" but who will be excluded from the kingdom because they were not earnest in their faith and did not bear fruit that was the evidence of true faith. Meanwhile, the inclusivist would say that there are some who had earnest faith and produced fruit, but who did not know or understand to call upon the name of Christ.

The inclusivist perspective seems both more consistent with the character of God revealed in Jesus and more just. It allows human beings to reject salvation, but also allows God's mercy to judge everyone according to their heart and their faith. It removes the idea that there is a magic prayer that must be spoken and if only you say the right words, you will be accepted to heaven, while billions who earnestly sought to love God and neighbor yet did not know to call upon the name of Christ will be tormented eternally in hell.

I believe John 14:6b is about what Christ does to affect our salvation, not what we as humans do in receiving that salvation. I believe that God can and does distribute the gift of salvation made possible by Christ to anyone he chooses, based not upon their deeds but upon the faith he sees in them—a faith that is seen by one's deeds. They thus come to the Father through Jesus, who is the way, the truth, and the life, even if they did not, in this life, know him or understand that he was in fact the Savior.

There were those in the early church who held this view, including Justin Martyr. John Wesley, the founder of Methodism, seemed to have held this view. C. S. Lewis and John Stott, twentieth-century luminaries in the evangelical world, held this view. This is the official position of the Roman Catholic Church and the unofficial position of many mainline churches.

Some have said, "If the inclusivist position is true, why would we send missionaries around the world, or why even tell our neighbors about Christ?" My response is that I share Christ with others not because I believe all who don't know him will be eternally tormented in hell. I share him with others because I believe that in Christ we see the clearest picture of who God is and what

God longs for from humanity. I share Christ because I believe it is in knowing, loving, and serving him that we find the fullest and most authentic life possible. I share Christ with others because I believe God wants all people to know the good news of Jesus Christ. I share Christ because I believe he is the way, the truth, and the life.

CHAPTER 27

Women Need Not Apply

In the summer of 2013, newly elected Pope Francis met with reporters and responded to their questions. The world was anxious to know more about the pope's views on a wide range of issues of importance in the Church today. One reporter asked the pope what he thought about the possibility of ordaining women. He noted that women are important in the Church and there is a need to develop a greater theology related to women. But then he responded clearly and directly: "With reference to the ordination of women, the Church has spoken and says, 'No.' John Paul II said it, but with a definitive formulation. That is closed, that door."[1]

The "no" of John Paul II he was referring to was a letter dated May 22, 1994, to the bishops of the Catholic Church, in which the pope gave a clear and definitive declaration that women could not be ordained.[2] John Paul II quoted Pope Paul VI, who had offered the following reasons why the Church does not ordain women:

The example recorded in the Sacred Scriptures of Christ choosing his Apostles only from among men; the constant practice of the Church, which has imitated Christ in choosing only men; and her living teaching authority which has consistently held that the exclusion of women from the priesthood is in accordance with God's plan for his Church.[3]

The essential argument is that Jesus did not choose any woman when choosing the twelve apostles; therefore Jesus must have felt that no woman should ever be ordained as a pastor or priest. Women need not apply. I wonder, did Jesus really have this in mind when he chose twelve male disciples? Or was he choosing his apostles based upon who might have the greatest likelihood of receiving a hearing and becoming accepted leaders in first-century Judaism?

First-century Judaism was steeped in eighteen centuries of patriarchy. Women played an important role in society and particularly in the home, but they were clearly subordinate to men. The first-century Jewish historian Josephus wrote, "The woman, says the Law, is in all things inferior to the man. Let her accordingly be submissive, not for her humiliation, but that she may be directed; for the authority has been given by God to the man" (*Against Apion* 2, 201). A morning blessing within Judaism that originated from, if not the first century, then not long after that, is still said by some Jewish men every morning: "Blessed are you O God, King of the Universe, Who has not made me a woman."

For many conservative churches, it is not the fact that Jesus did not choose a female apostle that keeps them from allowing women to serve as pastors or even lay leaders in the church. It is what the apostle Paul wrote in his letters. In 1 Corinthians 14:33b–35, he writes, "As in all the churches of the saints, women should be silent in the churches. For they are not permitted to speak, but should be subordinate, as the law also says. If there is anything they desire to know, let them ask their husbands at home. For it is shameful for a woman to speak in church." Or again, as Paul writes in 1 Timothy 2:11–12, "Let a woman learn in silence with full submission. I permit no woman to teach or to have authority over a man; she is to keep silent."

Paul has to mention this in two letters because it was likely becoming a "problem" in some churches that women had recognized the egalitarian nature of the gospel, as Paul so eloquently stated in Galatians 3:28: "There is no longer Jew or Greek, there is no longer slave or free, there is no longer male and female; for all of you are one in Christ Jesus." Paul recognizes a number of women who are leaders in the church. In Romans 16, Paul names numerous women who were co-laborers in the gospel with him. These include Priscilla, described as a fellow worker who, with her husband, risked her life for him. Mary is said to have "worked very hard for you." Junia, Paul's relative, had been imprisoned with him and was said to be, with her husband, "outstanding among the apostles." Tryphene and Tryphosa "work hard in the Lord." The list goes on.

Why, then, does Paul not permit women to speak in the church?

Paul grounds his prohibition against women speaking in the second Creation story found in Genesis 2 and the story of the Fall in Genesis 3. This is what he says following his statement that it is "shameful" for a woman to speak in church: "For Adam was formed first, then Eve; and Adam was not deceived, but the woman was deceived and became a transgressor" (1 Timothy 2:13–14).

Let's return to the Creation stories in Genesis 1–3. The first Creation story, in Genesis 1, is egalitarian: "So God created humankind in his image, in the image of God he created them; male and female he created them. God blessed them, and God said to them, 'Be fruitful and multiply, and fill the earth and subdue it'" (Genesis 1:27–28). There was no patriarchy. They were created at the same time, and neither was given dominance; they were partners in subduing the earth. And God saw that it was good.

The second Creation story gives us a different approach. The woman was made after the man. In Genesis 2:18, God says, "I will make him [Adam] a helper as his partner." This idea of helper has often been misunderstood. The Hebrew word is *ezer*. It does not signify a weaker individual meant to serve another, but rather a strong individual coming to the aid of someone weaker. It appears twenty-one times in the Old Testament, sixteen of which refer to God coming to the aid of his people. In this passage, the word is used twice to refer to Eve.

In Genesis 3, things begin to change. We speak of this story as "the Fall."

As I suggested earlier, this is not a reporter's account of what happened in the Garden of Eden. Neither was it written to satisfy the curiosity of readers about the first pair of humans. The story is archetypal, meant to teach us about ourselves. We are Adam and Eve in this story. The man would have to work by the sweat of his brow, and he would one day return to the dust from which he came. The woman would henceforth experience pain in childbirth; God also said to her, "your desire shall be for your husband, and he shall rule over you" (Genesis 3:16).

These were the consequences of sin coming into the world. Paradise with its beautiful partnership between man and woman was lost. Adam would rule over Eve because of her poor judgment in leading them to eat the fruit. Whether you take this story literally, or archetypally and figuratively as I do, it is clear that male dominance was a result of sin and the Fall.

We see this tragic new relationship throughout the Old Testament. When our youngest daughter was eight-years-old she was given her third-grade Bible. She decided to read it from cover to cover. We talked about each chapter or story at night before we said her bedtime prayers. After three weeks of reading, she said, "Daddy, this book is almost all about boys, and when there are girls, they aren't treated very nicely." I asked her to explain, and she told me that the boys had names, but the girls had no names (there are a few exceptions I pointed out to her, but she is generally right that women are not named). She told me the stories were all about boys. She had read how Abraham had given his wife Sarah away, twice, pretending she was his sister, in order to save himself. Lot's wife had become a pillar of salt. And Sarah's slave girl was forced to produce a child for Abraham. And this was just the first twenty chapters of Genesis. I finally told her, Rebecca, let's skip ahead to the Gospels!

Had she kept reading, she would have read that in the Law a woman is worth half of what a man is worth. Women were ceremonially unclean for fourteen days after they gave birth to a girl, but only seven days after they gave birth to a boy. Women were counted as the property of their husband. Fathers were allowed to sell their daughters into slavery. In Judges 19, there is the story of a man giving away his virgin daughter to be gang-raped rather than handing over the male stranger who was staying overnight. In the same story, the male stranger saves himself by throwing his female concubine out the door so the men of Gibeah could rape her all night. She dies on the doorstep of the home the next morning. If you're not convinced that the Old Testament view of women was one of subordination and male dominance, keep reading in Judges 19–21 to see how various women are treated.

Today we still see the impact of the Fall on how women are treated in our world. Parents sell their daughters to human traffickers, who find a ready market among men. Shocking stories appear in the news of men kidnapping women and keeping them chained up for years. A woman is sexually assaulted every two minutes in the United States. Physical and emotional abuse is a regular part of life for many women. When women are murdered, 40 percent of the time the perpetrators are their husbands or boyfriends. Less than 7 percent of men that are murdered are murdered by a girlfriend or spouse.[4] These are all manifestations of sin and the Fall.

John's Gospel offers a powerful perspective on what Jesus did while on the cross. But you have to read John carefully to see the point. John begins his Gospel, "In the beginning . . ."—words that are meant to point the reader to the Garden of Eden. Then, in John 19:41, he gives us a detail no other Gospel gives us: "Now there was a garden in the place where he was crucified, and in the garden there was a new tomb in which no one had ever been laid." Jesus is crucified in a garden, and buried in a garden. He is raised in a garden and, when Mary Magdalene first sees the resurrected Christ, she doesn't recognize him, because he looks like the gardener. Here's the point: Jesus came to reverse the curse of Eden. Part of that curse is the subordination of women.

The curse has been addressed in Christ. Paul told us that women were to keep silent in the church because of Eve's sin and, by implication, the curse placed upon her. Even if you take that story literally, Christ came to reverse the curse and to heal paradise. In the beginning, God's will was partnership. Sin brought patriarchy. Shouldn't the ideal of redemption be a return to partnership and an end to the subordination of women? And if this is the case, is it not time to recognize that Paul's words about women remaining silent do not reflect God's timeless will for the role women are to play in the church?

CHAPTER 28

Is It Okay to Get a Tattoo?

I received a Facebook message as I was sitting down to complete the last few chapters in this book. A college student wrote to say, "Adam, what do you think about tattoos? I was thinking about getting one, but I looked in the Bible for guidance and found this verse in Leviticus 19:28: 'You shall not make any gashes in your flesh for the dead or tattoo any marks upon you: I am the LORD.' So, is it wrong for me to get a tattoo?" What would you tell this young man?

You might be thinking, "Seriously, Adam, with all the important topics you could take on, you've included a chapter on tattoos?" But my interest is not so much in tattoos as it is in recapping what we've learned about the Bible and how we're to read it. So consider this a test.

I took a quick look online and found a host of websites saying that tattoos were clearly against God's will. "You shall not tattoo any marks upon you." How much clearer could God be?

Yet we've learned that scripture was not dictated by God but rather written by men seeking to express what they believed was God's will. They were writing in a given time and culture, and they were writing to address the needs of the people of their time. While they generally wrote under the prompting of the Spirit, this does not mean that every word of scripture was chosen by God or equally inspired by God. We've learned that some scriptures correct others, and that clear teaching in scripture does not always reflect the timeless will of God. We also learned that in Acts 15 the apostles set aside most of the requirements of the Law, saying they were no longer binding on Gentile Christians.

Thus deciding what is a "biblical lifestyle" is more complicated than finding a scripture and following it. In fact, the more we learn about the Bible, the more it appears not to be the kind of "rule book" that we might wish it were.

A. J. Jacobs is an editor-at-large of *Esquire* magazine. He's also an agnostic Jew who decided to spend a year following the Law of Moses as literally as possible. He documented this in a humorous book called *The Year of Living Biblically*. One thing he learned was that those Jewish and Christian fundamentalists who purport to take the Bible literally still pick and choose what they follow.

One of the important lessons he learned while practicing the positive ethical teachings of scripture was that doing good things actually changed how he thought. Often we believe that we change our heart and that changes our behavior. While this is often true, Jacobs learned that the converse was true: changing your behavior often changes your heart.

Jacobs noted that his wife became frustrated with him for following literally Leviticus 15:19–23, which states that you are not to sit on something a menstruating woman has sat on. If you do, you have to wash your clothes and take a bath. You also cannot sleep in the same bed with a menstruating woman; if you do, you must wash your clothes and take a bath. He said that his wife, in protest over this passage, would sit on every chair in the house during her period, forcing him to stand until he purchased a portable chair he could carry with him!

I loved something Jacobs said in a TED talk. He noted that it is impossible to literally do everything the Law says you must do. Everyone must pick and choose. Then he said, "The important thing is picking and choosing the right things." I think he got it exactly right: pick and choose the right things.

Leviticus 19:28 says, "Don't get a tattoo." But the verse just before it, Leviticus 19:27, says, "You shall not round off the hair on your temples or mar the edges of your beard." I have a friend who insists that getting tattoos is wrong. I want to say to her, "I don't see ringlets on your husband's temples, and he has no beard! Why do you insist on taking verse 28 literally but not verse 27?"

My response to the young man on Facebook was to say, in essence, "To appropriately interpret this scripture, it would be helpful to try to understand why Moses was forbidding tattoos." My guess is that they were used in pagan rituals marking someone as belonging to the local deity. It is also believed that slaves were branded just like animals. If this is so, Leviticus 19 may have been written to discourage people from permanently marking their bodies as a way of honoring a pagan god.

I also said to this young man, "Regarding the Law of Moses, the Council at Jerusalem in Acts 15 made a declaratory decision that much of the Law of Moses was no longer binding upon Gentile Christians—it was a covenant God made specifically with Israel in ancient times. God made a new covenant with the world through Jesus Christ. Paul says the Law now functions as a guide. Jesus summarized what he expected from his disciples with these words:

'Love the Lord your God with all your heart, soul, mind and strength; and love your neighbor as you love yourself.' So I'd ask, will your getting this tattoo in any way diminish your love for God or your ability to love your neighbor?"

We examine all the rest of what scripture teaches in the light of these two great commandments. I mentioned earlier in the book that these function like a colander. Would getting a tattoo affect your capacity to love God and neighbor? Recognizing Jesus is God's definitive Word, we would do well to ask if he says anything about marking one's body with tattoos. He does not.

My final response to the young man was that it would appear that the prohibition against tattoos may be more about motive than the act itself. It was likely a prohibition against a practice indicating ritual devotion to a pagan god. So perhaps the real question comes down to motivation for us as well. Why do you wish to permanently mark your body? What does the mark mean to you? What statement, if any, are you trying to make to others? Are your motives and markings in keeping with, or at least not opposed to, a desire to love God and love your neighbor? As a parent of two twenty-something daughters with tattoos, there's one more question you might want to ask, at least if you are still on your parents' payroll: WDMDT—What do Mom and Dad think? ☺

CHAPTER 29

Homosexuality and the Bible

If a man lies with a male as with a woman,
both of them have committed an abomination;
they shall be put to death; their blood is upon
them. —LEVITICUS 20:13

God gave them up to degrading passions.
Their women exchanged natural intercourse
for unnatural, and in the same way also
the men, giving up natural intercourse with
women, were consumed with passion for one
another. Men committed shameless acts with
men and received in their own persons the due
penalty for their error. —ROMANS 1:26-27

Over the last fifteen years, I've had more questions asked of me about homosexuality and the Bible than about any other topic in this book. It is the most divisive issue facing Christianity in the West today. Americans and Europeans have experienced a shift in attitudes and perspectives on this issue, and that shift spans all generations, though it is most pronounced among young adults. While mainline and Catholic churches wrestle with the question of homosexuality more than evangelical churches, changing attitudes toward homosexuality are being felt in evangelical churches as well.

Gallup found in 2001 that 40 percent of Americans felt homosexual relations were morally acceptable. By 2013, 59 percent of Americans believed that homosexual relations were morally acceptable.[1] I do not mention these statistics to suggest that Christians should determine what is morally or ethically acceptable by using opinion polls. But the polls show us that our culture, including many Christians in our culture, is questioning the Bible's teaching regarding homosexuality. Hence Christians, particularly pastors and church leaders, will find themselves in an increasing number of conversations about homosexuality and the Bible. In this chapter, I'd like to offer some reflections on homosexuality and the Bible as I've sought to make sense of this issue.

The issues we've described up to this point—about the Bible's humanity, what precisely is meant by its divine inspiration, and how we make sense of the Bible's difficult passages—bear directly on the issue of the handful of verses in the Bible that speak about same-gender sexual relations. If every word in the Bible was virtually dictated by God, as suggested by those who hold to verbal, plenary inspiration, it would *seem* clear that God finds homosexual intimacy to be, in the words of the Law, an "abomination" and in the words of Paul, a "degrading," "unnatural," "shameless act" worthy of divine punishment. Though I reject this concept of inspiration, I believe that even those who hold this view have grounds for rethinking the church's traditional interpretation of the biblical passages related to same-sex intimacy.

I'd like to begin our conversation about homosexuality and the Bible by inviting you to think with me about what precisely Moses had in mind when he commanded that a man who "lies with a man as with a woman" must be put to death.[2]

There is no record in the Torah of two men seeking to share their lives together as companions and lovers. There are two instances in the Torah of men lying with men as with a woman. It seems likely to me that when Moses commands the death penalty for a man lying with a man that he was addressing these practices that are described in two separate passages in the Torah. Let's consider each of these two passages.

In Genesis 19, we read the story of Sodom, from which the terms "sodomy" and "sodomite" are drawn. In this story, two angels (in both Hebrew and Greek the word "angel" means "messenger") came from God, and visited the town of Sodom. Lot, Abraham's nephew, invited the men to lodge with him for the night. Here's what Genesis says: "Before they had gone to bed, all the men from every part of the city of Sodom—both young and old—surrounded the house. They called to Lot, 'Where are the men who came to you tonight? Bring them out to us so that we can have sex with them.' Lot went outside to meet them and shut the door behind him and said, 'No, my friends. Don't do this wicked thing. Look, I have two daughters who have never slept with a man. Let me bring them out to you, and you can do what you like with them. But don't do anything to these men, for they have come under the protection of my roof'" (Genesis 19:4–8, NIV).

Once again we see the strange patriarchal world in which the Bible was shaped, as Lot offers his two daughters to be raped by the men of Sodom rather than giving up the strangers he's just met (a story virtually identical to the one that occurs in Judges 19 with the Levite's concubine and the men of Gibeah).

But here's the question I would ask related to this story: is this story really about loving, committed homosexual relationships?

Had the town's men gang-raped Lot's daughters, would this story be about loving, committed heterosexual relationships? Of course not. Did the men of Sodom consider themselves homosexual? All of them? Or was their attack upon these strangers a way of demonstrating power over them, humiliating them, while violently gratifying their own sexual desires?

I'm reminded of the story of Scott Howard, who was repeatedly raped by members of a prison gang called 211 Crew while serving time in the Colorado Department of Corrections.[3] The 211 Crew was known for a vocal hatred of homosexuals. Yet they raped men in prison suspected of being gay. Rape was a means of demonstrating power over others. What relationship does this kind of gang-rape have to loving, committed relationships between two people of the same sex? None that I can see.

I doubt any of the men of Sodom would have considered themselves homosexual by our definitions today. Genesis 18 tells us the people of Sodom regularly practiced evil. This attempted gang rape was just the latest in a long line of horrible things the people of Sodom had done.

Centuries later, God would say through the prophet Ezekiel, "This was the guilt of your sister Sodom: she and her daughters had pride, excess of food, and prosperous ease, but did not aid the poor and needy. They were haughty, and did abominable things before me; therefore I removed them when I saw it." Among the abominable things they did was to attempt to gang-rape two strangers who had come to town, in addition to having pride, hoarding food, and not aiding the poor and needy.

It is worth noting that the story of the attempted gang rape in Sodom is the only example of same-sex sexual activity in the Torah up to this point. Could this have been the backdrop to Leviticus 18:22 and 20:1? Given that this is the only occurrence of a "man lying with a man" is it at least possible that Leviticus 18:22 and 20:13 were condemning homosexual rape rather than anything approximating two people sharing their lives in a loving relationship?

It is also possible that Moses was condemning the pagan use of "sacred" or temple prostitution in Leviticus 18:22 and 20:13. Deuteronomy 23:17–18 says, "None of the daughters of Israel shall be a temple prostitute; none of the sons of Israel shall be a temple prostitute. You shall not bring the fee of a prostitute or the wages of a male prostitute into the house of the Lord your God in payment for any vow, for both of these are abhorrent to the Lord your God." We know little about this practice, but it appears to either have been some kind of fertility ritual or sex for pay with the payment going to support the temple of the pagan deity for which the prostitute worked. If this was the model for sex between men, then Moses's commands in Leviticus 18 and 20 may have been prohibiting Israelite men from visiting pagan male temple prostitutes and thus practicing idolatry. Once again, this practice was a far cry from two people of the same gender sharing their lives together.

There's another possible way of understanding the thinking behind Leviticus 18:22 and 20:13. The Torah classifies a variety of things as natural and unnatural, normal and abnormal. Natural is normative and, by virtue of its normative status, "clean." What is not "normal" is "unclean." Other words used in place of "unclean" in the Old Testament are detestable, or a practice, act, or animal might be considered an "abomination." Homosexuality did not conform to the norm for sexual relations, and hence it was unnatural, unclean, detestable, or an abomination.

There are a host of things described by the Law of Moses as unclean or an abomination that we would not consider unclean or abnormal today.[4] Eating pork, or rabbit, or any seafood that does not have scales (lobster, crab, clams) was detestable and an abomination. Yet we don't consider eating these things an abomination today, nor a violation of God's will. Is it possible that the backdrop for Moses's condemnation of a man lying with a man as with a woman was this sense that something was either clean or unclean, acceptable or detestable based upon whether it was "normal" (i.e. conforming to the norm) or abnormal?

My point in all of this is that we too quickly assume we know what Moses was condemning, but if we look at the only two examples in the Torah of men lying with men as with women—gang rape and temple prostitution—we find practices that have virtually nothing to do with two people sharing their lives in a loving, committed relationship. Likewise, Moses's way of determining that some things were abnormal, therefore unclean, therefore off limits, therefore an abomination is not how we determine what is acceptable or detestable today.

When Paul takes up the issue of same-sex relationships in Romans, he seems to have in mind at least two of the three ideas I've just described from the Old Testament: ritual sexual encounters tied to pagan worship/idolatry and the idea that what was natural or normative was clean, and what was not natural was unclean and sinful. We see this in the way Paul contrasts natural versus unnatural in Romans 1:26–27, "Their women exchanged natural intercourse for unnatural, and in the same way also the men, giving up natural intercourse with women, were consumed with passion for one another." We hear echoes of the Old Testament view of clean and unclean, natural and unnatural, acceptable or detestable. Likewise these verses describing same-gender sex are set in the context of Paul's condemnation of idolatry (see 1:25). It has been thought by many that Paul was describing, as Moses may have been, ritual prostitution practiced in some of the pagan temples. One final same-gender practice that might have been behind Paul's condemnation of same-gender relationships in Romans 1 was pederasty. This was the practice of mature men taking on pubescent boys as students and lovers, a practice we would still condemn today.

Again what I am hoping to demonstrate is that we might explain the condemnations related to same-sex intimacy in the Bible as pertaining to these kinds of situations: gang-rape, temple prostitution, idolatry, and pederasty. If this is what the scripture writers were condemning, I suspect most of us would agree with their condemnations of these practices. But these practices, and the motivations behind them, are very different from two people sharing their lives together in a covenant relationship.

In the rest of this chapter, I'm going to offer an alternative approach for making sense of the biblical condemnations of same-sex relationships. I'd like to suggest that the handful of verses in Moses and Paul may be similar to other verses in their writings that seem out of sync with God's will as we understand it today, verses that condone violence, accept slavery, or subordinate women.

Before considering this last point, I want to say a word about Jesus. Some are quick to point out that while Jesus never addresses homosexual relationships, he does describe heterosexual marriage as God's will. That is true, but the context of these passages is never in references to loving same-sex relationships. The context of his reference to heterosexual relationships is, if I remember correctly, always about divorce. I don't think we can take Jesus's silence on this issue as approval of same-gender relationships. But it is important, given that Jesus is God's definitive Word by which all other words about God are judged, that he does not speak to this issue at all. That, for me, leaves open the possibility that Moses and Paul did not accurately capture God's will concerning same-sex relationships.

I have suggested above that the handful of passages in the Bible that seem to speak directly to a prohibition against same-sex marriage and companionship could be prohibitions against something entirely different from what we mean today when we talk about two people sharing their lives as loving companions. But even if they are directly condemning same-sex relationships, we've seen already that not everything explicitly taught in scripture captures God's timeless will. Some scriptures seem clearly shaped by the cultural norms and the theological and social presuppositions of their authors. They do not seem to reflect the heart of God revealed in Jesus Christ. We have seen that the New Testament church took the bold step of acknowledging that much in the Old Testament did not reflect God's continuing will for his people, setting aside circumcision, kosher laws, and much more.

Among the biblical teachings that many question today are those we've discussed so far: the propensity toward patriarchal norms that devalue women and even command that they remain silent in the church, and the tragic violence said to be committed in the name of and at the command of God. In addition, slavery is allowed and even regulated in scripture, though we recognize today that it is contrary to God's will.

Let's spend a few minutes on the topic of slavery before coming back to the Bible and homosexuality. Though the defining story of the Israelite people was that they were once slaves who, by the liberating power of God, were set free, the Israelites continued to embrace the practice of slavery. It would be more than two millennia before human beings would finally understand that slavery was wrong. Moses didn't see this as he gave laws, in the name of God, that allowed Israelites to sell their children into slavery, to purchase slaves, and even to beat their slaves.

Sometimes those defending biblical inerrancy and verbal, plenary inspiration say that slavery in the Bible was not like American slavery, as though somehow the biblical form of slavery was more morally acceptable. But when you read passages in the Bible related to slavery, this does not appear to be the case. Consider for instance, Exodus 21:20–21: "When a slaveowner strikes a male or female slave with a rod and the slave dies immediately, the owner shall be punished. But if the slave survives a day or two, there is no punishment; for the slave is the owner's property." The Israelite is allowed to beat his slave with a rod provided the slave doesn't die within two days from the beating? Do we really believe this was ever God's will for human behavior? Yet Exodus 21:20–21 purports to be the command of God. How do we explain this if not by recognizing that cultural norms played a role in shaping scriptural norms?

Here's the point: There are things commanded in the Bible, in the name of God, that today we recognize as immoral and inconsistent with the heart of God. Rather than attempting to justify such things, we should loudly condemn these teachings and commands and make clear that this did not ever reflect the will of God.

Hundreds of verses in the Bible refer to slavery. These appear in both Testaments. It seems that Paul and Peter could not imagine a world without slavery. The New Testament authors command runaway slaves to return to their masters. Though there were slave owners in the church, they were not commanded to let their slaves go free (though Paul asked Philemon to free his slave Onesimus, this is not commanded elsewhere by the apostles). Instead, Christian slave owners were to treat their slaves justly.

As we read and interpret scripture, I'd suggest that there are three broad categories—let's call them buckets—that biblical passages fit into. There are passages of scripture—I would suggest the vast majority—that *reflect the timeless will of God for human beings*, for instance, "Love your neighbor as you love yourself." There are other passages that *reflect God's will in a particular time but not for all time*, including much of the ritual law of the Old Testament. And there are passages that *reflect the culture and historical circumstances in which they were written but never reflected God's timeless will*, like those related to slavery. The question regarding loving and committed relationships between same-sex people is, in which of the three buckets do the handful of verses that speak about same-sex intimacy belong? Conservatives on this issue believe they fit in the first bucket. Many moderates and progressives believe they fit into the second or, most likely, the third bucket.

Interestingly, most conservatives I know agree that at least half of one of these scriptures fits into the second or third bucket. Leviticus 20:13 states, "If a man lies with a male as with a woman, both of them have committed an abomination; they shall be put to death; their blood is upon them." Does God really want gay men to be put to death? I don't know anyone, not even Topeka's Fred Phelps, who advocates that homosexuals be put to death. Even conservatives see this as a bucket 2 command. Progressives would put it in bucket 3, but no one sees it as a bucket 1 command.

So here's what I want you to notice: First, it is possible that the biblical passages where same-sex intimacy is mentioned could be describing something very different from the loving monogamous relationships that we're currently considering in conversations about homosexuality. The practices Moses and Paul forbade likely were quite different from the idea of two same-sex people sharing their lives. Second, even if Moses and Paul were able to conceive of concepts like sexual orientation, what they wrote does not necessarily reflect the heart and character of God. Ultimately, where you come out on this issue is not a matter of biblical authority. Serious Christians on both the left and the right believe the Bible speaks with authority in our lives. Likewise, Christians on both sides recognize that some biblical passages don't capture God's timeless will or reflect God's heart and character. Which bucket we put scriptures in, or how we see them in the light of their culture, is not a matter of biblical authority but a matter of biblical interpretation.

My understanding of the nature of scripture has changed over the years. After coming to appreciate the Bible's humanity and recognizing its complexity, I no longer feel compelled to defend passages attributing violence to God. I also no longer make the case that Old Testament slavery "really wasn't that bad," and I've been grateful to welcome ordained women in leadership and preaching roles in our church.

For years I felt compassion for gay and lesbian people. I welcomed them into our church. But I told them that I believed it was not God's will that they share their lives with another person of the same gender because the Bible taught that same-sex intimacy was wrong. (Though I refrained from telling them the Bible called them an "abomination" and commanded their death.) I told them that I understood that this prohibition was a hard saying, but if they wanted to be deeply committed Christians they needed to remain celibate. I was telling them, in essence, that they needed either to change or to forgo romantic love and companionship for the rest of their lives.

This bothered me, in part because I was asking them to give up what was so life-giving to me. I have been married to LaVon for thirty-one years. We married right out of high school. Our relationship is not primarily about sex but companionship. We are each other's helper and companion. I can't imagine life without being able to hold her hand, kiss her lips, sleep next to her in bed, or share romantic moments. On the merit of a handful of verses of scripture, whose historical background and alternative interpretations I had not fully explored, I was telling people who wanted to follow Christ

that they needed to forgo romantic companionship in order to faithfully follow Jesus. I was asking of them something I was not sure I
could do myself, and which I was not required to do as a heterosexual Christian.

As I listened to and read the stories of hundreds of gay and lesbian people, I came to love them, to feel compassion for them, and
to question whether these biblical passages actually reflected what
God would say to his gay and lesbian children. But it was only as I
began to recognize the complexity of scripture, its humanity, and
the various "buckets" into which its passages fit that I was able to
see that the prevailing position within much of Christianity may
not, in fact, reflect God's will for homosexual people.

Are there homosexuals who are emotionally broken and in need
of help? Of course, just as there are heterosexuals who are the sexually and emotionally broken and unhealthy. Are there perverse and
unhealthy expressions of homosexuality? Of course, just as there
are perverse and unhealthy expressions of heterosexuality. But just
as there are healthy heterosexual relationships, I've witnessed
healthy homosexual relationships.

The Bible informs my relationship with my wife, and it should
inform how two homosexuals share their life and love. And just as
heterosexuals are called to fidelity in marriage and celibacy in sin-
gleness as the highest ideal, so too are homosexual Christians called
to such ideals. One doesn't get a pass for immoral behavior by being
homosexual, but most homosexuals I've met are not looking for a
pass to be immoral; they are looking for a blessing to share their life
with another person as "companion and helper."

I'm told that there is less monogamy and more sexual and rela-
tional dysfunction among homosexuals. I don't know if this is true
or not. What I know is that most churches are unwilling to teach
what healthy sexuality and romantic relationships look like for

homosexual people. Since it was unacceptable and sinful to the church, many were left to live out these relationships in unhealthy and illicit ways. But it is worth noting that the vast majority of illicit sexual behavior, sexual addiction, and sexual abuse is not related to homosexuality, but heterosexuality.

One more thing I feel compelled to mention: I've heard over the last ten years that homosexual marriage is somehow a threat to "real" marriage. I've never felt my marriage was threatened by the right of gay and lesbian people to marry. The threats to my marriage come from my own desires, from my failure to listen to and understand my wife, and from my workaholic tendencies, but whether homosexual people can marry or not has absolutely no bearing on the health of my marriage.

It is clear that the younger generation in our society sees this issue differently from those Christians who are older. There is greater acceptance of gay people among younger adults, and a greater willingness to read the scriptures that speak about same-sex intimacy in the same way we read scriptures about slavery or violence or women keeping silent in the church. This is true even among many younger evangelical Christians. As more and more states allow homosexual marriage, gay and lesbian couples who have been married for years, who have children, will show up at churches hoping to find Christ and a Christian community. Will churches ask these families to divorce and divide the children to be faithful followers of Christ? Or, as one pastor suggested to me, will the church allow the family to stay together but insist that the spouses live in separate bedrooms and no longer share any romantic dimension of their relationship?

I believe that within twenty years a large number of Christians, including conservative and evangelical Christians, will have come to see this issue differently—more grace-fully. The issue will lead many Christians to question their view of the Bible, asking the kind of questions we've been discussing in this book. Mainline churches will have resolved the issue ten years before evangelical churches. A large number of churches will hold to a more conservative interpretation of scripture on this issue, but they will seem increasingly unattractive to younger Christians and to nonreligious and nominally religious people who are drawn to Jesus but not to what will be increasingly perceived as bigotry.

I'm not suggesting that most Christians who are conservative on this issue are bigots or homophobes. While this is clearly true for some, I don't believe these terms apply to most of the conservative Christians I know. Most genuinely wish to love gay and lesbian people and to welcome them into their churches. For most, the issue is what kind of book the Bible is, what it means to call it inspired, and how to understand the Bible's humanity. For some earnest, deeply committed Christians changing their view of homosexuality feels tantamount to apostasy. Yet many of these same Christians already recognize the complexity of scripture as it relates to a host of other subjects. Somehow the issue of homosexuality feels different to them.

My own views on this issue changed as a result of thinking about the nature of scripture, God's role in inspiring it, the meaning of inspiration, and how we make sense of the Bible's difficult passages. As I came to appreciate the Bible's humanity, I found I could at least ask whether the passages in scripture about same-sex intimacy truly captured God's heart regarding same-sex relationships. But what really prompted me to look seriously at this issue and to wrestle with it were the gay and lesbian people I came to know and love, including children I had watched grow up in the church I serve.

I am a United Methodist pastor. My denomination currently

prohibits pastors from officiating in same-sex marriages, prohibits our churches from hosting same-sex marriages, forbids the ordination of "self-avowed practicing homosexuals," and notes that "the practice of homosexuality is incompatible with Christian teaching." I believe these ideas will become increasingly problematic in the years ahead, and as people wrestle with the nature of scripture, I think they will increasingly see the passages related to homosexuality as bucket 2 or bucket 3 scriptures.

Ultimately the key to finding our way forward on this issue will come from our ability to articulate a clear view of scripture that recognizes both its divine inspiration and its humanity. This view must give us tools and guidelines for knowing when we can question scriptures as no longer binding, and when and why others are not to be set aside. The earliest apostles made a dramatic decision at the Jerusalem Council that some scriptures were no longer binding. I think it is critical that we learn from them. I believe there are times when God calls us to ask questions of our Bible, and as we do, we set aside those things that may not reflect the timeless will of God, even as we recognize and guard against a temptation to set aside what is simply inconvenient.

My hope is that this book might aid in that conversation.

CHAPTER 30

Making Sense of the Book of Revelation

Are we living in the Last Days? Many Christians believe so. I'd like us to think together about one of the most confusing books of the entire Bible: the Book of Revelation. Grab your Bible. We're going to take a quick walk through one of the most enigmatic books in the Bible. Let's begin our study of Revelation in chapters 1–3, where we learn something about the original readers of this book and what precipitated John's writing of it.

Turn to Revelation 1:4: "John to the seven churches that are in Asia: Grace to you and peace." This is an interesting greeting—it is the same kind of greeting we find in other New Testament letters. Revelation, it turns out, is a lengthy letter (slightly longer than Paul's letter to the Romans) written to the churches and Christians of what is today central Turkey. You can see on the following map where the seven churches were located.

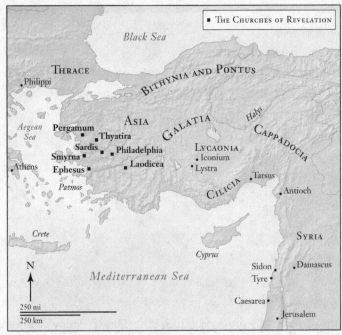

The Seven Churches of Revelation

Turn to chapters 2 and 3 of Revelation, and you can see that each of the churches is given a specific message. The author was familiar with these churches. Some are offered encouraging words, but several are warned sternly. Ephesus had lost its first love—its spiritual passion—and tolerated a group in the church that had embraced the values and practices of the pagan culture around it. Smyrna faced persecution from the Jews of the local synagogue; about the time Revelation was written, Christian Jews were being expelled from the Jewish synagogues. Pergamum was a center of pagan worship with its massive altar to Zeus, which now resides in a German museum. This may be the very altar John referred to as "Satan's throne." Here, too, people were compromising their faith by participating in the required homage offered to the emperor. In

Thyatira, a woman who was a false teacher taught that the people could eat food that had been sacrificed to the pagan gods. In Sardis, the people had a reputation for a vibrant faith, but John said their faith was actually empty and they, too, had "soiled" themselves in the world. The church of Philadelphia was being harassed by the local synagogue, and the church at Laodicea had become lukewarm in its faith.

Here's an important point to understand: everything John writes in this letter is aimed at addressing the problems he has described in these opening words. He will address the tendency to compromise with the world and encourage his readers to remain faithful in the face of adversity. This is very important. The visions John is about to convey were not meant to tell twenty-first-century Christians about the end times but to encourage and challenge first-century Christians living in what is now Turkey to stop conforming to the culture around them and to avoid anything that smacked of the worship of Rome, its emperor, and its gods. He assured them that, even if the decision were costly, they would be okay in the end, for Rome would be defeated and God's kingdom would prevail.

To convey his message, John adopts a form of writing well known among Jews and Christians of his time—we call it apocalyptic. This kind of writing communicates through visions and images that are powerful and evocative. It is not meant to be read literally. Instead, the images communicate in ways that a typical letter could not. For instance, in Revelation 17, the Roman Empire and its capital city are described through a vision of a "great whore" "drunk with the blood of the saints" and sitting upon a beast. What a vivid picture of the Roman Empire!

Not everything you read in apocalyptic literature has a one-to-one correspondence to something else. It is a literature of crisis or warning, though sometimes of comfort. When I think of apocalyptic literature, the closest modern equivalent to me is some of the work of Pablo Picasso. In 1937, Picasso drew a pen-and-ink series, like a comic strip, called "The Dreams and Lies of Franco." The images were grotesque, odd, and open to multiple interpretations. But it was clear that they served as a protest against General Francisco Franco's policies, actions, and megalomania. In essence, this is how apocalyptic literature, particularly the Book of Revelation, functions.

There are four views on how we are to read Revelation. The first view is called the *futurist* view. It is a favorite of TV evangelists and has become very popular in the last 150 years in the United States. This approach sees nearly everything in the Book of Revelation as pointing to the events of the last days before and just after Christ returns. The Left Behind series of books that was so popular a few years back was based upon this view of Revelation. Many people today, when they think of the Book of Revelation, believe that the book primarily describes events of the decade leading up to the Second Coming of Christ—and many of these believe we're living today in the last days.

The second view is called the *historicist* view. This approach sees Revelation as foretelling the future, starting from the time of John, so that each vision is about a time to come, starting around AD 95. For example, chapters 6, 7, and 8 are said to describe the decline of Rome and the spread of Christianity. Chapter 9 is said to describe the rise of Islam. Chapter 10 describes the Protestant Reformation. This view was held by many Christians up to the 1800s.

The third view is called the *preterist* view. "Preterist" means "past," and this approach sees most of the events described in Revelation as pertaining to the people who lived in John's time, with the visions describing events in the Roman Empire of the late first and early second centuries. Most mainline and a large number of evangelical scholars today hold this view.

A fourth view is the *idealist* perspective. This view sees most of revelation as describing the perpetual struggle between good and evil, the perpetual challenges of living for God in a pagan culture, and the hope God offers to all who are persecuted for remaining faithful. Every age and generation can find itself somewhere in the book.

I've got ten commentaries on Revelation in my library, written by some of the foremost scholars to study this book, and every one of them holds some combination of the preterist and idealist perspectives. This is in stark contrast to the views of most television evangelists and many conservative preachers, who favor the futurist view. Most mainline scholars see the book as describing events of the author's day.

With this in mind, let's walk through the Book of Revelation to see it as the original recipients likely understood it. By the way, a couple of short books you might find helpful in making sense of the entire book of Revelation are Warren Carter's *What Does Revelation Reveal?* and Bruce Metzger's *Breaking the Code*, both of which were written for laypeople and clergy.

A bit more about the historical context of the Book of Revelation might be helpful as we begin our walk through the book. Around 195 BC in the town of Smyrna (the location of one of the churches to which the Letter of Revelation was addressed), the first temple was erected to the goddess Roma. Roma was a female deity, and the Roman Empire sought to embody her qualities. Sixty years after this temple was built, the lands around Pergamum (the location of another of Revelation's churches) were bequeathed to Rome, and temples to Roma were dedicated throughout the region.

Historians tell us that the practice of honoring emperors as deities began with Emperor Augustus (reigned 27 BC to AD 14). Typically temples to Augustus, who had assumed the title of Lord, were located next to the temple of Roma. Much of this had its origins, or was practiced most strongly, in Asia Minor, where the original readers of the Book of Revelation lived.

So the conflict behind the Book of Revelation pitted worship of and allegiance to God against worship of and allegiance to Rome. Some in the churches thought they could navigate carefully and do both. John is telling us that God alone is worthy of our worship; he's warning that Rome's interest is power and control, and that ultimately pledging allegiance to her is idolatry.

Turn in your Bible to Revelation chapters 4 and 5. John's visions begin in the heavenly throne room, where God is shown in all his majesty and creatures around the throne sing songs of praise:

> Day and night without ceasing they sing, "Holy, holy, holy, the Lord God the Almighty, who was and is and is to come." And whenever the living creatures give glory and honor and thanks to the one who is seated on the throne, who lives forever and ever, the twenty-four elders fall before the one who is seated on the throne and worship the one who lives forever and ever; they cast their crowns before the throne, singing, "You are worthy, our Lord and God, to receive glory and honor and power, for you created all things, and by your will they existed and were created." (Revelation 4:8c–11)

Revelation begins with this powerful picture of God's kingdom and the true and rightful King. The ensuing chapters paint a picture of the goddess Roma's kingdom and the devastation she brings. They announce the ultimate destruction of Rome and, at the same time, the salvation of those who remain faithful.

In Revelation 13:15–18, we find the infamous "mark of the beast":

> [He will] cause those who would not worship the image of the beast to be killed. Also it causes all, both small and great, both rich and poor, both free and slave, to be marked on the right hand or the forehead, so that no one can buy or sell who does not have the mark, that is, the name of the beast or the number of its name. This calls for wisdom: let anyone with understanding calculate the number of the beast, for it is the number of a person. Its number is six hundred sixty-six.

This mark of the beast—666—is an interesting brand or mark. In Revelation the number seven represents completeness, wholeness, or perfection. The Holy Spirit is described as the sevenfold spirit. Jesus is described as a lamb with seven eyes and seven horns. The number six is one less than perfection—it symbolizes imperfection, and 666 symbolizes utter imperfection. But beyond this in Hebrew, Greek, and Latin letters represented numbers. Various names have been associated with the numbers 666. Among them is Nero Caesar.

Nero was the emperor who had murdered the leading apostles in 65 AD. Nero committed suicide in 68, but, as was the case with Hitler at the end of World War II, many did not believe it and expected him to return. Nero represented Rome at its most evil.

Chapters 17 and 18 make clear that the antagonist in this book is Rome. Rome is referred to as Babylon, a code word Christians used for Rome because Babylon had destroyed Jerusalem and the Temple of God in 586 BC, just as Rome had done in AD 70. Here the city of Rome is portrayed as a prostitute. She rides on a seven-headed beast. Look at Revelation 17:9: "This calls for a mind that has wisdom: the seven heads are seven mountains on which the woman is seated." Rome was known as the "city on seven hills."

Chapters 19–22 include the battle between good and evil and the final triumph of God. They are among the most beautiful chapters in the Bible, speaking of a truth that we can never forget. They make clear that good will always ultimately triumph over evil. God will ultimately triumph over Satan. And the day will come when there will be a new heaven and a new earth, and death, suffering, and pain will be banished forever.

I've given you just a glimpse of how this letter was read and understood by the Christians of Asia Minor. But what does it mean for us today?

In every age, there is a temptation for the state to deify itself. And every nation has values and practices that are contrary to those of the kingdom of God. The state at times seeks to be worshipped and served (it seldom uses these words, but it demands the allegiance of the heart). And God's people may be tempted to give in and compromise and to accept the state's values. The question Revelation raises is, will you worship God or will you give your primary allegiance to the state?

Likewise the "emperors" throughout the ages have often longed to be worshipped alongside the state. We have many examples in the last hundred years: Stalin in the Soviet Union, Hitler and his Nazi Party, Franco in Spain, Mussolini in Italy. There was Pol Pot in Cambodia, and at least forty beasts in Africa since the end of colonialism, including people like Idi Amin. In the Middle East there have been Gaddafi, Saddam Hussein, Hosni Mubarak, and Bashar al-Assad. The giant statues, the plastered pictures or images of leaders on the sides of buildings—do you see how this situation is that of John's day repeated a hundred times in the last hundred years?

In the United States, we've built in some safeguards— representative democracy, for one—but there is still a tension one feels at times. I love going to Washington, D.C., and seeing the various monuments by night. The Lincoln Memorial does in many ways what the temples to Augustus did in the time of Revelation. It is patterned after the Greco-Roman temple, and Abraham Lincoln sits where the sculptures of the deities and emperors sat in temples dedicated to them. Worshipping Roma or Augustus was an act of pledging allegiance and offering a sacrifice—a kind of melding of patriotism and religion—not unlike American civil religion. Our form of government, our political parties, our economic system are all at odds sometimes with God's kingdom. I've known many Christians for whom, when push comes to shove, their primary allegiance seems to be to civil religion rather than to God's kingdom.

Perhaps the gods we're more likely to be tempted by today are the trinity of money, sex, and power. But here's the point I want you to get—the real point of Revelation: It is not aimed at telling us when the end will happen. It is aimed at telling us that *in the end, none of these gods will be left standing, and that Christians are called to give our hearts and our allegiance only to one God, who is worthy of our praise.*

Revelation challenges us to examine our hearts and place God first there. It challenges us to be careful when it comes to the state, even in America. We are meant to influence the state as salt and light, but we are clear that neither our nation nor our politics, nor even our economic system, should sit in the place of God in our hearts. Ultimately, Revelation tells us that resisting evil may come at a cost to us, but even if that cost is our very lives, we'll find ourselves a part of Christ's glorious kingdom. The day will come when every nation falls. Every political party will come to an end, and the kingdoms of this world give way to the kingdom of God.

CHAPTER 31

Toward an Honest and Reverent View of Scripture

W e've come to the end of our conversation about the Bible. I'm aware that there is so much more that could be said about scripture, and so many more questions that could be addressed. But I'd like to end our conversation by recapping the reasons I wrote this book, offering a brief history of what has come to be called the "battle for the Bible," and by restating my answer to the question, "What is the Bible?"

This book was born out of the conversations I've had with Christians and non-Christians alike concerning the Bible. It disturbed me that often the content of the Bible itself was the stumbling block that kept them, or turned them, from the Christian faith. They were not turned off by Jesus's words in the Gospels. They found Jesus quite compelling. But other things in the Bible left them confused.

These people had been told that every word of scripture was chosen by God, that one must read the Bible literally and accept it without question. This left some feeling that they had to choose between science and Christianity. Others felt that the Bible's description of a God who called for the genocide of entire tribes of peoples in the ancient Near East was part of the very "problem of religion." Still others were convinced that the Bible and the church that followed it were to blame for the subordination of women or persistence of slavery in countries with majority Christian populations.

In the last few years, homosexuality has become a focal point in American society. A 2013 Pew Center poll found that 70 percent of millennials support same-sex marriage.[1] For many of these young adults, scriptures like Leviticus 20:13—"If a man lies with a male as with a woman, both of them have committed an abomination; they shall be put to death; their blood is upon them"—don't sound like a God of love they would wish to follow. One young woman named Dannika Nash captured what many other young adults have felt when she wrote in her blog, "I was forced to choose between the love I had for my gay friends and so-called biblical authority. I chose gay people, and I'm willing to wager I'm not the only one."[2] Dannika was clear that she was not choosing between Christ and loving gay people; she was choosing between a certain view of the Bible and loving gay people.

The underlying issue in making sense of these and other troubling passages of scripture is the question of what kind of book the Bible is. A significant number of conservative and evangelical Christians believe in verbal, plenary inspiration with its conclusion of biblical inerrancy and infallibility. This, and similar views of scripture, place such a strong emphasis on God's role in composing scripture that there is little room left to wrestle with the Bible, or to question its troubling passages. The only course of action is to justify these passages and, in many cases, to insist that they are still valid expressions of God's will.

While I love my conservative Christian friends and consider myself evangelical, their view of scripture seems to me an inaccurate way of describing the Bible. It is not difficult to demonstrate inconsistencies in the Bible, and there are a host of problematic passages in which the Bible either teaches or accepts behavior that we consider immoral today (slavery, the subordination of women, concubinage, genocide, and the death penalty for crimes we would never deem worthy of death today).

Some of those on the left solve this dilemma, I believe, by going too far in the opposite direction. The Bible, for them, becomes primarily a human book, with little room for God's involvement in it at all. The Bible has antiquity on its side, but it is not in any meaningful sense words from God.

Instead of assuming that the Bible is the result of God's word-for-word inspiration of its authors, or that the Bible is merely a human book, I've suggested that the scriptures were written by human beings who were inspired by God yet wrote in the light of their own experiences, the scientific knowledge they had access to, and the historical circumstances in which they lived. They sought to address the needs of the communities to whom they wrote. They were shaped not only by the Spirit but by their own theological and moral convictions, assumptions and presuppositions.

I've sought to help you see that the Bible is far more complex than is often supposed. We considered in earlier chapters both the way biblical documents were written and the process by which they were canonized. We learned that the New Testament canon was finalized more than three hundred years after the time of Jesus, and that the Protestant Reformers still questioned whether some of the New Testament books should be in the canon nearly 1,500 years after the death of the apostles.

We also learned that the Bible is not a theological textbook, a book of promises, or an owner's manual. It is a compilation of various types of literature, including short stories, poetry, wisdom sayings, prophetic warnings, gospels and letters written over the course of 1,400 years. This compilation begins with the Old Testament, which tells of Israel's story and bears witness to her faith in, and experience of, God. The New Testament tells the story of Jesus, whom Christians believe is the Messiah, the Savior and Son of God. It includes letters written to help early Christians as they sought to understand and live their newfound faith.

While affirming that that the Bible is inspired by God, a key premise of this book is that the Bible's authors were inspired by the Spirit *in the same way* and *to the same degree* as many contemporary preachers and prophets and even ordinary Christians have been inspired by the Spirit in every age. You've likely felt moved by the Spirit, and you've likely heard God speak to you as you listened to a sermon or a song, or read an inspirational book. I believe the inspiration experienced by the biblical authors was not different from our own experience of inspiration.

This is disconcerting to many Christians who *need* the Bible to be inspired to a greater degree than ordinary Christians are inspired by the Spirit. But the fact that we want or need something to be a certain way does not make it so. Some ask, "How then is the Bible any different from contemporary Christian writings that are widely read and found to be inspiring among Christians today?" This is an important question.

What makes the Bible more authoritative than contemporary inspirational writings is not a different degree of the Spirit's inspiration but the proximity of the biblical writers to the events that they were recording and the fact that the church experienced God speaking through these words, felt they contained the essentials of the faith and found them helpful or useful during the opening centuries of the Christian era. The church came, over a long period of time, to consider these the essential writings ("writing" is, as you will recall, the meaning of the word "scripture"). These documents together became known as "the Books" (*ta biblia* in Greek from which we have our word, Bible).

A BRIEF HISTORY OF
THE BATTLE FOR THE BIBLE

As the Anglicans affirmed in 1563, "Holy Scripture containeth all things necessary to salvation: so that whatsoever is not read therein, nor may be proved thereby, is not to be required of any man, that it should be believed as an article of the Faith, or be thought requisite or necessary to salvation." There is nothing in this statement about inerrancy or verbal, plenary inspiration. It says that no doctrine or practice can be insisted upon by the church if it is not proved or supported by scripture. That was as far as the Anglicans (and later the Methodists) went in a formal doctrinal statement concerning scripture. In essence, they said that the writings of the Old Testament and New Testament authors offer us the essentials of our faith.

This is far more *elastic* than the "creeds" of conservative Christianity today. It allows room for us to question things that are in the scriptures (as Luther and Calvin themselves did, regardless of how they themselves referred to scripture).

This statement is consistent with the Reformation principle of *sola scriptura* ("scripture alone"), by which the reformers and those who followed meant that scripture contains, in essence, all that is essential for our knowledge of God and God's will. The reformers recognized that some scriptures were confusing or raised legitimate questions. These scriptures were to be interpreted in the light of the clearer texts. I suggested earlier that those scriptures which lead some of us to scratch our heads should be interpreted in the light of the scriptures that Jesus said summarized the Law and the Prophets—the Great Commandments to love God and love neighbor, and the Golden Rule. In addition, and even more importantly, Jesus is *the* Word by which all other words of scripture should be interpreted and understood.

Following the Reformation, the proverbial pendulum exalting scripture above the tradition of the Catholic Church swung farther and farther. By the mid-1600s, the Westminster Confession of Faith had moved scripture from the Sixth Article of Religion to the very first statement in its confession of faith. And instead of simply having two articles or statements devoted to scripture, as the 1563 Articles of Religion had, the Westminster Confession of Faith has ten articles or statements devoted to scripture, all of which come before any statement about God.

The seventeenth century marked the beginning of the Enlightenment, when philosophers, intellectuals, and scientists began questioning faith and the traditions and beliefs long held by many in society. Critical thinking was brought to bear, more than ever before, on the Bible, its composition, canonization, and teaching. This threatened traditional church teaching and the doctrinal formulations of the church. The Enlightenment placed an ever-increasing emphasis on reason as the revealer of truth. In response to perceived threats to Christianity and to traditional understandings of the Bible, many in the church gave even greater emphasis to the divine origin of scripture.

In the nineteenth century, modernism emerged as the successor to the Enlightenment. Like its predecessor, it raised serious questions about traditional doctrines within Christianity and insisted on critical study of scripture and religion. Those Christians who embraced the critical approach of the Enlightenment and then modernism were often known as "liberal" or "modernists."

Modernists or liberals sometimes discounted the role of the Spirit in the formation of scripture. They tended to set aside the miraculous elements described in the Bible, given that such elements were not observable, testable, nor consistent with modern experience. They raised serious questions about Christian doctrines like the virgin birth, the miracles of Jesus, the deity of Christ, and the resurrection of Christ. Efforts to reconstruct a merely human Jesus, known as the "historical Jesus," are a legacy of modernism.

The modernist movement brought about a strong reaction from the church in the late nineteenth and early twentieth centuries. Christian theologians and biblical scholars produced a series of essays, ninety in all, that defended traditional Christian doctrines. These were published as a twelve-volume set called *The Fundamentals*. In addition to strongly defending traditional or "orthodox" Christianity, they critiqued modernism and the historical-critical method of studying scripture. These essays gave rise to the term *fundamentalist*, used to describe those who insisted not only on adherence to the historic essentials of the Christian faith but on rejection of historical-critical methods of studying the Bible and their conclusions. Fundamentalists also insisted on verbal, plenary inspiration and inerrancy.

Ultimately, five "fundamentals" were considered critical to demonstrating orthodoxy: Biblical inspiration and inerrancy, the virgin birth of Jesus, the belief that Christ's death was an atonement for sin, the physical resurrection of Jesus from the dead, and belief that the miracles described in the Gospels actually happened as described. While the concepts of verbal, plenary inspiration and inerrancy existed prior to the fundamentalist-modernist controversy, they were popularized and widely embraced as an essential Christian belief among conservatives as a result of this controversy.

Much of the twentieth-century church was defined by this struggle between fundamentalists and modernists, or conservatives and liberals. The worst insult, if you were a fundamentalist, was to be called a liberal! The worst thing you could call a liberal was a fundamentalist! As is often the case, these two ends of the debate did not speak for all Christians. Many Christians leaned one way or another but did not fully accept either approach. A significant number of Christians, to the present, find themselves somewhere between the black-and-white of the liberal-conservative dichotomy.

I'm one of these Christians. I generally accept as reliable the data and perspectives found in scripture, except when there is a compelling reason to question its teaching. But I also believe it is acceptable to raise questions and to wrestle with the Bible when something in its teaching seems inconsistent with, among other things, the character of God revealed in Jesus Christ.

Of the five "fundamentals" of the fundamentalists, I accept four and a half! I believe Jesus was born of a virgin, that Christ's death atones for our sin and reconciles us to God,[3] that Christ was physically raised from the dead, and that Jesus actually performed miracles when he walked on the earth. But I reject that the Bible is inerrant and that every word or idea was virtually dictated by God. There are places where the biblical authors were limited in their knowledge, were shaped by their culture and times, or actually misrepresented God and God's will (for instance, slavery or the subordination of women). Making use of historical-critical methods for studying the Bible can help us discern how culture and historical circumstances shaped the biblical authors and can guide us to the profound truths of scripture while making sense of its confusing parts.

To reiterate the basic premise of this book: You are not dishonoring God by asking questions of scripture that seems inconsistent with modern scientific knowledge or geography or history. And you are not being unfaithful to God if you ask questions of a verse that seems inconsistent with the picture of God seen in the life, teachings, death, and resurrection of Jesus. This is possible because you recognize that the Spirit's inspiration of the human authors of scripture was similar to the Spirit's work in your own life. The Holy Spirit prompts you but does not dictate. The Spirit whispers to you, but you don't always hear correctly. The Spirit's work in your life does not make you inerrant or infallible.

You are not judging God by wrestling with the Bible; you are asking questions of the human authors of scripture. Jesus and the New Testament apostles also wrestled with the Bible. But when you wrestle with scripture, recognize both the weight of scripture's authority and our tendency to discard what is inconvenient. Christians are meant to wrestle with and interpret difficult passages in the Bible in the light of the Bible's clearer passages, with the help of the church's teaching and consensus, the reflections of her scholars and leaders across the course of history, and our own intellect and experience of the Spirit in our lives.

I've devoted much of this book to describing challenges and confusing portions of the scriptures. I would like to have devoted an equal amount of time to drawing attention to the profound ways that God speaks through the Bible, and the profound truths that it bears witness to. Daily I hear God speaking to me as I read the scriptures. Its words, with a few exceptions, are life giving.

The Bible contains the theological, spiritual, and ethical reflections of God's people. It offers the earliest and most reliable testimony to the life, teachings, death and resurrection of Jesus Christ. It contains the earliest Christian reflections on the meaning of his life for the ordering of our lives. Through the Bible, God has spoken and continues to speak to the human race. It contains every truth we need to know God and God's will for our lives.

I begin each day reading the Bible. I end each day reading from its pages once more. Its stories are the defining stories of my life. Its precepts daily shape my life. With Paul, I believe the Bible is God-breathed and "useful for teaching, reproof, correction, and training in righteousness." I love the Bible . . . and sometimes I wrestle with it.

CHAPTER 32

Postscript: Reading the Bible for All Its Worth[1]

I've devoted much of this book to describing how *not* to read the Bible. I offer this postscript with a few words about how *to* read scripture. These suggestions are not original to me but are things I've learned along the way that have helped me not only to make sense of the Bible but to hear God speak through it. But before I offer specific suggestions, I'll say it one last time: *it's okay to wrestle with the Bible.*

I would encourage you to ask questions when you come across something that seems inconsistent with the teachings of Jesus or the larger witness of scripture. Yet recognize as you do that there may be another explanation you simply don't yet have.

With that in mind, let's consider eight suggestions for reading the Bible for all its worth—that is, for hearing God speak through scripture.

1. SEE YOURSELF IN THE STORY

When reading the Bible's narrative stories, I find it helpful to step into the story. I try to imagine what the individuals were feeling, thinking, or doing. I ask, "Which of these characters would I be?" "In what ways is their story similar to my story?"

I recently preached a series of sermons called Messages from the Wilderness. The wilderness in the Holy Land is the desert. It is both a real place, but also a metaphor for those times in life that are difficult. Each week we looked at a different Old Testament character who had both been in the literal wilderness, the desert, but who was also in an emotional or spiritual wilderness.

One week we studied Elijah the prophet. In 1 Kings 19 we read that Queen Jezebel planned to kill Elijah. He was afraid, felt all alone, and fled to the wilderness. Verse 4 of 1 Kings 19 notes that Elijah "went a day's journey into the wilderness, and came and sat down under a solitary broom tree. He asked that he might die: "It is enough; now, O LORD, take away my life, for I am no better than my ancestors." I invited the congregation to imagine a moment in their own life where they were afraid, under attack, or just felt overwhelmed by how hard life was. I asked if they had ever felt like praying, "It is enough; now, O LORD, take away my life." I remember one of my parishioners who told me she prayed every night that she would die in her sleep.

When you read the narrative stories connect the dots between the experience of the biblical character and your own life experience. In the case of Elijah, God came to him, speaking to him in the "sound of sheer silence" (the King James called it the "still, small voice" and the NIV refers to the "gentle whisper").

As I preached on this text I helped our congregation to see themselves in the story and to remember times when they felt like giving up. We talked about how God speaks to us in the silence, yet how little of it we get anymore. Father Richard Rohr notes that "we are a toxically overstimulated people." We spoke of becoming quiet and listening for God in the silence. As we studied Elijah's story, his story became our story.

2. DISCOVER THE SITUATION IN WHICH THE SCRIPTURE WAS WRITTEN

A good study Bible will include an introduction to each book that gives you scholars' best thinking about the situation of the author and the people to whom he was writing. As an aside, three study Bibles I really appreciate: *The Harper Study Bible*, *The TNIV Study Bible* (TNIV is *Today's New International Version*), and the *CEB Study Bible* (the CEB is the *Common English Bible*).

This can be really helpful, as we learned earlier in the book when we studied the words of Paul in Galatians. Another example is Philippians. Paul wrote this letter while in prison awaiting news of whether he would be executed. It may have been written while he was imprisoned in Rome. Knowing this makes the letter all the more astounding. Philippians is often called Paul's "epistle of joy" because he commands joy and rejoicing multiple times in the letter. That he writes these words while sitting in prison awaiting execution adds to the power of his call to me to rejoice in all circumstances.

3. THREE QUESTIONS TO ASK

As I read both narrative stories and other forms of literature in the Bible, I often ask these three questions: 1. What does this passage teach me about humanity? 2. About myself? 3. About God? As I ask these questions, I often take notes. In reflecting upon the answers to these questions, the scriptures, and God through them, speak to me.

Let's consider Luke 17:11–19:

> On the way to Jerusalem Jesus was going through the region between Samaria and Galilee. As he entered a village, ten lepers approached him. Keeping their distance, they called out, saying, "Jesus, Master, have mercy on us!" When he saw them, he said to them, "Go and show your-selves to the priests." And as they went, they were made clean. Then one of them, when he saw that he was healed, turned back, praising God with a loud voice. He prostrated himself at Jesus's feet and thanked him. And he was a Samaritan. Then Jesus asked, "Were not ten made clean? But the other nine, where are they? Was none of them found to return and give praise to God except this foreigner?" Then he said to him, "Get up and go on your way; your faith has made you well."

Jesus is on his way to Jerusalem, where he will be crucified. Lepers, according to the Law of Moses, were required to avoid direct contact with people and to announce aloud that they were lepers as they approached others in public. They were required to keep their distance because leprosy was thought to be highly conta-gious. When I think of leprosy, I think of diseases that are common today and thought to be communicable. I think of MRSA, a form of staph infection that is resistant to antibiotics. I knew a young man who was nearly fired when his employer learned he had MRSA. His employer was afraid and not adequately informed about the disease.

In Jesus's day, lepers had any number of skin disorders that left people afraid of contracting the disease. Jesus routinely stops to help lepers and even touches them. In this story, Jesus has compas-sion on the lepers, all ten of them.

I wonder what it felt like to be a leper who was ostracized from the people in the village, no longer welcome in the temple, and made to feel like a pariah? What does this story tell me about human beings who ostracize those we fear? How does Jesus's response to lepers call me to treat those with potentially communicable diseases today? And what does it tell me about the character of God that Jesus shows compassion upon and stops to help the lepers of his day?

Finally, notice that while all ten lepers were healed by Jesus, only one returns to give thanks, and this one is the Samaritan (Jews considered Samaritans to be unclean and heretical). What does it tell me about humanity that nine never returned to find Jesus and thank him for their healing? About myself? And what do I learn from the one who did return? These questions help me see myself in the story, and they help me understand how the story is meant to speak to the reader. I hear God speaking to me as I read this text.

4. PRAYING THE SCRIPTURES

When I read the scriptures every morning, I usually read the passage I wish to focus on once, using the practices I've described above. Then I read it a second time, sometimes aloud, inviting God to speak to me through the passage. Finally, I pray the scripture. Here's how this works. Let's take Romans 12:1–2:

> I appeal to you therefore, brothers and sisters, by the mercies of God, to present your bodies as a living sacrifice, holy and acceptable to God, which is your spiritual worship. Do not be conformed to this world, but be transformed by the renewing of your minds, so that you may discern what is the will of God—what is good and acceptable and perfect.

As I prayed this scripture in the morning, I would go through it line by line, praying something like this, "Lord, help me to live these words of Paul. Help me present my entire body to you as a living sacrifice. I pray that in what I do and what I say you may be glorified. I invite you to guide my steps, and to use me to do your will. May my words and actions be an act of worship to you. Lord, help me not so much to be shaped by the world but to be used by you to shape the world. By your spirit, renew my mind—my heart, my values, and my way of thinking. Shape me as a potter shapes the clay. And help me to know, in every situation I encounter, what your will is, and then give me the boldness and courage to pursue it. In Christ's name. Amen."

Another way I might allow this scripture to shape my prayers would be simply to take one small part of it and memorize it, then pray it multiple times throughout the day. I might choose the phrase "Be not conformed to this world," and decide to pray each hour, "Lord, help me not to be conformed to this world." These short prayers are often called "breath prayers," as they can be prayed with one breath.

5. MEMORIZING SCRIPTURE

One of the things I value about my early experience in the Pentecostal Church was the emphasis on memorizing scripture. I memorized dozens if not hundreds of scripture verses. Those scriptures remain in my subconscious, and they seem to come to mind for me when I need them the most. Over the years I've encouraged our congregation members to memorize scripture. We take a particular verse that ties into the sermon for a given week and place it on a small card, about the size of a business card. I invite members to place the card on the dash of their car or tape it to the mirror where they brush their teeth, and to say the verse aloud twice each morning and twice each night. I encourage them to pray the scripture verse as we learned above. At the end of the week, they will have memorized the verse.

6. STUDY SCRIPTURE WITH OTHERS

Perhaps the most powerful way of reading scripture is to read it with others in a small group. I've participated in multiple Bible studies over the years. I find that God speaks to me and helps me see biblical texts in new ways as I hear others reflect upon the words of scripture. A great Bible study group will include people who read the scriptures from different vantage points. It is a safe place to ask questions and offer different interpretations. Members usually come prepared, having read the scriptures and any study materials carefully before arriving to study. In these study groups, we've used all the other models for studying scripture. These groups have produced rich friendships and have helped me hear the Bible in fresh ways, for which I am profoundly grateful.

7. BRING THE SCRIPTURE INTO
YOUR LIFE SITUATION

I was at the hospital recently to see a woman who had had a severe infection, which required that her leg be amputated to save her life. As we spoke, she told me the scriptures that had been most helpful to her while in the hospital were the lament psalms (psalms in which the writers complain to God about their life situation and ask God to deliver them). Most of these psalms speak of enemies, and some harshly call for God to destroy the psalmist's enemies. I've always appreciated the complaint or lament psalms for their honesty. Life is sometimes painful and hard, and we need to complain to God at times. These psalms tell us it is okay to complain to him.

But one of the things that has always troubled me about these psalms is how incongruous they sometimes are with the teachings of Jesus. They call for the destruction of enemies, whereas Jesus calls us to love our enemies. When I read these psalms to others or for myself, I skip over what I've always considered to be sub-Christian themes of destroying the enemy. But she told me that when she prayed them, she saw her illness as the enemy, and she was both complaining to God and asking God to slay her infection. Suddenly these bits of psalms I previously considered a bit embarrassing took on a powerful new meaning.

8. IMAGINE WHAT MIGHT HAVE BEEN

When reading narrative stories in the Bible, it is sometimes helpful to ask what might have happened if the figure in the story had chosen a different course of action.

Several years ago, I was in Jerusalem and I asked my guide to take me to the Potter's Field (also known as the "Field of Blood")—I had seen it many times from a distance but never up close. This is the place where tradition says that Judas hung himself after betraying Christ. There are the remains of an old Crusades-era church on the site, and what may be Byzantine tombs. And there in the center is a tree, a reminder that Judas hung himself. As I stood on the site reading the story in Matthew 27:1–10, I began to wonder what would have happened if Judas had waited just three

days before deciding to take his own life. Would not Jesus have for-
given him? Can you imagine the sermons Judas might have
preached across the Roman Empire—of how he had betrayed
Christ for thirty pieces of silver, and how, in regret, he had contemplated taking his own life. But then how, after the resurrection,
Christ forgave even him! Judas could have preached this message
of redemption, grace, and hope around the world, if he had only
waited three days.

I think about this text and reading it there in the Potter's Field
every time I'm with someone who is suicidal. This idea, captured
by seeing in the text what could have happened, has touched hundreds of people as I've shared it with them.

❧

I want to conclude this conversation with you by encouraging you
to actually read the Bible. The Bible is Israel's story. It is the church's
story. It is God's story. And as we read it carefully, we see that it is
our story. When we read with ears and hearts open to hear, God
speaks and the scriptures convey to us "wonderful words of life."

Bibliography

Abraham, William J. *The Divine Inspiration of Holy Scripture*. New York: Oxford University Press, 1981.

Allert, Craig D. *A High View of Scripture? The Authority of the Bible and the Formation of the New Testament Canon*. Grand Rapids, MI: Baker Academic, 2007.

Bruce, F. F. *The New Testament Documents: Are They Reliable?* Grand Rapids, MI: William B. Eerdmans, 1981.

Carter, Warren. *The Roman Empire and the New Testament: An Essential Guide*. Nashville, TN: Abingdon Press, 2006.

Countryman, L. William. *Biblical Authority or Biblical Tyranny? Scripture and the Christian Pilgrimage*. Harrisburg, PA: Trinity Press International, 1994.

Efird, James M. *How To Interpret the Bible*. Atlanta, GA: John Knox Press, 1984.

Fee, Gordon D., and Douglas Stuart. *How to Read the Bible for All Its Worth: A Guide to Understanding the Bible*. Grand Rapids, MI: Zondervan, 1982.

Fretheim, Terence E., and Karlfried Froehlich. *The Bible as Word of God in a Postmodern Age*. Eugene, OR: Wipf & Stock, 1998.

Geisler, Norman L., ed. *Inerrancy*. Grand Rapids, MI: Academie Books, 1980.

Hodgson, Peter C., and Robert H. King, eds. *Christian Theology: An Introduction to Its Traditions and Tasks*. Philadelphia, PA: Fortress Press, 1985.

Jones, Scott J. *John Wesley's Conception and Use of Scripture*. Nashville, TN: Kingswood Books, 1995.

Keck, Leander E., Walter Brueggemann, Terence Fretheim, Walter Kaiser, ed. *The New Interpreter's Bible: A Commentary in Twelve Volumes*. Vol. 1, *Genesis to Leviticus*. Nashville, TN: Abingdon Press, 1994.

Marxsen, Willi. *The New Testament as the Church's Book*. Philadelphia, PA: Fortress Press, 1972.

McDonald, Lee Martin. *The Biblical Canon: Its Origin, Transmission, and Authority*. Peabody, MA: Hendrickson, 2007.

Metzger, Bruce M. *The New Testament: Its Background, Growth, and Content*. 3rd ed. Nashville, TN: Abingdon Press, 2003.

Montgomery, David R. *The Rocks Don't Lie: A Geologist Investigates Noah's Flood*. New York: W. W. Norton, 2012.

Niditch, Susan. *War in the Hebrew Bible: A Study in the Ethics of Violence*. New York: Oxford University Press, 1995.

Placher, William C., ed. *The Essentials of Christian Theology*. Louisville, KY: Westminster John Knox Press, 2003.

Seibert, Eric A. *The Violence of Scripture: Overcoming the Old Testament's Troubling Legacy*. Minneapolis, MN: Fortress Press, 2012.

Stark, Thom. *The Human Faces of God: What Scripture Reveals When It Gets God Wrong (and Why Inerrancy Tries to Hide It)*. Eugene, OR: Wipf & Stock, 2011.

Sullivan, Clayton. *Toward A Mature Faith: Does Biblical Inerrancy Make Sense?* Decatur, GA: SBC Today, 1990.

Wright, N. T. *The Last Word: Beyond the Bible Wars to a New Understanding of the Authority of Scripture*. New York: HarperOne, 2005.

Acknowledgments

Several people have played a critical role in the writing of this book. First, I would acknowledge the outstanding professors who taught me the scriptures, first in college at Oral Roberts University and then in graduate school at Perkins School of Theology at Southern Methodist University. They are not responsible for the errors in my thinking, but whatever is good in this book is in part shaped by them. I am grateful for the people of the United Methodist Church of the Resurrection, who have shared their lives, questions, and doubts with me. It is through nearly twenty-five years of pastoral ministry with them that the views of scripture described in this book took shape. They were also kind enough to allow me a sabbatical leave to write this book. The Lilly Clergy Renewal Program provided funding for my sabbatical, during which most of this book was written. Roger Freet, at HarperOne, has been my conversation partner and very patient editor. His partnership has been invaluable to me. And finally, I want to acknowledge my wife, LaVon. She is my companion and my best friend. She's been on a journey with me these last thirty-one years as I've tried to make sense of the Bible. Her willingness to tolerate the stacks of books around our house and to give up hundreds of hours together as I wrote made this book possible.

Notes

Chapter 2: A Biblical Geography and Timeline

1. Technically we're still in an Ice Age, but we're currently in an interglacial period known as the Halocene. I mention the end of the Ice Age because this is thought to have had a significant impact upon the development of human civilizations, and it was also a period of widescale flooding, which we'll talk about in Section 2 related to Noah.

Chapter 3: The Old Testament in Fifteen Minutes

1. No one knows for sure when Abraham lived, but the commonly used dates are somewhere between 2200 BC and 1800 BC.

2. I'm using traditional dating here. Scholars disagree about some of the dates, particularly for the book of Daniel, where conservatives take the book at face value and date it during the 500s, whereas more critical scholars date it in the second century BC. In addition, in writing for a Christian audience, I'm using the traditional designations BC and AD rather than BCE and CE, which are more helpful in secular and scholarly work. Christians mark time from the birth of Christ, just as Muslims mark time from Muhammad's emigration from Mecca to Medina, and Jews from the Creation.

CHAPTER 4: Who Wrote the Old Testament, When, and Why

1. There is some disagreement on dating, so that some place the destruction of the temple in 587 BC and others in 586 BC.

CHAPTER 5: Which Books Made It into the Old Testament and Why

1. Martin Brecht, *Martin Luther*, trans. James L. Schaaf, 3 vols. (Minneapolis, MN: Fortress Press, 1985–93), 3:98.

CHAPTER 8: The New Testament in Fifteen Minutes

1. There is some variation in counts in part because some verses were originally included in older Bible translations but have now been reduced to footnotes after ancient manuscript discoveries demonstrated that the verse in question was likely added at a later date.

2. There is some debate as to whether Paul was put to death at the end of this imprisonment or if he was let loose for a brief time and later returned to Rome for another trial and his execution. Hence dates for Paul's death are usually given as either 64/65 or 67/68.

CHAPTER 9: Reading Someone Else's Letters

1. This is true of eight of Paul's thirteen letters. Many mainline scholars suggest that five of the letters were written after his death by followers.

2. Conservatives tend to date books earlier, liberals later, and these are approximate ranges.

3. How is it that Jesus was born four years *before Christ?* That was a bit of a mistake on the part of a brilliant (and short) monk known as Dionysius Exiguus. He lived in Rome in the 500s and is responsible for changing how time was measured in the empire, and ultimately much of the world. Using the information at his disposal, he fixed the year of Jesus's birth and noted it as Anno Domini, "the year of our Lord," meaning the number of years since Jesus was born. He was remarkably close when he fixed the year that would become AD 1, but based upon the information we now have, we know that Jesus was actually born several years earlier. Rather than fixing the calendars and renumbering the years back to the eighth century, we simply acknowledge that Jesus was likely born somewhere around 4 BC. and died somewhere around AD 29–30. (Luke 3:23 tells us that Jesus was "about thirty years of age" when he began his public ministry, and since the Gospels record three Passovers during Jesus's public ministry, it is thought that he was about thirty-three when he died.)

4. This summary of Paul's preaching is based on Luke's account in Acts 17 of Paul's message to the Gentiles in Athens.

5. Centers for Disease Control, "Trends in In-Hospital Newborn Male Circumcision—United States, 1999–2010," Morbidity and Mortality Weekly Report 60, no. 34 (2011), www.cdc.gov/mmwr/preview/mmwrhtml/mm6034a4 .htm?s_cid=mm6034a4_w.

CHAPTER 11: How, When, and Why the Gospels Were Written

1. Aramaic is a Semitic language that has much in common with Hebrew.

2. This tradition may have begun with a misunderstanding of something the early second-century bishop Papias said about Matthew, but it was thought by many of the church fathers to be an accurate statement, namely, that there was an early version of Matthew's Gospel written in Hebrew.

3. All four Gospels are anonymous; they never claim authorship. The early church tells us that Matthew, Mark, Luke, and John were the authors. John gives hints as to the author's identity, but the others are truly anonymous.

4. As I've noted elsewhere in the book, evangelical and many mainline scholars accept this tradition, while more critical or skeptical scholars reject it. I find it plausible.

5. I am aware that some discount this line of reasoning. I leave it to the reader to decide. It is certainly true that I look back at events in the past with a different perspective today than I had at the time. I sometimes forget this or that detail, or occasionally remember it slightly differently than another might remember it. But what is interesting, as I approach fifty, is that while I can't recall what I ate for lunch yesterday, I remember fairly accurately even small details of things that happened decades ago.

CHAPTER 12: The Perplexing, Puzzling, and Profound John

1. Eusebius, *Ecclesiastical History* 6.14.5–7, translated by Arthur Cushman McGiffert.

2. Did John really live into his 80s or 90s and write this Gospel or was it written by a disciple seeking to accurately convey the story and theological reflections as he heard them from John? I don't know, but in the absence of more information, I tend to let the tradition stand that John penned these words himself in his old age.

3. When scholars speak of a developed or "high" Christology, the assumption is that the church's assessment of Jesus and the meaning of his life, death, and resurrection, as well as the understanding of his identity, developed over time. In the

earliest preaching and teaching, he was seen as the long-awaited Jewish messiah and savior. But over the first few decades of the church's existence, as Christians reflected upon the identity and work of Jesus, the language they used to describe him grew more glorious. Matthew, Mark, and Luke all point to Christ's divinity, but this idea is found on nearly every page of John's Gospel.

CHAPTER 13: Which Books Made It into the New Testament and Why

1. Clement's willingness to boldly instruct and correct the church at Corinth points to an emerging role for the bishop of Rome. The seeds of the papacy are seen in this act, emerging before the end of the first century. Additionally, Clement claims to write under the inspiration of the same Spirit he claims Paul was inspired by.

2. Most mainline scholars believe 2 Peter was written long after Peter's death, perhaps as late as the early second century.

3. Or some believe it was 70 to 155.

4. Saint Justin Martyr, "First Apology," trans. Alexander Roberts and James Donaldson, http://www.logoslibrary.org/justin/apology1/67.html.

5. It is surprising to many twenty-first-century Christians that music and singing is not mentioned, though we know that early Christians did sing "psalms, hymns and spiritual songs" to one another (Ephesians 5:19).

6. Some date the Gospel of Thomas to the middle of the first century, though most date it around 100 or later.

7. Lee Martin McDonald in *The Biblical Canon* (Peabody, MA: Hendrickson, 2007), 296. F. F. Bruce in *The Canon of Scripture* (Westmont, IL: InterVarsity Press, 1988), 180ff, notes that it was Tertullian who first used this phrase to designate a collection of books.

8. The other epistles are often grouped together under the name General Epistles or Catholic Epistles.

9. "Thirty-Ninth Festal Letter of Athanasius," www.ntcanon.org/Athanasius .shtml#Festal_Letter

10. There are a number of verses in Acts that are often called the "we passages," where Luke describes Paul's journeys using the term "we" as though he himself were present for that portion of the journey.

11. Preface to Revelation in Luther's 1522 edition of the Bible, quoted in "Luther's Treatment of the 'Disputed Books' of the New Testament," *Bible Research*, www .bible-researcher.com/antilegomena.html.

12. I have sought to summarize in this chapter hundreds of pages of more detailed descriptions of the process of canonization. I find the history of canonization fascinating. If you would like to know more, two of the best books I've read on the subject are Lee Martin McDonald, *The Biblical Canon: Its Origin, Transmission and Authority* (Peabody, MA: Hendrickson, 2007); and F. F. Bruce, *The Canon of Scripture* (Westmont, IL: InterVarsity Press, 1998).

CHAPTER 14: Is the Bible Inspired?

1. Scott Barry Kaufman, "Why Inspiration Matters," *HBR Blog Network*, November 8, 2011, http://blogs.hbr.org/cs/2011/11/why_inspiration_matters.html.

2. Paul is the stated author of 2 Timothy, but as we noted earlier, many mainline scholars believe 2 Timothy was written after Paul's death by one of his students.

3. Words that appear only once in a document, type of document, or language are referred to by scholars as *hapax legomenon* (something said only once).

4. Hebrews 4:12 speaks of the "word of God" but is likely referring to the variety of ways that God speaks, including scripture but also how we hear God speak to us in the "still small voice" of his Spirit as we pray, listen to sermons, sense God's promptings, and hear God through others.

5. This view of inspiration is in some ways similar to that proposed by Karl Barth and the neoorthodox movement in the twentieth century.

6. As with 2 Timothy, most mainline scholars believe that 2 Peter was written after Peter's death, though some believe these texts drew upon his ideas and things he had said while he was alive.

7. Craig D. Allert, *A High View of Scriptures?* (Grand Rapids, MI: Baker Academic, 2007), 185–88. This is an excellent book on the nature of scripture.

8. The actual wording of Article V of the Methodist Articles of Religion (based upon Article VI of the Anglican Church's Thirty-Nine Articles) reads, "The Holy Scripture containeth all things necessary to salvation; so that whatsoever is not read therein, nor may be proved thereby, is not to be required of any man that it should be believed as an article of faith, or be thought requisite or necessary to salvation." The Evangelical United Brethren Church noted, "We believe the Holy Bible, Old and New Testaments, reveals the Word of God so far as it is necessary for our salvation. It is to be received through the Holy Spirit as the true rule and guide for faith and practice. Whatever is not revealed in or established by the Holy Scriptures is not to be made an article of faith nor is it to be taught as essential to salvation." Both were accepted when the two churches merged to form the United Methodist Church in 1968.

CHAPTER 15: Is the Bible the Word of God?

1. Though our primary knowledge of Jesus comes through the gospels and epistles which were written by human authors.

2. The exception is his first sermon in Nazareth, where Jesus read from Isaiah 61:1–2, after which he said, "Today this scripture is fulfilled in your hearing." They then took him and tried to throw him off a cliff. Aside from this, Jesus's preaching does not appear to be an exposition from an Old Testament text.

3. Steve Jobs was the cofounder of Apple Computer, Walter Isaacson the chairman of CNN and the managing editor of *TIME*. The biography was released just after Jobs's death.

4. Karl Barth was one of the great Protestant theologians of the twentieth century.

CHAPTER 16: How Does God Speak to and Through Us?

1. There are three possible exceptions: one could make a case that portions of the Law of Moses were dictated by God, and that some of the Prophetic writings in the Old Testament were audibly given to the prophets, and that portions of Revelation were conveyed orally. But even here I would suggest that it is likely that Moses, the prophets and the author of Revelation heard God in the ways I'm describing in this chapter.

2. The term "charters" was first used of early Christians for Jesus himself and later the documents that bore witness to him.

CHAPTER 17: Is the Bible Inerrant and Infallible?

1. Letter 82, i, 3, in *Letters of St. Augustine: The Nicene and Post-Nicene Fathers of the Christian Church*, ed. Philip Schaff, first series, vol. 1 (Grand Rapids, MI: Eerdmans, 1994), 348.

2. "Chicago Statement on Biblical Inerrancy with Exposition," *Bible Research*, www .bible-researcher.com/chicago1.html.

3. Paul Feinberg, "The Meaning of Inerrancy," in *Inerrancy*, ed. Norman Geisler (Grand Rapids, MI: Academie Books, Zondervan Publishing House 1980), 294.

4. This same idea of a special grace of the Holy Spirit that ensures infallibility is used by Roman Catholics regarding papal infallibility. They suggest that when the pope speaks *ex cathedra*, that is, when he is issuing an official pronouncement on doctrine or morals, he is given a special grace from the Holy Spirit that protects him from error.

5. Some inerrantists do not argue that God chose the word order, suggesting instead

that God allowed the authors to use their own vocabulary and grammatical style, yet still ensured that each word was precisely what God intended. This still defies logic, at least to me.

6. It is sometimes reported as a three-day walk, but I've actually walked portions of this journey, and while it may be theoretically possible, it would not be typical. A BBC reporter walked it several years ago with a donkey, to retrace the journey Luke describes Mary and Joseph making before the birth of Jesus. It took him ten days to travel from Nazareth to Bethlehem.

CHAPTER 18: A High View of Scripture?

1. Glen Miles is the senior pastor at Country Club Christian Church in Kansas City, Missouri, who shared this metaphor of the colander with me. I believe he received it from a seminary professor of his.

2. This James is thought to be the same James who wrote the epistle in our New Testament and who describes himself as "the servant of the Lord" and also the one named in Matthew 13:55 as a brother of Jesus.

CHAPTER 19: Science, the Bible, and the Creation Stories

1. The dating for creation among Young Earth Creationists varies but the traditional dating was that creation occurred around 4000 BC.

2. Frank Newport, "In U.S., 46% Hold Creationist View of Human Origins," *Gallup Politics*, June 1, 2012, http://www.gallup.com/poll/155003/hold-creationist-view-human-origins.aspx.

CHAPTER 20: Were Adam and Eve Real People?

1. I like how the *Encyclopedia Britannica* article "Homo Sapiens" states, "It seems appropriate to conclude that a latent capacity for symbolic reasoning was present when anatomically modern Homo sapiens emerged and that our forebears discovered their radically new behavioral abilities somewhat later in time. A cultural 'release mechanism' of some sort was necessarily involved in this discovery, and the favoured candidate for this role is language." *Encyclopædia Britannica* (Chicago: Encyclopædia Britannica, 2013).

CHAPTER 21: Were There Dinosaurs on the Ark?

1. Susan Klebold, "I Will Never Know Why," *O, The Oprah Magazine*, November 2009, www.oprah.com/world/Susan-Klebolds-O-Magazine-Essay-I-Will-Never-Know-Why/4#ixzz2alDdVRhA.

2. Geologist David Montgomery's *The Rocks Don't Lie: A Geologist Investigates Noah's Flood* is a great place to start if you're looking for an interesting read that expresses appreciation for the story of Noah and recognizes its importance in shaping the field of geology, while still offering an introduction to the evidence against a recent global flood.

3. There is a wide range in the reporting of total deaths due to war and genocide in the twentieth century. Including atrocities governments committed against their own people, I've seen numbers as high as 200 million.

4. Address by President Dwight D. Eisenhower, "The Chance for Peace," delivered before the American Society of Newspaper Editors, April 16, 1953.

CHAPTER 22: God's Violence in the Old Testament

1. As an example of actually carrying out this penalty, see Numbers 15:32–36, where a man was found gathering sticks on the Sabbath, and God instructed Moses to have the community stone him to death for this crime.

2. According to this text, this is why the Levites were set apart for the priesthood and service to the Tent of Meeting and later the temple: for their willingness to put their brothers, friends, and neighbors to the sword to protect God's honor. For their willingness to kill their friends and family, they "brought a blessing" upon themselves. This is a further example of the problematic nature of these texts.

3. The land of Canaan comprised roughly the areas that are today Israel and Palestine, and parts of Jordan, Syria, and Lebanon.

4. http://biblehub.com/hebrew/2763.htm.

5. See Clay Jones, "Killing the Canaanites: A Response to the New Atheism's 'Divine Genocide' Claims," *Christian Research Journal* 33, no. 4 (2010), www.equip.org/articles/killing-the-canaanites/.

6. See Eric Seibert, *The Violence of Scripture: Overcoming the Old Testament's Troubling Legacy* (Minneapolis, MN: Fortress Press, 2012). Throughout the book, Seibert gives multiple examples of the patterns of Old Testament violence and justifications repeated throughout history.

7. This translation is William Albright's published in *The Ancient Near East: An Anthology of Texts and Pictures*, Edited by James Bennett Pritchard (Princeton, NJ: Princeton University Press, 2011), 288.

8. For a survey of ways in which violent passages of the Bible have been invoked to support aggressive wars, see Siebert, *The Violence of Scripture*, chap. 2.

CHAPTER 23: Suffering, Divine Providence, and the Bible

1. Readers often feel disturbed by the fact that God allowed Satan to do these terrible things to Job merely to test him. It is helpful to remember that Job is an epic poem. It is, in some ways, a lengthy parable set to verse. As such it is a story, not the report of an actual series of events or conversations.

2. The NRSV adopts an alternative reading and, in my opinion, ruins the verse. It has, "So he will kill me; I have no hope." The NIV mirrors the KJV.

3. I included this same clipping in my book *Seeing Gray in a World of Black and White* (Nashville, TN: Abingdon Press, 2008).

CHAPTER 24: Can We Trust the Gospel Accounts of Jesus?

1. I'll use the term "reasonably reliable" throughout this chapter. By it I mean that the Gospels offer an accurate portrait of the things that Jesus said and did—that they are trustworthy as means of knowing who Jesus is, what he did, what he stood for, and what contemporaries understood his life to mean.

2. There are newer books that have been written on the subject, some better than others, but I think Bruce's is an excellent and relatively short text.

3. None of the Gospel writers give us their names, but leaders in the early church told us the names of the authors.

4. F. F. Bruce records the ways in which small details in Luke and Acts have been confirmed by archaeology in chapter 7 of *The New Testament Documents*.

CHAPTER 26: "No One Comes to the Father Except Through Me"?

1. I've addressed the topic myself in *Christianity and World Religions* (Nashville, TN: Abingdon, 2005); and in chapters in my books *Seeing Gray* and *When Christians Get It Wrong*.

2. C. S. Lewis, *The Problem of Pain* (San Francisco: HarperOne, 2009), 77.

CHAPTER 27: Women Need Not Apply

1. "Pope Francis' Press Conference during the Papal Flight on Sunday, July 28, 2013," Catholic News Agency, www.catholicnewsagency.com/news/full-transcript-of -popes-in-flight-press-remarks-released/.

2. See "Apostolic Letter, Ordinatio Sacerdotalis, of John Paul II to the Bishops of the Catholic Church on Reserving Priestly Ordination to Men Alone," www .vatican.va/holy_father/john_paul_ii/apost_letters/documents/hf_jp-ii_ apl_22051994_ordinatio-sacerdotalis_en.html.

3. Ibid.

4. Elizabeth Flock, "WHO Study: Forty Percent of Murdered Women Murdered by Their Partners," *U.S. News and World Report*, June 21, 2013.

CHAPTER 29: Homosexuality and the Bible

1. Frank Newport, "In U.S., Record-High Say Gay, Lesbian Relations Morally OK," *Gallup Politics*, May 20, 2013, www.gallup.com/poll/162689/record-high -say-gay-lesbian-relations-morally.aspx.

2. While many mainline scholars believe the laws of Leviticus come from a time long after Moses lived, conservatives typically accept that these laws in Leviticus were handed down by God to Moses.

3. Alan Prendergast, "Prison Sexual Abuse Survivor Speaks Out," *Prison Legal News*, Nov. 30, 2013, www.prisonlegalnews.org/displayArticle.aspx?articleid=2 4068&AspxAutoDetectCookieSupport=1.

4. See Leviticus 11 for a comprehensive list of forbidden animals and Deuteronomy 14:3 where the eating of these animals is said to be, in Hebrew, *towebah* – the same word used to describe a man lying with a man as with a woman in Leviticus 18:22.

CHAPTER 31: Toward an Honest and Reverent View of Scripture

1. http://www.pewresearch.org/daily-number/seven-in-10-young-adults-favor -same-sex-marriage/.

2. "An Open Letter to the Church from My Generation," Dannika Nash, April 7, 2013 found on Dannika's blog at http://dannikanash.com/2013/04/.

3. A number of different theories have been put forward for how Christ's death atones for our sin and reconciles us to God. I describe several of these in *24 Hours That Changed the World* (Nashville, TN: Abingdon, 2008).

CHAPTER 32: Postscript: Reading the Bible for All Its Worth

1. The title of this chapter is borrowed from Gordon Fee and Douglas Stuart, *How to Read the Bible for All Its Worth* (Grand Rapids, MI: Zondervan, 1982). I read the book nearly thirty years ago, and I don't know that any of what is in this chapter is drawn from there, but the title captured well what I hoped to convey in this final chapter.

Index